Oracles
and Divination

Edited by
MICHAEL LOEWE AND CARMEN BLACKER

With contributions by
LAMA CHIME RADHA, RINPOCHE
MICHAEL LOEWE   CARMEN BLACKER
J. S. MORRISON   HILDA ELLIS DAVIDSON
O. R. GURNEY   J. D. RAY   J. R. PORTER
R. B. SERJEANT

SHAMBHALA
Boulder 1981

SHAMBHALA PUBLICATIONS, INC.
1920 13th Street
Boulder, Colorado 80302

Distributed in the United States by Random House
and in Canada by Random House of Canada Ltd.

Printed in the United States of America

Library of Congress Cataloging in Publication Data
Oracles and divination.

   Includes index.
   Contents: Tibet / Chime Radha—China / Michael
Loewe—Japan / Carmen Blacker—The Classical
world / J.S. Morrison—The Germanic world / Hilda
Ellis Davidson—(etc.)
   1. Oracles—Addresses, essays, lectures.
2. Divination—Addresses, essays, lectures.
I. Loewe, Michael. II. Blacker, Carmen. III. Lama
Chime Radha, Rinpoche.
BL613.O73   291.3'2   81-50968
ISBN 0-87773-214-0 (pbk.) AACR2
ISBN 0-394-74880-8 (Random House: pbk.)

Acknowledgements

The editors are glad to record their thanks to the following individuals and authorities for permission to reproduce illustrations of items in their collections or from their publications: Dr Stephan D. R. Feuchtwang; *Monumenta Nipponica;* Dr Masanao Sekine; Heibonsha Limited, Tokyo; the History and Philosophy of Science Syndicate, Cambridge; Kadokawa shoten, Tokyo; Ishiyamadera; the Staatliche Museen, Berlin, DDR; the National Museum, Aleppo; the Trustees of the British Museum; the American Schools of Oriental Research; the *Biblical Archeologist;* the Oriental Institute, the University of Chicago; Professor Franz Rosenthal; Princeton University Press; Routledge and Kegan Paul, London. Thanks also are due to Peter Wilkie for his kind permission to reproduce his photograph of objects used in Tibetan divination.

Contents

Illustrations

Introduction

By divination we mean the attempt to elicit from some higher
power or supernatural being the answers to questions beyond
the range of ordinary human understanding. Questions about
future events, about past disasters whose causes cannot be
explained, about things hidden from sight or removed in
space, about right conduct in a critical situation, about the
time and mode of religious worship and the choice of persons
for a particular task – all these have from ancient times and
in all parts of the world been the subject of divinatory
enquiry.

The following nine chapters seek to show how in various
civilizations such questions were put, and how the answers,
which we call oracles, were transmitted and interpreted. The
nine chapters, with a single exception, originated in a series
of lectures delivered in Cambridge University in 1979.

No attempt has been envisaged in this book to cover the
whole field of divinatory practice, neither in any one culture
nor in the world as a whole. The book is perforce limited to
nine areas only. These nevertheless range in space from
Iceland to Japan, and in time from the third millennium
B.C. to the present day. Nor was the book conceived as an
exercise in comparison or contrast. Each contributor was
encouraged to treat on its own merits the subject as it
appeared in his own field.

A notable range of different methods nevertheless presents
itself. In nearly all cultures specially gifted people, seers or
mediums, are recognised as affording the necessary link with
the supernatural world. Such people may transmit the
utterances of the oracle, as with the Greek Pythia or the
Japanese *miko*, or may 'see' in clear images the answer to the
question, as with those in Tibet possessing the faculty of *Tra*.
Oracles come frequently in the form of dreams. In Mesopotamia, Greece, Israel, Japan and among the Norsemen,
oracular dreams were solicited by means of incubation in a
sacred site. Other common methods involve the inspection
by the seer of some kind of pattern, as with the cracks on
the turtle shell in China, the entrails of sacrificial animals in

Babylon, or the flight of birds in the sky in Greece. Again frequent are methods in which the element of chance is held to be directed by the invisible oracle, as manifested in the fall of dice, the outcome of lot, or the behaviour of birds or cows.

Our contributors have drawn on a wide variety of types of evidence: relics of the practice itself such as inscribed bones or the clay models of livers; painted vases; literary records of questions put and answers given; manuals used for guidance and instruction; critical essays by sceptics like Cicero and lampoons of satyrists such as Aristophanes.

These combine to show how universal and pervasive the practices have been. In the monotheistic cultures of Israel and Islam they continued despite the prohibitions of the Old Testament and the rebukes of Muhammad. In the polytheistic society of Athens, long regarded as the abode of reason and enlightenment, they retained a prominent place. In China divination gave rise to the earliest written records of a great civilization; its principles found a place in both the Taoist and the Confucian ways of life, and in the sophisticated philosophies of the Sung period. In the Germanic world the practice was closely associated with the runes and the predictions of bards and seers.

Many of our contributors describe the phenomenon noted by Plutarch in the 1st century A.D., the decline of the oracles. With it goes a decline in divinatory practices. The cause may lie in the disappearance of the seer, whose intuitive utterances give way to the pronouncements of an ungifted scribe, or in a shift in world view. Where no higher source of wisdom is recognised as existing outside the human world, the practices become meaningless and 'superstitious'.

Where any conviction remains in the existence of a supernatural order, however, mantic practices are likely to persist. They are likely to flourish in proportion to men's recognition of their own weakness and consequent need for help in solving problems beyond the scope of human competence.

M.L.
C.B.

Cambridge, 1980.

I

Tibet

LAMA CHIME RADHA, RINPOCHE
Head of the Tibetan Section, British Library

Divination has been a normal and unquestioned part of life in Tibet and neighbouring countries and regions which share its culture, right up to the present day. A variety of methods of foretelling future events has been widely employed, of varying degrees of sophistication and complexity. The study of divination in Tibet, therefore, whether it is regarded as a sociological or psychological phenomenon, as the exercise of a human faculty of which modern industrial societies have lost the use, or in some other way, is not a matter of purely historical research, confined to ancient and mysterious texts of which the exact meaning and interpretation must always remain to some extent a matter of conjecture. On the contrary, divination and other magical (or non-scientific) modes of knowledge and activity are a living part of the everyday experience of the Tibetans and their neighbours in Sikkim, Bhutan, Ladakh and Nepal. As such, they can be examined with an immediacy and freshness which may make them of especial interest.

When I refer to non-scientific modes of knowledge and activity, I do so as a Tibetan and in no disparaging sense. I use the word 'scientific', not as relating to knowledge or truth in their widest meaning, but as denoting that materialist view of the universe, dominant in the modern Western world, which tends to the analysis and explanation of all phenomena in terms of the interactions of sub-atomic particles. From the 'scientific' point of view it would of course be possible and even necessary to explain away the belief in divination and other magical operations as a mere superstition having no correspondence with objective reality, and of relevance only to the social anthropologist. More sympathetic explanations might invoke the concept of synchronicity, the inter-connectedness of all objects and events in space and time, whereby in states of heightened awareness it becomes possible 'to see a world in a grain of sand and a heaven in a wild flower'. Or one could hypothesise that the external apparatus of divination, whether it is a crystal ball, the pattern of cracks in a tortoise shell, or a complex system of astrology, is essentially a means of focussing and concentrat-ing the conscious mind so that insights and revelations may arise (or descend) from the profounder and perhaps supra-individual levels of the unconscious.

Innumerable other explanations would no doubt be possible, depending on the fundamental axioms and assump-tions on which is based one's interpretation of the world of experience. The Tibetans themselves would certainly regard the visions and predictions of seers and diviners as mind-created, but then in accordance with Buddhist philosophy so they would regard everything that is experienced either sub-jectively or objectively, including entities of such seemingly varied degrees of solidity and independent existence as mountains, trees, other beings, sub-atomic particles and waves. In what follows I shall try to describe various methods of divination used in Tibet as far as possible in the terms in which they are accepted and understood by the Tibetans themselves, leaving the reader to evaluate and interpret what is described according to his own preferences and beliefs.

LAMAS AND TULKUS

Recourse to divination might be had about any of the important events and decisions of life: the arranging of marriages, the birth of children, the undertaking of journeys and affairs of business, the choice of site for building a house, the treatment of sickness and disease, the outcome of legal disputes, the recovery of lost articles and animals, social relationships, plans and ambitions of all kinds, and indeed any matter about which a person felt sufficiently anxious to wish to have some reassurance or forewarning in advance of the actual outcome of events. It was a common experience in Tibet for people to travel many miles to consult a respected *mopa*, or diviner, on some question of importance to them or their families. The Buddhist religion coloured and sustained every aspect of the life of Tibet, and the *lamas*, or religious teachers (who might or might not also be monks) were everywhere revered. The greatest number of divinations were carried out by the lamas, especially the re-incarnate lamas or *tulkus*, who are believed to incarnate through a succession of lives in order to continue their spiritual work. The *tulku* best known in the Western world is the Dalai Lama, who is the Tibetan Head of State; the discovery of his present incarnation through divination is described later in this article. Each monastery had at least one incarnate lama at its head and one could estimate that, prior to 1959, there were perhaps six or seven hundred *tulkus* throughout the whole country, although it would never have occurred to Tibetans to count them, since the quantitative approach to life had no place in their outlook. Many *tulkus* were regarded as embodying in their essential nature the qualities of some important spiritual principle; the Dalai Lama, for example, is acknowledged to be an emanation of Chenrezig, the Bodhisattva or divine being who personifies the principle of compassion. To the extent that the *tulkus* succeeded in making themselves at one with eternal spiritual principles they could be said to have a dual nature, both human and transcendent. Thus, it was natural to consider that they had a greater understanding of both the world of objective experience and the inner world of thought and feeling than ordinary people, and a greater insight into the ultimate truths transcending the mundane view of reality. It follows that the more important *tulkus* were considered to be the most skilled and completely accomplished *mopas* or diviners.

Most, though certainly not all, *tulkus* regularly performed divination. For example, four *tulkus* were associated with my monastery of Benchen in East Tibet, and between them they performed divination almost as a daily occurrence. Provided that no special ceremonies or periods of meditation in retreat were taking place, visitors had completely free access. When lamas visited the house of someone who had just died in order to carry out the lengthy ceremony prescribed in the Tibetan Book of the Dead for guiding the consciousness of the deceased to a favourable re-birth, then a donation to the monastery was expected, but ordinary acts of divination were performed quite gratuitously as part of the normal course of events. Those who visited a lama or *tulku* for spiritual advice or for a blessing would also raise questions about matters affecting their daily lives and ask for a prediction of their outcome. To provide this was an accepted part of a lama's duty towards his spiritual charges, and such requests were never refused.

PROFESSIONAL DIVINERS AND ASTROLOGERS

There were no restrictions or laws on who could or could not act as a *mopa*. Not all divinations were performed by re-incarnate lamas. Anyone who possessed the necessary aptitude could practise divination, and as their skills developed and they acquired the reputation of being a successful *mopa* people would increasingly seek their services. Most often it was older people, and in particular 'wise women' who were noted and sought after for their powers of divination. They were much in demand: it was not the custom to perform divination on one's own behalf, and people felt it more appropriate and effective to consult someone else whom they believed to have the necessary power.

Although most divination was performed by lamas and lay people as an adjunct to their normal vocation or occupation, there were some *mopas* who earned their living by divination and the practice of astrology. These two activities were closely associated as means of foretelling the future. Every year, almanacs which showed favourable and un-favourable times for various undertakings were drawn up on a strict mathematical and astronomical basis by professional astrologers. Tibetan astrology derived partly from Indian and partly from Chinese sources, and over the centuries it had evolved into a system of its own. Probably the Chinese influence was the stronger of the two; we had a saying that *cho* (religious doctrine) came from India and *tsi* (astrology) from China. Our system of marking the years by the names of animals and of elements – Fire Dragon, Water Horse, and so on – was derived originally from China. Astrological almanacs were used by large numbers of people. Members of the aristrocracy and important officials employed their own diviner-astrologers. Matters of military strategy were also referred to astrology and divination; and this continues to be done in the independent Himalayan kingdoms adjacent to Tibet. During the final conquest of Tibet by the Chinese army, the impression was strongly held in East Tibet that the Chinese, despite official disapproval of astrology, were conducting their campaign in accordance with the almanacs. It was noticeable, and if merely a coincidence then a striking one, that during those months regarded as unfavourable for military operations the Chinese launched no offensives.

The career of professional diviner was a somewhat insecure way of supporting oneself and one's family. Anyone whose prophecies were not confirmed by events would quickly lose his reputation, and his trade would suffer accordingly. There was thus a certain pressure on diviners to express their predictions with some degree of ambiguity and inexactitude, in order to minimise the possibility of error. A high degree of tact and diplomacy was a necessary part of the diviner's skills, just as in the days of private medicine in Western countries a good bedside manner was as essential to a doctor as his professional competence. Nevertheless, within these constraints, some diviners were trusted as being honest and genuine, while others had the reputation of being charlatans and were not respected.

THE RELIGIOUS DIMENSION

Besides its application to all aspects of secular life, divination also played its part in religious activities. Indeed, in Tibet it was never really possible to separate the religious and the secular. Buddhist values had permeated so deeply into the consciousness of Tibetans that all the activities and experiences of life were seen as having a spiritual dimension and

significance. Even folk songs and love poetry were possessed
of a spiritual symbolism as well as their immediate outward
meaning. In addition to the involvement of the lamas in the
general practice of divination and the production of divinatory texts, religious observances and rites were recommended
as a means of averting misfortune of all kinds. Divination was
used during initiation ceremonies to determine the spiritual
'family' to which the candidate belonged, and thus to
indicate which religious exercises and practices were most
conducive to his spiritual development. It was also of great
importance in the discovery of newly re-born *tulkus* or re-
incarnate lamas, following their death at the end of their
previous existence. This last instance could perhaps be
regarded as a special case in the religious sphere of the general
application of divination to the recovery of lost objects of any
kind.

PARTICULAR METHODS

Having thus described the general background and scope of
the use of divination in Tibet, I shall discuss some particular
methods of divination. These are:

  (i)   PRA (Tra) – signs or visions;
  (ii) MD'-MO (Dahmo) – divination by arrows;
  (iii) 'PHREN-BA (Tring-ba) – the use of the *māla* or
        rosary;
  (iv) ŚO-MO (Sho-mo) – the throwing of dice;
  (v)   SMAN-GSAL-MAR-ME-BRTAG-PA-LDEB (Mar-
        me-tag-pa) – the use of butter lamps;
  (vi) BYA-ROG-KYI-SKAD-BRTAG-PA   (Bya-rog-kyi-
        kad-tag-pa) – interpretation of bird behaviour.

(i) *Tra Divination*
Divination by *tra*, or the reading of signs and visions, is one
of the more esoteric of the divinatory arts of Tibet. Normally
one needs to acquire the skill from someone else who already
possesses it, and not everyone has the gift to practise it
successfully. The diviner or *tra-pa* focusses his attention, free

from particular thoughts and images, by gazing into a small mirror (*Me-Lon'*) made of polished stone or metal, or into the still waters of a lake (*Tsho*), or into the clear sky (*Nam-Mkh'*). Having addressed himself to the question or problem to which he seeks the answer, he empties and concentrates his mind, usually by reciting *mantras*, or sacred formulae associated with particular divinities or spiritual principles. The divinity who is most especially associated with *tra* divination is the *Mahakali* (divine protectress) Palden Lhamo. As the *trapa*'s concentration and absorption deepen, a certain current of consciousness begins to flow, and a vision appears before him. In the ultimate analysis, the vision would be regarded as a creation of mind, but from a more relative point of view it seems solid and substantial and often is visible to people other than the *trapa* himself.

The ball of the thumb (*The-bon*) can also be used for *tra* divination. It is painted red and dipped in soft wax so that it becomes covered with a film of it. All light is shut out of the room and only a single butter-lamp is left burning. The *trapa* holds up his thumb and to everyone present it appears to grow in size and become like a large screen. On this screen appear visions of various symbolic objects – it may be of trees, lakes, people, or other concrete forms. The visions then have to be interpreted according to the question which was asked. If the interpretation is doubtful or uncertain, the *trapa* asks again in his mind and another vision appears. If he asks yet again, then letters appear on the thumb-screen. After that, the visions fade. Three seems to be regarded throughout the world as a significant number in magical operations, as in the three wishes that are often granted in Western fairy stories and folk tales. Certainly in Tibet it was the expectation that only three sets of visions would appear in *tra* divination.

Discovery of the Dalai Lama by Tra. Tra was used in order to discover the whereabouts of the present incarnation of the Dalai Lama. After the death of the previous (thirteenth) Dalai Lama (1933), the Regent who was acting as head of state went in the company of other high officials and spiritual leaders to a lake near Lhasa which is sacred to Palden Lhamo. This lake had been recognised as holy by the second Dalai

Lama, many centuries earlier. Future events are indicated by signs and images which appear on the surface of its waters. At the time when the twelfth Dalai Lama was being chosen, clear details had been seen in the lake of the place where he was born. On the present occasion, the Regent and his companions went to the holy lake and prayed for guidance. After some while, the clearly visible picture of a monastery with a golden roof appeared in the lake; east of it was a road leading to a small village containing a house with a blue roof. Also there appeared in the lake the letters 'Ah', 'Kha', and 'Ma'. These visions were kept secret at the time.

Invocations to the State Oracle (see pp. 27f below) and other official oracles had already produced several indications that the new incarnation was to be sought for in the east, and it was suggested that the letter 'Ah' might stand for Amdo province in East Tibet. Small groups of messengers were sent from Central Tibet to search in that region. In a number of areas children were found who had been born with various significant marks and physical characteristics. One search party, disguised as three merchants on pilgrimage, went to Kumbum monastery in the Ta-tse region of Amdo, a monastery which has a gilded roof. Some distance to the east of the monastery lay a village containing a house with a blue roof. Nearby was a small monastery founded by the fourth Karmapa Lama, Rolpe Dorje. In the light of subsequent events, it was assumed that the letters 'Kha' and 'Ma' in the vision at the holy lake represented the name Karmapa. The supposed pilgrims called in search of refreshment at the blue-roofed house. As a further precaution, the leader of the party, a lama and high official who had known the previous Dalai Lama well, changed clothes with one of the others and acted in a subordinate position. Round his neck he wore a rosary which had belonged to the previous Dalai Lama. A little boy was living in the house with his family. When he saw the rosary he immediately wanted it. Asked by the wearer if he knew him, the child promptly identified him by name, and also named a second member of the party correctly. A series of tests was carried out, which included the recognition by the child of a number of other possessions of the thirteenth Dalai Lama. Eventually the officials were satisfied beyond all doubt that the new incarnation had been found, and in due course the boy was taken back to Lhasa and enthroned as the fourteenth Dalai Lama.

These events throw a revealing light on much earlier happenings. When the Potala Palace in Lhasa had been redecorated in 1920, the thirteenth Dalai Lama had asked that in one room a blue bird should be painted on the west wall and a white dragon on the east. The artists were surprised at his request, as there was no traditional precedent for these images. Their probable significance only became apparent later, when it was realised that the thirteenth Dalai Lama had died in Lhasa in the year of the Water Bird (1933) and that the new incarnation was born in East Tibet in the year of the Iron Dragon (1935). By his own order, the thirteenth Dalai Lama was enshrined in a *stupa*, or reliquary shrine, in the Potala Palace facing eastwards.

Other Examples of the Use of Tra. A lady well-known to me in East Tibet told me that before her marriage she consulted a *trapa* to discover how many sons would be born to her. Using a mirror, the *trapa* had a vision of three flowers: one red, one yellow, and one white; the white one was slightly damaged. He explained that she would have three sons, one of them being a reincarnate lama, represented by the yellow flower, since yellow was the colour associated with the Buddha and also the distinguishing colour in the robes worn by *tulkus*. The red flower represented a son who would become an ordinary monk, since red was the colour of the robes worn by Buddhist monks in Tibet. The third son was represented by the imperfect white flower; he would not enter the religious life, as white was associated more with the dress of the laity, and was probably destined to suffer from ill-health and physical affliction. All these prophecies were in fact fulfilled. Her second son was recognised as a *tulku*; and of his two brothers the elder became a monk, and the younger was disabled through being hit in the knee by a Chinese bullet during their escape from Tibet in 1959; he also suffered serious illness which at one time put his life in danger.

During the conquest of Tibet by the Chinese, many lamas fled across the Himalayas to India to escape imprisonment or execution. The use of *tra* became an important aid on these difficult and dangerous journeys. One well-known lama from my own region of East Tibet was travelling with a party of companions through completely unknown territory to the north of the Tibetan border with Assam. The way was almost entirely blocked by dense forest and large boulders, and there seemed no hope of further progress. Most of the party spoke in favour of turning back, but the lama decided to have recourse to his power of *tra*. He gazed into the sky, and received the vision of a path further ahead. Encouraged by this, his companions were persuaded to struggle on, and in a short while they emerged from the rock-strewn forest on to a definite roadway, altogether unsuspected in that desolate area.

I travelled from East Tibet to Lhasa during the latter stages of the Chinese take-over of the country and from there I escaped to India. A lama of my acquaintance similarly made the journey from Lhasa to freedom and safety in India. Before setting off, he consulted his cousin, a very expert *trapa*, about his journey. Using the ball of his thumb in the way I have described earlier, his cousin had a vision of three dogs playing happily together. The three dogs then became one dog, and this dog crossed a bridge over a wide and deep river; the bridge was perilous and narrow, and the dog had to proceed warily and with great caution. The *trapa* explained the symbolism of his vision thus: the lama, fleeing from the evil times which had ended the former period of peace and happiness, would lose most of his companions on his way to safety and would go through great dangers, but if he exercised the utmost vigilance his journey would at last be safely accomplished. According to my lama friend, his cousin's prophecy proved to be an entirely accurate description of the flight of his party to India.

Evaluation of the Phenomenon of Tra. These examples of the application of *tra* to a number of different problems and questions perhaps will give the reader some idea of the variety of circumstances in which this method of divination might be invoked. In fact the power of *tra* might be made use of in any matter of uncertainty, religious or secular, personal or public, where a need was felt for guidance as to the outcome of present or future events. One can scarcely expect that these examples will be totally convincing to someone who has never experienced the reality of divination in his own life, and whose culture conditions him to an almost instinctive and unthinking rejection of everything relating to magic, mystery and the operation of forces and principles which are_not at present recognised by modern Western science. The sceptical reader will perhaps turn automatically to concepts such as coincidence and mass hysteria as a way of accommodating the phenomena I have been describing within his existing view of the world. But such explanations would seem inadequate and unconvincing to a Tibetan brought up in a culture which accepts mind and mental phenomena as the underlying basis of all reality, and surrounded from birth by manifestations of powers such as divination which, although far from commonplace, are regarded as a normal and natural part of everyday life.

Of course similar powers have survived here and there in remote and undisturbed communities in the Western world until quite recent times: one thinks immediately of the well-known gift of second sight in the Scottish Highlands. Perhaps Jungian psychology, with its concepts of the supra-individual reaches of the unconscious mind, and of intuition as a function of equal validity to that of reason, offers the easiest way for the modern sceptic to arrive at an intellectually respectable position. This would allow him to come to terms with these disturbing phenomena, produced as they are by people who at one and the same time live in the same world as himself and yet experience a quite different reality, without either dismissing the validity of their experience or abandoning his own scientific view of the world. For it is noticeable that the signs and visions of *tra* possess an oblique or indirect quality similar to that which characterises dreams and other manifestations into consciousness of the unconscious. They do not speak to us directly in reply to the conscious questions which evoke them, but in terms of symbols and hidden meanings, often apparently unconnected with the subject in hand, which have to be interpreted by a skilled practitioner. Tibetans share the traditional Eastern view that sense, experience and reason form only part of our means of knowing reality. The totality of mind is seen as including modes of being and functioning from which the power of reasoning itself derives, and which it can therefore never succeed in encompassing or understanding. From this point of view there must of necessity always be more things in heaven and earth than are dreamed of in any rationalist philosophy. But with such reflections we pass from the field of secular scholarship into the intuitive domain of poets, the sphere of religion with its truths accessible only to revelation and faith, and the world of mysticism with its knowledge gained in immediate apprehension transcending the dualistic relationship of subject and object.

(ii) *Dahmo Divination* (see Plate 1)

Although speaking in symbols, *tra* was one of the more concrete forms of divination used in Tibet, for its revelations were expressed in visual images. *Dahmo*, or divination by arrows, although having an obviously symbolic basis, is more abstract in its detailed mode of operation. Two arrows are used: one has a white, and the other a black, scarf tied around its shaft. These arrows represent the fundamental polarity of affirmation and negation, light and darkness, good and evil, positive and negative. A white woollen cloth is placed on a table, and on top of it is piled a heap of barley. The two arrows are thrust point downwards into the barley. The diviner seats himself in front of this divinatory apparatus, brings to mind the question to be asked, and concentrates his mind by reciting *mantras*, in the manner already described in connection with *tra* divination. Once his mind is sufficiently concentrated, he enters into some kind of paranormal relationship with his magical apparatus which could be explained in Western scientific terms only on the basis of such phenomena as *telekinesis*. For the two arrows begin to move without any apparent physical force being applied to them. They may go round each other, come together, or move in a variety of ways; one may even knock the other over. The diviner interprets the pattern of their movements in accordance with traditional texts which explain their significance in detail. *Dahmo* divination is regarded as being under the protection and inspiration of Gesar Dahmo, a hero of ancient Tibetan legends.

(iii) *Tring-ba Divination* (see Plate 1)

Tra and *dahmo* involve phenomena somewhat out of the

ordinary, and the use of special objects, such as mirrors and arrows. The method of divination most common in Tibet, however, was *Tring-ba*, which requires the use of nothing more exotic than the *māla*, the Buddhist rosary of 108 beads, which every Tibetan carries with him constantly in order to carry out his daily devotions. Preparation for the act of divination is made in a way similar to those already considered; the rosary is held between the hands, the question on which guidance is sought is asked mentally, and then, with no preconceptions about what the answer should be, the mind is allowed to become still, concentrated and open to the flow of events in the present moment. The diviner then grasps his rosary in two places, isolating a number of beads between them. These are then counted off, in one method commonly practised four to the right, four to the left, and so on, until a number between one and four are left. It is also possible to count off in threes, fives, or sixes, and to be left at the end with six beads instead of four. The counting off is done three times, and so builds up a sequence of three numbers between one and four (or between one and six). The general meaning of the primary numbers is as follows:

(1) good fortune, but it may not come immediately;
(2) misfortune;
(3) whatever is happening, whether good or bad, will occur very quickly;
(4) moderately good fortune, but with some difficulties.

The triple sequences allow different combinations of these possibilities to be built up which give more variable answers to particular questions. For example, 1, 1, 1 would greatly reinforce the idea of eventual good fortune achieved only after considerable delay, whereas 1, 3, 3 would indicate that the good fortune would arrive immediately. 1, 2, 3 suggests eventual good fortune, unless there are immediate problems, in which case the outcome is likely to be unfavourable. 2, 2, 3 would be a very grave sequence, indicating immediate disaster.

In addition to these general meanings, there exist texts which give detailed answers on particular questions for each combination of numbers. These could run to hundreds of pages. In my monastery a text called 'Tsod-med-bzi' (or 'the Four Limitless Divinations') which had been composed there, was used. The four limitless states referred to by this text are the four divine abodes, basic to all schools of Buddhism, of friendliness, compassion, sympathetic joy, and equanimity. Such texts grew out of previous models, enlarged and enriched by spontaneous composition in states of meditative inspiration. They were thus the products of a dynamic, living and growing creative process operating within a fundamentally defined and established tradition. Whatever elements of novelty and originality they contained, they were faithful to an overall system derived mathematically from the principles of astrology.

The art of *Tring-ba* divination is to combine the primary answers suggested by the numbers and the received texts with an intuitive feeling for the situation. It is in this operation that something that might be called creation or inspiration enters the process of divination; this is an opening up to the mysterious and the noumenal, whereby truths and insights of which one was not previously aware enter into consciousness – whether one thinks of them as emerging from one's own consciousness or superconsciousness, as being revealed more or less externally, or in some other way. To the sceptic who regards such explanations as highly unsatisfactory and nebulous, one can only say that however the phenomena are theoretically accounted for they are found to be effective in practice. If divination in Tibet had not been sufficiently successful in the results it produced, it would not have been practised so widely or over so long a period of time. When it is taken seriously and sustained effort is made to acquire the necessary skills, then the results become correspondingly impressive. With deepening experience, one's sensitivity to the creative or intuitive element grows, and strikingly accurate predictions may be made.

One of the young *tulkus* at my own monastery was once consulted by some local people who had lost a horse. Using his rosary, the *tulku* divined that the horse would be found in the middle of some water and advised its owners to search accordingly. The lama who was his tutor was surprised at the *tulku*'s rashness in not presenting his advice in more safe and non-specific terms. In the event, however, the young

diviner's confidence proved justified; in the locality was a
wide and very shallow lake containing a small island covered
with trees and scrub; the wandering horse was discovered to
have caught its bridle on one of the branches as it skirted
the island, and to be standing in the water, unable to move.

(iv) *Sho-mo Divination* (see Plate 1)
Throwing dice, or *Sho-mo* divination, was another method
widely used in Tibet. The protecting deity associated with
this form of divination is again Palden Lhamo. Three dice are
normally used, giving rise to a total of sixteen different
numbers between 3 and 18 which may be arrived at in
various combinations (e.g., 6, 1, 1; 5, 2, 1; 4, 2, 2; 4, 3, 1;
and 3, 3, 2; and so on). These numbers are interpreted in
accordance with traditional texts arranged under a number
of different headings relating to the main areas of human
experience in which the aid of divination is most commonly
sought. There are sixteen such headings in one widely-used
text, with detailed readings under each one against each of
the sixteen numbers which the throw of the dice may produce.
This text was originally written by Gedun-gyaltsho, the head
of the *Gelugpa* school of Tibetan Buddhism to whom the title
of Dalai (Ocean of Wisdom) Lama was first awarded by the
Mongol rulers of Tibet in the fifteenth century. It was later
condensed by Nagwan-dno-drub. Here, by way of example,
is an indication of the readings given under the various
headings against the number 11, which in general is an
auspicious number.

(1) *Khyim-Phya:* Domestic Affairs (home and family).
Prosperity prevails, life blossoms and is fruitful.
However, the nature spirits are not entirely at peace,
and could cause problems for the household. To
propitiate them, *pujas* (religious ceremonies) should
be carried out, including fire purifications and the
making of offerings.
(2) *Khan-pa-'m-yul-sa:* House and Property Matters. If
moving to a new home is being considered, the
circumstances are extremely favourable.
(3) *Grog-sa:* Fortune. Good fortune attends one's efforts,
which should result in success and accomplishment.

(4) *Nor-sa:* Wealth, Affluence. The present situation is auspicious, and any property or financial dealings should go well.

(5) *Don-Phya:* Purpose. There may be difficult and uncomfortable situations to go through, but the final outcome will be successful.

(6) *Kha-Mchu-Rtsob-pa:* Lawsuits and Contentions. Circumstances are obstructive and progress will be slow and heavy.

(7) *Nad-sa:* Illness. If suffering from a particular illness or disease, one will recover. If feeling unwell, health will be regained.

(8) *Srog-Phya:* Danger (threats to life). There are no dangers to be feared in one's life at present.

(9) *Gdon-Phya:* Mental Obstacles (set-backs from unexplained causes). There are obstructions caused by nature spirits (whom one may have provoked inadvertently; for example, by interfering with a spring belonging to the Nagas, or water serpents). To remove the difficulties, one should perform *pujas* and make offerings.

(10) *Sman-sa:* Medical Treatment, etc. If one is undergoing medical treatment or about to receive it, the outcome will be favourable but one must be careful to follow the doctor's instructions conscientiously.

(11) *Srid-Phya:* Political Activities, Worldly Ambition. Present plans will produce good results and be crowned with success.

(12) *Dgra-Phya:* Military Affairs. Fortune is favourable; if engaged in battle, one will be victorious.

(13) *Mgron-Po:* Visits by Friends. One will receive a visitor in the immediate future, but perhaps accompanied by bad tidings.

(14) *Tshon-Phya:* Business Matters. Success demands immediate action. Any delay will result in failure.

(15) *Lam-Phya:* Journeys. Small obstacles and difficulties may be experienced, but in general one will have a safe and comfortable journey.

(16) *Bor-Stor:* Lost Property. By searching in the direction of the east one will find what is lost, but attempts to recover it may involve legal dispute.

(v) *Mar-me-tag-pa* (*Divination by butter lamp*)

Butter lamps could also be used for divination. I quote below an extract from a text explaining the method which was discovered in a cave in 1364 by Sangye-Lingpa, a famous lama who lived from 1340 to 1396 AD. In Tibet many hidden texts were discovered in this way. They are called *terma*. A few specially gifted lamas, known as *tertons*, have the ability of knowing through dreams or through the power of immediate insight where they are to be found. Hidden treasure of gold or silver has also been discovered in the same way. We believe that such texts were concealed by great teachers of the past until the time was ripe for them to be revealed to succeeding generations. To the suspicious rationalist mind, this might sound like an elaborate subterfuge for passing off modern forgeries as the work of hallowed masters of the past. To believe that, however, would be completely to misunderstand the Tibetans' reverence for their religion, which would make such blatant deception unthinkable to them. More sympathetic Western critics have seen the phenomenon of *terma* as a means by which Tibetan Buddhism has kept itself a living and growing tradition, able to adapt and re-present its essential teachings to meet the changing needs of each generation. Such scholars would suggest that the *terma* are composed by the lamas who discover them in states of genuine religious inspiration, when from the spiritual point of view their consciousness is essentially at one with that of the great masters to whom the composition of the texts thus revealed is subsequently attributed; these attributions are therefore to be regarded as symbolically rather than literally true. Such explanations may make it easier for the modern mind to accept the existential validity of the phenomenon of *terma*. But I am bound to say that they would seem quite unnecessary to Tibetans: we have no difficulty in believing in the literal explanations of the discovery of *terma* texts, any more than in the other phenomena described in this chapter which we are satisfied are abundantly confirmed by our own experience of them.

The extract from the text discovered by Sangye-Lingpa is as follows:

The method of divination by butter lamp is to study the movement of the flame. It should be performed on the eighth or tenth day of the month, or on the day of the full moon or the half moon. Take a small sliver of wood from the yew-leafed fir tree, wrapped in cloth (which acts as the wick), place it in the lamp, and pour the butter around it.

If the lamp burns brightly, with a slender, sharp flame, white in colour, then, whether you are a person of note or an ordinary man or woman, you will be prosperous.

If the lamp burns white or red, with a slightly uneven flame, then perseverance will enable you to overcome any difficulties you may be going through; in case of illness, recovery is assured.

If the flame is shaped like a banner of victory, you will enjoy fame and respect.

If the flame is gold in colour and shaped like a lotus, there will be success in business.

If the flame is very bright, there will be success.

If the flame burns for a long time, there will be good fortune.

If the wick burns down to a shape resembling a small lotus, your possessions will be increased.

If the wick burns away completely, there will be no obstacles.

If the lamp gives off a pleasant smell, whatever you do will be successful.

If the lamp burns with a little spluttering sound ('tap, tap, tap'), love will develop.

If the flame goes straight up like a spear, you will become very clear in your mind.

If the flame forms the shape of a lasso, you will have great power.

If the flame is in the shape of the crescent moon, you will enjoy peace and tranquillity.

If the flame is very pale, resembling a clear fruit, there will be hindrances caused by past actions (karma).

If black smoke is present, your vision is obscured and subject to delusion.

If the flame is dark red mixed with black, there are emotional conflicts.

1. Objects used in Tibetan divination: arrows, dice, rosary, mirror and divination text, by courtesy of Peter Wilkie.

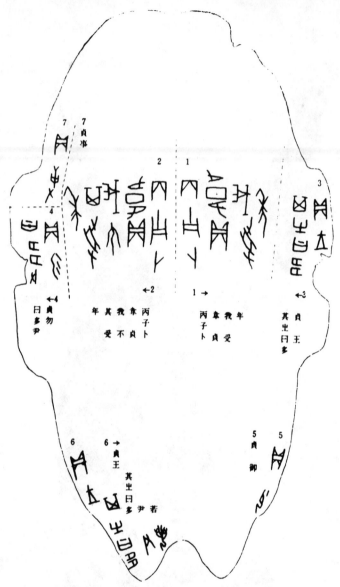

2. Turtle's plastron, used in divination during the Shang Dynasty (traditional dates 1766–1122 BC); overall measurements 20 by 12 cm. Some of the seven separate inscriptions should be taken in pairs, and the main question, or 'charge', is given in positive and negative form, as nos. 1 and 2, i.e.:

1 On the day *ping-tzu* shell cracking took place. Wei put the charge 'There will be a harvest'

2 On the day *ping-tzu* shell cracking took place. Wei put the charge 'There will not be a harvest'

It may be noted that some of the characters of these two inscriptions, which are engraved symmetrically along the central line of the plastron, were written in mirror fashion. The original piece is now in Taipei; reproduced from *Shodō zenshū* volume 1 (Heibonsha, Tokyo, 1954), Plate 1, by courtesy of Heibonsha.

If separate flames arise in ugly colours, there is loss of vitality.

If sparks rise from the lamp, someone is wishing you evil.

If the lamp is difficult to light and burns feebly, you will lose all your fortune and power.

If the flame flickers suddenly, with a 'Lhap, Lhap' sound, an enemy is approaching or a messenger will be forced to return.

If the wick falls over, hindrances will arise.

If the butter overflows, you will be unsuccessful in business and suffer loss.

(vi) *Bya-rog-kyi-kad-tag-pa* (*Bird Divination*)

In many parts of the world, diviners have studied the flight, calls and other behaviour of birds. In Tibet we also did this. The most highly regarded bird was the crow. Crows were never killed, as it was believed that they were messengers from the *Mahakalas*, or divine protectors. Every morning the crows came to our houses, and we always watched them and listened to their cries. After some experience, it became possible to understand the meaning of these calls and to know if anything unusual was happening. It was rather like a mother with her baby. To the outsider, all crying babies sound much the same, but the mother not only recognises the sound of her own baby but can tell at once whether it is hungry, whether it is in some other genuine discomfort, or whether it is just bored or irritable.

While we were escaping from Tibet to India, my companions and I on several occasions appeared to receive warnings of danger from the unusual behaviour of crows. Once, we were on our way up a mountain pass. Many crows were circling around, and their position in relation to us was unfavourable. One flew very close to us and seemed to be trying to make us turn back. As we were confident from the earlier reports of scouts that no enemy troops were in the vicinity, however, we continued on our way. Finally the crow that was most active in its attentions to us actually alighted on the head of my horse and pulled with its beak at the bridle. Immediately afterwards we arrived at the top of the pass and below us we could see two hundred or so Chinese soldiers approaching from the opposite direction. To escape them our party had to split up and scatter, and was reunited only much later. Had we heeded the warning behaviour of the crows, we could have avoided these difficulties and dangers.

There are several texts which deal in a precise way with the meaning of the behaviour of crows. One such is found in the *Tanjur* itself, the traditional collection of commentaries on the Buddhist scriptures and writings on learned subjects translated into Tibetan from Sanskrit. This demonstrates the importance and antiquity of the regard given to the crow. It is called in Sanskrit *Kakajariti* ('On the Sounds of the Crow'), and is to be found in the Sutra section of the *Tanjur*.[1] It was translated into English by Berthold Laufer as 'Bird Divination Among the Tibetans'.[2] In his monograph (much of which is philological in its considerations), Laufer quotes an observation of a nineteenth century English traveller, Thomas Manning, which is a very accurate description of the cry of the Tibetan crow or raven:

> Many of the ravens . . . emit a peculiar and extraordinary sound, which I call metallic. It is as if their throat was a metal tube, with a stiff metal elastic musical spring fixed in it, which, pulled aside and let go, should give a vibrating note, sounding like the pronunciation of the word *poing*, or *scroong*.

After a brief description of the different types of crows, the *Kakajariti* runs as follows:

> The following holds good for the different kinds of tones emitted by the crow. The layman must pronounce the affair, the truth of which he wishes to ascertain, simultaneously (with the flight of the bird).
> When in the first watch a crow sounds its notes in the east, the wishes of men will be fulfilled.
> When it sounds its notes in the south-east, an enemy will approach.
> When in the south . . . a friend will visit.
> When in the south-west . . . unexpected profit will accrue.
> When in the west . . . a great wind will arise.

When in the north-west . . . a stranger (guest) will appear.
When in the north . . . scattered property (lost possessions) will be found.
When in the north-east . . . a woman will come.
When in the zenith (the abode of Brahma) . . . a demon will come.

The text continues with similar lists of prophecies for the other three watches of the day, and for the time of sunset. After this five-fold division of the hours of daylight, when crows are active, the text continues with the interpretation of the cries and other behaviour of crows seen while one is making a journey. It concludes with explanations of the meaning of crows' nest-building activities and of some additional cries, and with a word of advice on the propitiatory offerings which should be offered to crows to avert misfortune.

This precise ordering and identification of the directions of space and the divisions of time is typical of Tibetan divinatory texts. For example, in *Daki-Las-Tshog-Rtan-'drel-Mo-Rtsis-Kyi-Skor* we find:

From the abyss (nadir) to the highest heaven (zenith), all beings live in the five elements. The causes and conditions are wood, fire, metal, water and earth.
    The essence of wood is the Vajra (thunderbolt) *dakini*. She abides in the East and her colour is blue.
    The essence of fire is the Ratna (jewel) *dakini*. She abides in the South and her colour is red.
    The essence of metal is the Padma (lotus) *dakini*. She abides in the West and her colour is white.
    The essence of water is the Karma (action) *dakini*. She abides in the North and her colour is black.
    The essence of earth is the Buddha (wisdom) *dakini*. She abides in all-pervading space and her colour is yellow.
    To each of these elements, if one is the mother, then a second is the son, a third is the friend, and the fourth is the enemy.
    If wood is the subject, then water is the mother, fire is the son, earth is the friend, and metal is the enemy.

If fire is the subject, then wood is the mother, earth is the son, metal is the friend, and water is the enemy. (And so on.)

The first, sixth, eleventh, sixteenth, twenty-first, and twenty-sixth days of the month are the Vajra *dakini's* days.

The second, seventh, twelfth, seventeenth, twenty-second, and twenty-seventh days of the month are the Ratna *dakini's* days.

The third, eighth, thirteenth . . . etc.

You must not confuse these days.

SUMMARY OF FOREGOING

What is the author of this text and the traditional symbolism on which it is based trying to achieve or convey? The search is not merely for a way of foretelling specific events, but for the expression of an underlying world order, embracing both natural and supernatural realities. The *dakinis* (sky-maidens) are the celestial female embodiments of spiritual wisdom and power recognised by the *Vajrayana* or Tantric school of Buddhism, and therefore are of Indian conception. The system of five elements derived originally from China. These two conceptual systems are wedded to produce a unified view of reality which enables man and the world (or worlds) within which he lives to be understood, and appropriate action to be taken in the light of what is seen as the purpose and fulfilment of human existence. The synthesis of these two originally foreign elements took place within Tibet itself, aided by the creative discoveries of the *tertons*. One result of this process was the development of purely Tibetan systems of divination, inspired by and in harmony with orthodox Buddhist principles. The elaboration of this symbolism would be work for a much longer study than this present chapter. The system built up may seem at one and the same time both naive or simplistic and over-elaborate or artificial. To the consciousness conditioned by modern industrial society it is likely to appear alien and archaic. To such criticism one can only say that by their fruits shall ye know them, or more prosaically that the proof of the pudding is in the eating. As one works with the symbolism and penetrates more deeply into its meaning, one learns by its aid to arrive at an integrated view of the world, to see the one in the many, the highest in the lowest, the infinitely great in what is infinitesimally small, and to recognise behind all phenomena the unifying Emptiness which is void of all self-qualities and yet the creative source of all existence and relativities. In doing so one develops an intuitive insight into the workings of the world of nature, which reflect these universal principles, and that insight is the basis of the art of divination.

ORACLES

Divination and prophecy through the utterances of oracles were a familiar part of the traditional life of Tibet. These oracles manifested through the trances of human mediums when possessed by the spirit or consciousness of various deities belonging to the phenomenal order of existence. These deities are thought of as existing and functioning on the level of multiple appearances which constitutes the world of empirical experience and, therefore, as having a relative existence which is no less real or less illusory than that of their human auditors. They form part, in Buddhist doctrine, of that extended range of modes of conditioned existence which includes the everyday world of human experience, but which also includes realms of existence both higher and lower than the human.

Anthropologists have noted the obvious similarities between the trances and operations of oracular mediums in Tibet and those of the shamans of Mongolian, Siberian and Alaskan nomads and other peoples. Possession of human mediums (normally priests or priestesses whose lives were regulated by special rules of conduct) by deities speaking through them in elliptical language which required skilled interpretation, was of course widespread in the ancient Western world, and may be thought to reflect a level of human awareness and a mode of perceiving the surrounding world of experience more universal and far older than the perspectives of the great religions which have shaped men's beliefs and values in the last two or three thousand years. Such considerations have led many Western observers to see a dichotomy, if not an outright contradiction, between the higher doctrine of a supposed pure and original Buddhism, teaching an entirely spiritual way of developing and transforming human consciousness in detachment from the illusory phenomenal world, and the debased practices surviving from the pre-Buddhist indigenous religion of Tibet, by which men operate within the world of phenomena and seek by magical means to modify its events and manipulate the forces governing them to their advantage. Many of the beliefs and practices prevalent in Tibet may indeed be survivals of ancient and even archaic insights and understanding far older than those of Buddhism. But this does not of itself invalidate them or establish their incompatibility with Buddhist teaching.

While Buddhism is concerned primarily with transcendence and with enabling men and women to rise beyond suffering, illusion, desire and aversion through the recognition of the ultimate emptiness of all phenomenal appearances, it does not deny the relative order and consistency of the world of phenomena or the possibility of modifying and affecting it, with due caution, through understanding and co-operating with its governing laws and forces. Such, indeed, is what all men do on one level of reality by studying nature, growing crops, building houses, and practising arts and crafts and sciences. Such, on another less commonly experienced level of reality, is what Tibetans attempt to do in co-operating with and placating nature-spirits and local deities, and in seeking the advice and assistance of other divinities in the furtherance of their activities and enterprises. All these operations, in the world of psychical phenomena as in the world of physical phenomena, may be carried out either in awareness of their relative and ultimately illusory nature and with regard to their moral consequences, and therefore in compatibility with the teachings of Buddhism, or without that awareness and regard.

In Tibet, both men and women might act as oracular mediums, although the majority of them were men. Such people were often natural psychics or sensitives who, from an early age, showed themselves to be unusually open to communication with the world of spirits and unseen subtle forces. But it was by no means uncommon for mediumship or the power of prophetic trance to descend quite abruptly in adult life on some person who hitherto had shown no such aptitude, whose interests and activities were relatively mundane and who might be quite reluctant to accept his newly-acquired vocation. In such cases, the prophetic power visited upon the person concerned was regarded as being conferred by the deity, who had thus unexpectedly chosen him as the medium through whom to communicate with the world of men. Most oracular mediums, whether men or women, belonged to the laity and led the normal lives of married householders. The mediums through whom certain important oracular deities manifested, however, were ordained as monks and lived celibate lives. It was also common for lay mediums to abstain from sexual intercourse, meat, tobacco and alcohol before becoming entranced on any important occasion. However, some of the less reputable mediums made use of alcohol in order more easily to enter or simulate states of trance.

The chief and best known of all the oracles of Tibet was the State Oracle who resided at Nechung Gompa, a small monastery and shrine not far from Drepung monastery, one of the four great teaching monasteries of the dominant Gelugpa school of Buddhism in Central Tibet. Nechung Gompa was established during the reign of the fifth Dalai Lama (1617–1681). A number of different traditions exist of how the oracle came to take up residence there. Differences also exist in their identification of the deity manifesting through the oracle. The prevailing view among the Gelugpas is that this deity is *Pe Har*, one of the most important in the hierarchy of supernatural beings in the realms of conditioned existence. Another important oracle is *Dga-gdon*, a deity who first came into prominence at about the time that Nechung monastery was founded. (We have to remember that according to Buddhism the gods and other deities within the realms of conditioned existence are not eternal beings. For such a state is reserved for only the celestial Buddhas and Bodhisattvas who transcend all relativities and personify timeless and unchanging spiritual principles; gods and other deities, however, are subject to changes of state in accordance with their own previous actions, just as are men and all other beings within the world of becoming. Thus gods arise and again cease to exist, although their lifespan may be immeasurably long judged by the yardstick of human existence.)

To discuss fully all the various accounts of the history of the State Oracle at Nechung would be to generate material sufficient for a long article in itself. Here I will content myself by explaining something of the long association of the deity *Pe Har* with Tibetan Buddhism and the more recent rise to prominence of the Gelugpa protective deity, *Rdo-Rje-Sugs-Ldan*. Although introduced into Tibet earlier, Buddhism was really established securely in that country in the eighth century by Guru Padmasambhava, an Indian Tantric master who was specially invited to Tibet as the only teacher powerful enough to overcome the destructive supernatural forces that were opposing the spread of the new religion. Padmasambhava is known to the Tibetans as the second Buddha and revered by all schools of Tibetan Buddhism; he is especially venerated by the Nyingmapas, the oldest of the four main schools. The first monastery in Tibet was built at Samyé, but its construction met with innumerable setbacks and natural disasters until Guru Padmasambhava's intervention succeeded in subduing the nature spirits and demons who were causing these disturbances. Thereafter, the building of the monastery went forward without further interruption. The uniqueness and favourable qualities of the site received recognition in Padmasambhava's saying: 'There is no other place under the sun that is equal to Samyé.'

Samyé monastery having thus been built, it was necessary to appoint a supernatural guardian or protector who would defend it against any further attack by demonic or human agencies. This protector needed to be of a power and prestige commensurate with the importance of Samyé as the leading national shrine of the newly established religion. Through the power of his meditation, Guru Padmasambhava saw that a suitably awesome and ferocious deity named *Pe Har* was then dwelling as the guardian of a temple in Bhata Hor in Central Asia. As an emissary to persuade *Pe Har* to accept the task of guarding Samyé monastery and particularly its collection of scriptures and other treasures, Padmasambhava sent *Kuvera*, a deity in his service identified by his carrying a red spear. *Kuvera*, however, did not succeed in his mission.

Shortly after this, there was fighting in the Bhata Hor region and the temple where *Pe Har* resided was destroyed. A Tibetan merchant acquired one of the sacred objects from that temple and brought it with him on his return home. *Pe Har* followed this object into Tibet. At this time, Guru Padmasambhava was meditating in a cave. *Pe Har* (then still a destructive pagan deity, hostile to Buddhism, and leader of a band of powerful demons) came to attack him. A white stone fell from the sky above with great force on to the roof of the cave. The cave shook violently, the shrine was thrown into disarray, and Padmasambhava momentarily lost consciousness. Quickly recovering, he saw through his meditational insight that this destructive activity was the work of *Pe Har*. Padmasambhava transformed himself into a terrible scorpion with nine heads, nine pairs of eyes and horns, eight legs and additional eyes all round the body. Flames shot from this magical scorpion, burning *Pe Har* and his companions and threatening to consume them entirely. Screaming for mercy, *Pe Har* surrendered his life into Guru Padmasambhava's hands and offered to do whatever he ordered. When asked what work he could do best, *Pe Har* said in reply the protection of temples and *stupas* (reliquary shrines). Padmasambhava accepted *Pe Har's* submission, swore him to obedience and service to the Buddhist faith, touched his head with a *vajra* (thunderbolt sceptre) and put nectar on his tongue, and appointed him protector of Samyé monastery.

Pe Har said that now he had taken a vow of obedience to Guru Padmasambhava he would not renounce it, but that among his followers were five kinds of particularly dangerous and destructive demons – *bdud, btsan, gsin-rje, ma-mo, klu* – who might do great harm in the future, causing death and immense suffering to people when the Dark Age came. Guru Padmasambhava composed a number of Tantric texts which his consort, Yeshe Tsogyal, wrote down and which give instructions for overcoming these demons and averting the consequences of their evil actions. These texts were placed under the protection of Vairocana, his disciple. They were hidden in various places until the time comes for their rediscovery and use. Some of them were buried at Tokka tashi-ding in Sikkim. When the Dark Age comes and truth and righteousness are threatened with final destruction, Yeshe Tsogyal will again be reborn as an emanation of Guru Padmasambhava and will take the texts from their places of concealment for the benefit of sentient beings and the protection of the Dharma. These events are recorded in chapters 70–108 of the composite biography of Padmasambhava known as *Ma 'Ons Lun Btsan Gsal Ba'i Sgron Me*.

There are divergent traditions among the different schools of Tibetan Buddhism about the subsequent history of *Pe Har*. According to some views, he continued to dwell at Samyé monastery but, having been converted from a destructive demon to a defender of Buddhism and a disciple of Guru Padmasambhava, he developed so much in spiritual understanding and merit that he has attained a high degree of enlightenment and joined the ranks of the celestial Bodhisattvas who have gone beyond the limitations of conditioned existence. But the belief of the Gelugpa school is that when Nechung monastery was built, some nine hundred years or so after the establishment of Samyé monastery, *Pe Har* transferred to the new shrine and functions there as the State Oracle. A number of variants of this Gelugpa belief are mentioned by René de Nebesky-Wojkowitz,[3] several of them suggesting that *Pe Har* (or in one version his chief minister, *Dga gdon*) moved from Samyé to another monastery in Central Tibet on the banks of the Kyichu River. He displeased the monks there and was imprisoned in a box which was thrown into the river. This drifted downstream, and was retrieved from the water by or on the orders of the abbot of Drepung monastery; as soon as the box was opened, the imprisoned spirit flew out in the form of a white dove (or a flame, in another account) and took up habitation in a tree around which the shrine of Nechung was subsequently built. From a Tibetan point of view, there is no necessary inconsistency in believing on the one hand that *Pe Har* took an unbroken vow of obedience to Guru Padmasambhava to be the protector of Samyé monastery and on the other that with the rise to dominance of the Gelugpa sect, he transferred to Nechung and functions there as the State Oracle. For a Tibetan, it is entirely possible and reasonable that a powerful being like *Pe Har* should be able to manifest simultaneously in several different places and function in different ways through multiple forms, appearances or emanations of himself, all at the same time.

Another important oracle and protector of the Gelugpa School is *Rdo-Rje-Sugs-Ldan*, a deity who came to prominence relatively recently. The head lama of the Gelugpas reincarnated successively as the line of abbots of Drepung Loseling monastery, one of whom was called Penchin So-na Tak-pa. *Rdo-Rie-Sugs-Ldan* manifested himself to him and paid homage with the words, 'You are the most enlightened lama and yours are the most superior teachings, so I should like to act as their protector.' Penchin So-na Tak-pa accepted this offer. A subsequent incarnation was Sprul-sku Grags-pa rgyal-mtshan, a contemporary of the great Fifth Dalai Lama, during whose reign the shrine at Nechung was established. Sprul-sku Grags-pa rgyal-mtshan was prominent in both religion and politics. This made him enemies among those whose interests clashed with his policies and actions. Accusations were brought against him and the government made so many difficulties for him that eventually he took his own life, suffocating – or, according to another interpretation, hanging – himself with a white ceremonial scarf. His life having ended in this violent and inauspicious manner, his consciousness joined the ranks of the wrathful demons and he became known as *Rdo-Rje-Sugs-Ldan*. This whole area of Central Tibet was under the control of *Pe Har* and *Rdo-Rje-Sugs-Ldan* could stay there only with his permission. One view, although not favoured by the Gelugpa school, is that *Rdo-Rje-Sugs-Ldan* performed propitiatory rites to *Pe Har*, who by this time had reached a high degree of enlightenment and withdrawal from the things of this world, and obtained his permission to take his place as the chief protector of the Dharma or Buddhist teachings in Central Tibet. Viewed thus, it is *Rdo-Rje-Sugs-Ldan* rather than *Pe Har* himself who functions as the State Oracle at Nechung, which as we have seen was founded at the time that *Rdo-Rje-Sugs-Ldan* first came into prominence. *Rdo-Rje-Sugs-Ldan* is certainly one of the most popular protective deities among the Gelugpas, while receiving little or no recognition among the other schools of Tibetan Buddhism.

A Gelugpa account of the history of *Rdo-Rje-Sugs-Ldan* is given in the collected works of Pha bon Khapa, according to whom the following events succeeded the suicide of Sprul-sku Grags-pa rgyal-mtshan. The remains of the dead abbot were placed inside a *stupa* in his room. One month after his death, cries and screams were heard coming from this room, the walls and ceilings collapsed and the *stupa* fell over. A stream of white water flowed out of the room. Subsequently, many disasters occurred in the surrounding area of Central Tibet, with loss of life and property. The Dalai Lama and his chief monks made many attempts to placate the demonic spirit responsible for these calamities, who was discovered to be *Rdo-Rje-Sugs-Ldan*, but all their efforts failed. So they enlisted the aid of the head of the Sakyapa school of Tibetan Buddhism, Sakya Sonam Rinchen, who performed fire *pujas* (rituals) and succeeded in subduing the angry demon. *Rdo-Rje-Sugs-Ldan* appeared in the form of a monk with several eyes and, declaring himself to Sonam Rinchen, said, 'I am the destructive aspect of the Protector of the Gelugpas'. Having thus been overcome, *Rdo-Rje-Sugs-Ldan* was first made a protector of the main Sakya monastery near the Dor-ja River in Central Tibet (perhaps identical with the Kyichu River mentioned in the *Pe Har* legend). Someone who stole the ritual ornaments of the protective deity from this monastery died shortly afterwards in mysterious circumstances.

In attributing *Rdo-Rje-Sugs-Ldan's* submission to the head of the Sakyapas, Pha bon Khapa is perhaps accommodating history to Gelugpa susceptibilities and prejudices. Of the three older schools of Tibetan Buddhism, the Sakyas are the most congenial to the Gelugpas in doctrine and practice, but the weight of historical evidence strongly indicates that it was in fact the head of the Nyingmapa school who had to be called in to vanquish *Rdo-Rje-Sugs-Ldan*. Considerable research on this subject has been carried out by Dongthog, a Sakyapa lama now living in the U.S.A., and a copy of his findings is available at the British Library in London.

Pha bon K'hapa mentions other dire events that occurred in the period of *Rdo-Rje-Sugs-Ldan's* destructive activity before he was converted into a protector of the Dharma. At Nam-je ta-tsong near Drepung, the shadow of a hand was seen by many people and was followed by the death or sickness of most of those to whom it appeared. Further deaths followed upon the apparition of a monk with the body of a man and the head of a donkey. Some monks and lamas died after being visited by *Rdo-Rje-Sugs-Ldan* in the guise of a sick man seeking medical treatment. At this time, the Fifth Dalai Lama and his secretary, *Rje-drun*, were in meditation at the Potala palace and monastery in Lhasa. The Dalai Lama sent *Rje-drun* on a mission to visit *Rdo-Rje-Sugs-Ldan* in the spirit world and deliver a letter to him. He conferred upon the secretary two supernatural gifts: the power of psychic vision to see demons, ghosts and spirits, and a magic hat which made the wearer invisible. After a daunting journey through the spirit world, Rje-drun reached the awesome and forbidding palace of *Rdo-Rje-Sugs-Ldan*. His way was barred by two powerful Indian demons who refused him entry, but donning his magic hat he slipped past them unseen.

Passing through the palace, he came upon a room containing a throne upon which sat the imposing figure of a monk wearing three ceremonial robes. This was the human form of the abbot of Drepung who had taken his own life and become possessed by the demonic spirit of *Rdo-Rje-Sugs-Ldan*. Attendant spirits entered and, paying homage to their king, declared their intention of revenging themselves upon people for earlier wrongs that had been done to them. *Rdo-Rje-Sugs-Ldan* gave them a handful of white mustard seed which, when they threw it towards the earth, fell from the sky in the form of huge hailstones which completely destroyed the harvest. Taking off his hat, Rje-drun revealed his presence and handed over to *Rdo-Rje-Sugs-Ldan* the letter from the Dalai Lama. In graceful and conciliatory terms, this letter requested *Rdo-Rje-Sugs-Ldan* to be reconciled to the Gelugpa school and to become the divine protector of its teachings. Appeased, *Rdo-Rie-Sugs-Ldan* accepted this invitation and took up residence in a new temple built by the Fifth Dalai Lama near the Dorja River.

The visions and prophecies of the state oracle at Nechung have played an important part in Tibetan history, for example in the location and identification of the various incarnations of the Dalai Lama. There was controversy at the beginning of the eighteenth century over the choice of the Seventh Dalai Lama, partly provoked by Chinese interference, and the candidate eventually chosen was the one recognised by the Nechung oracle as the true incarnation. The Fifth, Seventh and Thirteenth incarnations are regarded as among the greatest Dalai Lamas, and all had strong connections with Nechung; the Fifth because it was during his reign and, according to some accounts, by his orders that Nechung Gompa was built; the Seventh and Thirteenth because of the part played by the oracle in their discovery.

After the death of the Twelfth Dalai Lama (1875), the Nechung oracle saluted several times towards the south-east, threw a scarf in that direction, and prophesied that the new incarnation would be found in that quarter of the country, near a river and a mountain shaped like an umbrella. The Thirteenth Dalai Lama was subsequently discovered in a village corresponding to the oracle's description, in the Pags-pa region of Lower Dakpo in East Tibet. There were many accompanying signs to indicate that this was indeed the Dalai Lama. Before that, the Nechung oracle had been consulted by the Regent and the chief lamas of Drepung monastery, and had said to them: 'Oh, little lamas and government officials! The incarnation of the Merit-Seeing Heavenly Teacher has been born in the east to a man named Kunga and a woman called Sgrolma. A worthy lama should be sent in search of him, and I will surely help you.' Afterwards he added: 'Lobsang Dargye, the former abbot of Ryud-sto monastery, should be sent to the holy lake and there he will certainly see a vision.' The lake referred to was the one near Lhasa sacred to the goddess *Palden Lhamo*. Lama Lobsang and his companions went to the holy lake and, although the weather was wintry, found it almost free from ice and as clear as a polished mirror. Pictures formed of a valley running east and west, with cultivated fields on the higher ground, and containing a village with a square compound, lying between an old monument and an imposing old house of several storeys.

These and other details corresponded with the locality of the village where the new Dalai Lama was afterwards found, and were recognised by Lobsang Dargye when he went there. The parents of the child were a young nobleman called Kunga-Rinchen and his wife Lobsang Sgrolma, who was of the family of Gampopa, the chief disciple of the great eleventh-century yogi, Milarepa. When the Nechung oracle heard the names of the parents of the supposed incarnation, he shouted in joy and saluted towards the south-east. Seers, astrologers and other diviners also identified the child as the Dalai Lama, and there were many signs and portents which confirmed this, including the usual test of recognition by the child of personal articles which had belonged to the previous Dalai Lama.

When the Thirteenth Dalai Lama reached the age of twenty, the second of the two Regents who had led the Government during the period of his minority wished to retire. The Nechung oracle was consulted about the wisdom of the young Dalai Lama's taking over the reins of office at this critical time (the treaty between Britain and Tibet following fighting on the borders of Sikkim had not yet been finally concluded). The words of the oracle were: 'Hri! Homage to Guru Padmasambhava who is the embodiment of all the countless Buddhas. Ever obedient to the commands of my teacher, I know that the lamas of the three monasteries under my care and the people of Tibet wish to know about the time for the inauguration of the Dalai Lama's reign. I and all the other gods agree that this is the proper moment. You should all request him to take charge of the government, and offer him the scarf which I am giving you. Hurrah! Hurrah!'

This advice accorded with the sentiments of the people and the views of the Emperor of China, and was put into effect. A year or two later the Nechung oracle gave warning advice in two separate prophecies which the Dalai Lama was careful to carry out exactly. The first of these was: 'Hri! This month you should go into retreat for meditation, to ensure the success of which the lamas should perform many religious rites. Next year in the first month you will be invited to the yearly assembly by the Khang-gsar Lama. There is danger of your meeting with an accident at that time, or you may fall sick owing to being in such a large gathering of people. You and the lamas should perform religious cere-monies six times a day. I will protect you.'

The second pronouncement of the oracle was: 'Hri! Homage to the wish-fulfilling tree of the Lord Buddha protected by the three precepts! You should repeat 100,000 times the mantra of Guru Padmasambhava. The sacrifices

for peace and prosperity should be performed, the whole of
the Kangyur (Buddhist scriptures) and Tangyur (commentaries on them) should be recited, and the life story of Guru
Padmasambhava should be read daily during the yearly
assembly. You should also perform a sacrifice to me. My
service to you is ever unfaltering and untiring. Today I offer
you this scarf.'

Lama Thubten Jampa Tsultrim Tenzin in his biography
of the Thirteenth Dalai Lama entitled *The Precious Rosary of
Jewels* (*No-tsha Rinpoche Phreng-wa*) describes how attempts
were made on the life of the Dalai Lama by black magic in
his twenty-fifth year. He refers to the part played by the State
Oracle in defeating them in the colourful words: 'to the
causes of all evil things the Nechung oracle was like a finger-
nail put on a louse.' He also quotes some relevant prophecies
by the oracle including the following: 'The scarves of the
fabulous Queen of Khongtse are of different colours. The
white, black and spotted threads are tied with twenty-one
knots. The life of my teacher is in danger. Are you lamas
not anxious? My friend *Shing bya chan* (*Pe Har's* minister of
the southern quarter) has warned you. My heart is heavy
and anxious. Now it has been made clear, you lamas should
consider it very carefully. I have many powers of wrathful-
ness and retribution, and these powers may take many forms.
But the part of you merciful lamas is to display kindness and
compassion. It is right to approach the matter with equanimity and without foreboding. We shall succeed in our
purpose, and you should perform rites for the life of my
teacher and for the safety of the monastery. But there is no
rite greater than the studying of profound texts. I, the form-
less one, will overcome heresy now and forever. You should
keep my words in your hearts.'

When his enemies were discovered, the Dalai Lama treated
them with great mercy and received these words of praise
from the State Oracle: 'Hri! This time my teacher has been
preserved from misfortune, with the help of the gods and the
Buddha. The evil-doers who resemble poisonous fruits of
beautiful colours have been treated with great compassion
by my teacher. This is the way of the Bodhisattva. I salute
thee for thy greatness.' When, some twenty-four years later,
the Dalai Lama was approaching death, an owl perched on

the roof of Nechung Gompa on two consecutive nights and hooted in a strange manner. Asked about this, the Dalai Lama himself said: 'You should understand the ill-omened sound of the owl to be a sign indicating that the time has now come.'

Finally, on a lighter note, we may recall the well-known story of the oracular medium of whose powers the authorities in Lhasa wished to test the authenticity. They sent him the following message, with a request that clear guidance should be given on it. 'A servant born under the sign of the sheep, is at his last gasp. What can be done about it?' To this, the oracle gave the answer: 'If possible, get new ones. Otherwise, have them repaired and they will last for some years yet.' This irrelevant-seeming reply proved to be entirely appropriate: the question referred to a pair of sheepskin bellows which were kept in the fireplace of a government office and had become torn.

Notes

1 Volume 123, Folio 221 (Narthang edition).
2 *T'oung Pao* XV (1914), pp. 1–110.
3 René de Nebesky-Wojkowitz, *Oracles and Demons of Tibet*.

2

China

MICHAEL LOEWE
Lecturer in Chinese Studies, University of Cambridge

INTRODUCTORY REMARKS

Of the many methods which have been used in China to practise divination or to consult oracles, three stand out conspicuously with especial significance. These are the roasting of animals' bones or turtles' shells and the induction of cracks upon their surfaces; the cast of the stalks of the yarrow plant as a means of forming linear patterns or hexagrams; and the recognition of inherent properties in the land with a view to determining its propensities for good or evil.

Of all the methods that have been practised in China these have been of the longest duration and the most widespread adoption. In exercising a profound influence on the growth of Chinese civilization they have formed a meeting place for religion, philosophy and science. For they were practised as a means of communication with sacred powers, by methods that lie beyond the normal perception of the human senses; they were seen as a manifestation of eternal, universal truths that transcend the ephemeral attainments or mundane purposes of the human intellect; and they were believed to demonstrate and explain the regular cycles of birth, decay and rebirth in the created world of nature.

A distinction may be drawn in Chinese thought and practice between divination, oracles and omens. Divination comprised a deliberate search by man for the answers to questions and included the artificial production of signs for the purpose. Oracles included questions that were put to signs already inherent in nature and recognisable to those gifted with certain faculties; but there is nothing in Chinese practice which may be compared directly with the Delphic Oracle, or the Sybill of Cumae. Omens are seen in the phenomena or portents of nature that are obvious to all, and that are of sufficient size and strength to demand explanation (e.g. eclipses).

These distinctions are broad, and must allow for the inclusion of intermediate methods and processes that lie, as it were, along a spectrum, bounded by divination at one end and omens at the other. The treatment of omens, or portents, forms a major element in the Chinese tradition, which will not be considered here. Moreover, it would be unwise in practice to insist on a rigid distinction between the terms 'divination' and 'oracles'; for the expression 'oracle bones' is used to denote objects which derived from divination; but it has too long a history behind it in Sinological writings to be discarded.

Divination, with which the greater part of this chapter will be concerned, may be regarded as an attempt to ascertain truth on a level other than that of verifiable analysis or quantifiable proof, and by means other than those which depend on reason. The process is possible thanks to the personal powers of an initiate to form a contact with eternal verities, by means, and towards ends, which he may or may not be able to control. Such is divination in its pure form and we shall quickly see that other considerations soon entered in, so far as China is concerned.

Consultation of oracles is seen in the observation of natural phenomena, be they of heaven or of earth, and the apprehension therein of signs that point towards the future. It was believed that the normal and smooth processes of natural change could comprehend signs of either the well-being or of the impending dangers that beset mankind. These signs could be recognised, for example, in the strength or direction of regular natural features such as winds or clouds, whose movements were thought to follow a pattern. As that pattern informed the whole fabric of the universe, recognition of its movements in one particular element or part of the cosmos could indicate just how the same pattern was affecting, or would affect, movements and activities elsewhere. Geomancy and some of its antecedents, as will be described below, depended on just such an understanding of nature.

Omens, or portents, derived from the abnormal, irregular or violent occurrences of nature, which were believed to indicate a rupture of the normal regular patterns. So far from conforming with those patterns, these events could be recognised as signs of cosmic upset which would reverberate in the different parts of the universe. This type of omen is exemplified in the appearance and course of comets, earth-quakes, the unexplained sound of voices, or the spontaneous uprooting of rocks and stones and trees.

At first sight, the interpretations of omens and some oracles may appear to be arbitrary. But on closer inspection it is seen that they often followed a systematic view of nature that depended on the theory of the Five Phases, or Elements.[1] Some interpreters of these events sought to identify move-ments in heaven or on earth as the direct analogues of similar movements in the realm of mankind. Frequently, in the records that we possess, they were construed with a direct bearing on dynastic or political fortunes.

There are two aspects of divination and oracles in China that appear to be contradictory but which are in fact complementary. The first depends on intuition or instinct and stands outside the sphere of rational activities; the second stems from the exercise of the human intellect. In considering the three main types of mantic practice below, we shall observe that there was a general tendency for spontaneous and intuitive divination to be overtaken by processes of regularisation or standardisation, or by intellec-tual advances. Thus, the creation of patterns on bones and shells came to follow a prescribed and regulated course. The interpretation of the patterns formed by the cast of the stalks became imbued with scientific explanations of the universe. Geomancy came to be practised in accordance with guide-lines laid down in handbooks, and with the use of a highly sophisticated type of magnetic compass. But despite these developments, time and again leading Chinese thinkers have reverted to the eternal and essential part played by intuition in these forms of divination, and stressed the failure of trying to understand the cosmos on rational grounds alone. Divination certainly stands in opposition, along a spectrum, to scientific measurement, experiment and verification; but in Chinese practice there is a wide middle ground wherein the two types of activity merge and affect one another.

A second characteristic of divination in China may be discerned in the importance placed on linear patterns, be they deliberately created on bones or through the medium of the stalks, or be they recognised as naturally informing earth, sky or cloud. This aspect of the subject has been of considerable significance in moulding Chinese thought, in fashioning the shape of Chinese cities and in imprinting certain features on the Chinese landscapes.

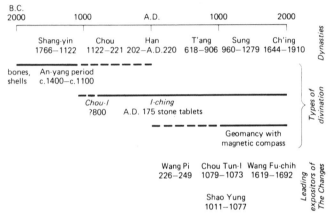

Figure 1. Chinese methods of divination; sequences in time.

The chronological sequence and time-scale of the three processes to be discussed are of some importance in placing divination and oracles in the context of Chinese cultural growth. The earliest of the three methods is the use of bones or shells, which may have started shortly after 3500 BC; it was practised as a regular observance in the palace of the Shang kings by *c*. 1400 BC. Probably this remained in fashion as the principal type of divination for some centuries, at least until *c*. 1000 BC. Thereafter it survived in a more restricted way and in company with a number of other methods. Perhaps from *c*. 1000 BC some Chinese were casting stalks, or using other unknown means, to devise the pattern of six parallel lines, or hexagrams, which have formed a characteristic feature of divination ever since, with constant intellectual and literary enrichment. Geomancy, in the form that we know today, may be traced back to about AD 1000, on the basis of antecedents known just before the Christian era.

At the time when the use of bones and shells took pride of place, a millennium or so had yet to elapse before the first appearance of named teachers and philosophers or the transmission of their doctrines in writing. In its formative stages this type of divination was thus not subject to those intellectual influences that can be traced in surviving literature, to the systematic theorising of philosophy or the accepted dogmas of scripture. That it became subject to standardisation may be seen in the use of verbal formulae and in the use of the material in as economical a way as possible. Texts such as the *Chou li* or *I li*, which were finalised after the Christian era, prescribe in minute detail the correct and standardised procedures for the ceremonies that accompanied their use.[2]

By way of contrast, comparatively soon after its inception, the use of yarrow stalks was being accompanied by the earliest known developments of Chinese philosophy and science and the first formulations of literary texts. Very soon the process gave rise to writings, some of which were later to be treated as scriptural; and throughout the historical period the method has given rise to new departures in Chinese thought with which it has become inextricably entwined.

Geomancy, with the use of the magnetic compass, is the youngest of the three methods to be considered here. The intellectual background against which its antecedents arose is that of the century or so before the start of the Christian era. This period witnessed the formulation of several schemes that explained the universe as a whole, with a place reserved therein for the exercise of imperial sovereignty. It also saw the compilation of a number of works on scientific subjects such as astronomy and medicine. The characteristic form of geomancy, which is current today, dates from one of China's most brilliant periods of cultural innovation, of the Sung Dynasties (960–1279). Since then it has been linked almost continuously with sophisticated theories of cosmology and science.

THE USE OF BONES AND SHELLS
(SCAPULIMANCY, PLASTROMANCY)

Since the beginning of this century, the learned world has
known of the existence of animals' bones and turtles' shells
that were deliberately used for divination and inscribed as
part of the process. The majority of the 100,000 pieces now
known derive from sites dated in *c*. 1400 BC, in China's
bronze age; some were found in sites of the neolithic periods;
and some come from sites of the Chou period (traditionally
1122–256 BC). The procedure involved the use of a heated
poker or some other instrument to drill, pierce or at least
weaken the bone or shell, so that when this was in its turn
applied to fire random cracks would be induced to appear
upon the surface. According to the frequency or shape
of the cracks, or perhaps some features of which we are now
ignorant, so depended the answers to questions which
were specifically defined by the diviner; very often this was
the king himself.

It is likely, and even probable, that in the first instance
animals' bones (e.g. ox, deer, pig, sheep or horse) were used
for the process; in one case at least part of a human skull
was used. As the shoulder blades of the animals were often
chosen for the process, this type of divination has been
termed scapulimancy. It was probably at a later stage that
shells of turtles, of which the majority of the material
evidence consists, were adopted in place of animals' bones;
divination of this type is sometimes termed plastromancy.

It is possible that divination with bones derived from
sacrificial rites. It has been suggested that the remains of
burnt offerings were inspected by the officiants; that the
type of cracks formed thereon was taken as an indication of
the acceptance or refusal of the oblation; and that from such
beginnings there followed the ritual practice of deliberately
inducing cracks on bones, for the specific purpose of putting
questions to this fount of wisdom.

Whatever speculation there may be regarding the origins
of the process, we possess far more certain information
regarding the practice itself. For the custom arose of inscrib-
ing texts on the bones and shells of three different types.
There was a record of the question, or 'charge'[3] that was

formulated; the prognostication, or answer, that had been reached by specialist interpreters was noted; and sometimes a record of the factual outcome was appended. The inscriptions vary in length, from a single character to several hundred characters. They were engraved on the material and subsequently coloured with black or red pigments. The precise method used to effect these extremely difficult tasks, of inducing the cracks and engraving the characters, has yet to be ascertained; it has defied a number of techniques of the twentieth century (see Plates 2, 3).

These inscriptions may well follow an earlier practice of painting a record on materials that were perishable. Owing to the durability of the bones and shells it has been possible to gain a radically new insight into the prehistory and early history of China, and to learn at first hand something of the procedures used and the questions put. Inscriptions engraved on over 40,000 pieces and now available in published form date from approximately 1400 to 1100 BC.[4] Many of the charges were concerned with the suitability of particular times for making sacrifice. Some concerned the prospects for the harvest, or the likelihood of rain or winds. Other enquiries fastened on the fortunes likely to attend the king or members of the royal house in the immediately ensuing period of ten days; or it might be asked whether projects for a hunting expedition, a military foray, or the establishment of a settlement were likely to meet with a successful outcome.

Specialists of various types with a number of different duties took part in the procedure, and the inscriptions yield the names of at least 130 men who acted as diviners, interpreters or other officiants. Sometimes the process of divination was repeated in respect of the same question, even up to ten times; very often the charge was framed as two statements, one positive and one negative, each awaiting the sign from the cracks (e.g. see Plate 2). Whether this type of repetition was intended to test the proficiency of the diviner, or to secure a majority verdict, or whether for other reasons, must remain open to question.

The technical terms that appear in the inscriptions as well as in much later literature testify to the ritualist nature of the procedures. These may have comprised several stages, such as the dedication of the bones or shells for the purpose, their purification of evil influences, and the formulation of the charge.

By the beginning of the Christian era, the Chinese – if one may risk a generalisation – had become well set in the habits of establishing regular forms and of standardising procedures and hierarchies for religious, social and political undertakings. This process had been developing for a number of centuries, at a time when other methods of divination had been coming into fashion. Scapulimancy and plastromancy continued to be practised, to an extent that cannot be determined. But of greater interest and significance than such an estimate is the evidence of literary and historical records of *c.* 100 BC and the ensuing century, and the light that they shed on the practice at that time.

Precise instructions, almost in the form of a manual, existed to determine the interpretation of the cracks[5]; detailed procedures, forms and rituals were prescribed for occasions of state when the imperial court required guidance from the bones or shells. Our texts include the formal invocation, which was solemnly recited by the officiant on these occasions, and which may be rendered somewhat loosely as follows: 'Commit unto us thy eternal truth, oh mighty turtle, that we, by thy power, may be guided in our choice . . .'[6]. The type of choice which is envisaged may have concerned the dates for undertakings such as a wedding or a funeral. Other questions that are mentioned include those of the correct circumstances for the succession of an heir to the throne, or the appropriate motives for building a city.

It may be asked for what reasons did the scholars, priests or philosophers of Han China ascribe to the turtle shell the power of revealing the true answers to these and other problems. Any answer that we may suggest must be regarded as a deliberate and anachronistic archaism by Chinese diviners of perhaps the first century BC, who were anxious to rationalise a practice that had been long hallowed in Chinese religion. Possibly the turtle may have been seen as a model of the cosmos, in the way that this was conceived in contemporary thought. For its shape comprised a square base below, surmounted by a dome, in the same way as the square earth was surmounted by the circular heavens.[7]

Sometimes the turtle was regarded as a means of prolonging life or achieving deathlessness.[8] But above all the virtue of the turtle may have been thought to reside in its longevity. It was known to be the longest lived of the creatures of the earth, and its age was sometimes quoted, in terms of Chinese hyperbole, at 3000 years.[9] For the instrument of divination must transcend the ephemeral vehicles of human life, and man must search for truth in bodies that appear to be permanent, such as the stars in their courses in the sky, or the turtle in his aeons of life upon the earth.

THE USE OF YARROW STALKS AND THE *BOOK OF CHANGES*

The second principal method of divination practised in China was destined to undergo considerable complication in its long continuous history, which has lasted until the present time. The practice became inextricably linked with one of China's scriptural texts, and it gave rise to a series of symbols that were to play a highly significant role in Chinese philosophy. It may be added that recent decades have shown how divination by stalks and the *Book of Changes* may appeal to the imagination and religious urges of the west, thanks largely to the pioneer lead of Richard Wilhelm and Carl Jung.[10]

The origin of the process and its earliest methods will probably never be known. It may perhaps have been believed that answers to questions could be brought forth from occult powers in the form of lines; that a single unbroken line signified a positive answer, and that a single broken line was negative. There can be no certainty how such lines were first imagined, seen or formed. But by *c.* 1000 BC, the process probably consisted in the evolution or the formation of a pattern of six lines, either whole or broken, and lying horizontally on top of each other. The total number of possible combinations, or hexagrams, is 64.

By the start of the Christian era at least the hexagrams were being fabricated with the use of the stalks of a particular plant. This was the yarrow plant, thought to possess magical and superhuman qualities in view of its longevity, the large number of stalks which sprang from a single root, and the great length of the stalks.[11] Owing to the second of these qualities the plant is sometimes described as 'milfoil'.

The complex procedure for divining with the use of stalks may be summarised, by way of simplification, as follows.[12] Beginning with a total of 50 stalks, the operator immediately discards one. The remaining 49 stalks are divided into two groups, at random; and each group is then further reduced, by removing four stalks at a time, successively. In accordance with the number of stalks that finally remain i.e. 0, 1, 2 or 3, the diviner is then entitled to form a line, usually in written form, of one of four types. In external appearance the line will be either whole (—) or broken (— —). But a further refinement, which leads to a further distinction, depends on an invisible quality, inherent in the mathematical property of the remainder. The line is regarded either as having been brought to completion, or as moving (or growing) towards completion. The four types of line are therefore:

Whole	Broken
(a) Fully mature	(c) Fully mature
(b) Moving towards maturity	(d) Moving towards maturity

When this process has been performed six times, the operator has been able to form a hexagram. However, if the hexagram includes one or more lines whose inherent value is 'moving', he must then form a second hexagram. Here, those of the lines that were previously determined as mature remain static; but the 'moving' lines are changed, a whole line becoming broken, and a broken line becoming whole. The significance of the transformation of one hexagram into another will be apparent below.

The hexagrams, then, were evolved deliberately for the purpose of divination. From the pattern of the lines, a specialist interpreter would surmise an answer to the question posed. It may be conjectured that, at the outset, such questions were of much the same type as those which were put to the cracks induced on bones and shells. But consultation of the stalks was probably not confined to the king or those who were acting directly on his behalf. Moreover, the questions could now concern not only straight issues requiring a positive or a negative answer, such as the prospects of rain, but also matters of choice or probability. For example, in 656 BC the stalks were consulted regarding the likely outcome of a marriage; in 535 BC the question which was raised concerned the selection of one of several sons to be an heir.[13]

Divination with the use of milfoil stalks started as an intuitive process which depended on the insight of a seer. But before long the human intellect began to play a role, as complex concepts arose and an urge towards standardisation accompanied the growth of philosophical implications. Perhaps from about 800 BC names were selected to identify the hexagrams, often in the form of material objects such as 'the cauldron' or 'the well', which would serve as mnemonics. Perhaps at the same time terse esoteric notes were committed to writing, in order to explain the significance of each hexagram, and to provide guidance for its interpretation. The earliest parts of the *Book of Changes*, which are entitled the *t'uan* and the *yao* and collectively known as the *Changes of Chou*, may well derive from such initial attempts or their descendants; for it cannot be told how far our present text corresponds with that of an original version.[14]

The language and terms of these early parts of the *Book of Changes* are technical; by the beginning of the Christian era they had become obsolete and their original meaning had probably been forgotten. We may presume that they had first been written down at the instance of certain masters of divination who were anxious to perpetuate their skills or, alternatively, at the request of apprentices who wished for an authorised doctrine which they could consult in times of perplexity. Whatever the origin may be, these early texts are phrased as formulae; the modern versions in translation may well bear little relation to the meaning of the original.[15]

Complexities shortly entered into divination by the yarrow stalks and the help of these texts, owing to scriptural, cosmological and metaphysical considerations. Already, by *c.* 600 BC, the texts of the *Changes of Chou* were being cited in their own right as an authoritative source of wisdom, regardless of whether or not a process of casting the stalks had actually taken place. In 136 BC imperial authorities arranged for this work, among others, to become the subject of special study, sponsored by the government. The process had started which was to lead to the inclusion of the book in the canon of scriptures, which were deemed to bear unquestioned authority.

However, the perplexities that the text occasioned had already given rise to the compilation of a number of supplementary or ancillary texts. These attempted to explain the original *t'uan* and *yao* in the light of contemporary thought, removed as this was by centuries from the time when the texts were themselves evolved. These ancillary texts, which came to be known as the *Ten Wings*, were destined in their turn to be coupled with the original *Changes of Chou* and likewise to attract the reverence due to scripture.

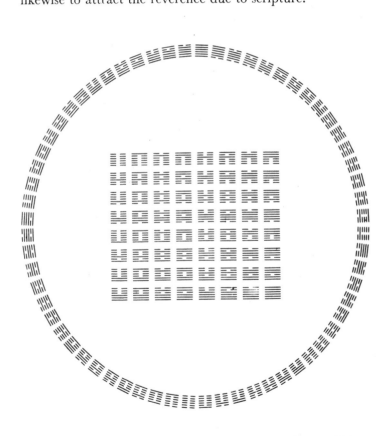

Figure 2. The sixty-four hexagrams, arrayed in two forms, which together symbolise the circular heavens and the square earth.

It has been observed that the process of casting the stalks could sometimes result in the production of two hexagrams, of which the second followed as the natural and inevitable consequence of the first. Behind this operation lay some profound principles of philosophy and natural science. It was probably believed that the only feature of the universe that could be regarded as constant was the fact of change, which perpetually underlies the workings of the heavenly, earthly and human realms. It was also believed that there was a direct interaction between those three worlds, such that the events and changes of any one corresponded with comparable changes in the other two. The 64 hexagrams, that were produced by the cast of the stalks, were conceived as symbols of the successive stages in the ever moving cycle of universal change. The throw that resulted in the production of any one hexagram, with or without its movement into the next, should not be regarded as a matter of chance; it took shape as an inherent and inescapable element of a particular moment of time, or of a particular occasion in the cycle. If it were to be interpreted correctly, that hexagram could reveal the major truths of the situation then prevailing in the cosmos; and if it carried with it a forward movement to the next hexagram, it could point directly to the situation that would inescapably follow.

By this means the cast of the stalks could be used as a means of ascertaining the major truths of the universe; and once those truths had been revealed, it would be possible to pose a particular question for an answer, that would be suitable first for the particular moment of cyclical change that had been identified, and, secondly, for its successor. A notable advance had occurred from the provision of a simple 'yes' or 'no' answer by means of divination, to a search for an answer that depended on the whole nature of cosmic being.

The 64 hexagrams, then, were being regarded as symbols in the stages of universal change; but difficulties soon arose. Long before the first century BC Chinese scientists had been accustomed to the observation of other rhythms and cycles in the world of nature, which could be measured in units of 5, 10, 12, 365 and 1/4, and 28.[16] Considerable intellectual effort was directed to reconciling these observed cycles of nature with the 64, enshrined by now in Holy Scripture. This same motive, of evolving a universal system within which all the different cycles could be comprehended, will recur below, in the consideration of some aspects of geomancy.

By the second century AD at least the *Changes of Chou* had become inextricably linked with their ancillary texts, and known collectively as the *I ching*, or *Book of Changes*. The book was no longer a simple, if esoteric, set of guidelines and explanations of the hexagrams and their individual lines; it now included amplifications that treated of philosophical principles. A more sophisticated stage was reached in the third century, when a brilliant young philosopher named Wang Pi (226–249) introduced a metaphysical element. He saw the hexagrams as a guide to that form of order (*li*; sometimes translated as 'reason') which determined the balance and relationship between the two states of being and non-being. By the eleventh century, when metaphysics was being taken to a much deeper level than previously, some of the Sung philosophers, such as Shao Yung (1011–1077), were fastening on the 64 hexagrams as the symbols of a fundamental binary system of being, which has been compared with the conclusions reached later by Leibniz. Other Sung philosophers, such as Chou Tun-i (1017–1073) saw the hexagrams as symbols in the process of material creation. This started from the unity of the Supreme Ultimate (*T'ai*

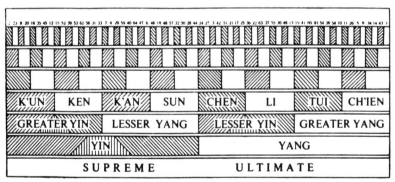

Numbers at top are those of Sixty-four Hexagrams
Names in middle are those of Eight Trigrams

Figure 3. The Supreme Ultimate and the sixty-four hexagrams; diagram of cosmic evolution (From Fung Yu-lan, *A History of Chinese philosophy*, volume II, translated by Derk Bodde, Princeton, 1953, p. 459).

chi), and proceeded by way of the interplay of the two forces of Yin and Yang to the construction of diversity from unity, and the creation of all matter in its requisite proportions; the 64 hexagrams marked the stages of the process.

However, the philosophers of the Sung age were by no means restricted to a view of the universe that was based solely on rational or theoretical considerations. If they saw the hexagrams as symbols that revealed the creation of multiplicity from unity, or of the regular interchange of two primal forces so as to create matter, they also saw the hexagrams as a vehicle for revealing truth intuitively. For they believed that some truths could only be sought by means of the random cast of the stalks and the evolution of the all informing hexagram; this was achieved by means that were anything but systematic or responsive to reason.

By way of summary it may be said that consultation of the yarrow stalks and their associated texts had moved a long way in two thousand years. Divination on the basis of a single full or broken line had changed to the deliberate formation of a pattern of six lines, by somewhat complex methods. Direct and intuitive recognition of the meaning inherent in a hexagram had moved to the need to ascertain its significance from sacred and authoritative writings. Those writings had themselves been extended from being un-explained formulae, to become a series of expository texts. The hexagrams, so far from being named as material objects whose shape could be recognised, had become symbols of the process of creation. Questions conceived in simple terms regarding, for example, the choice of a day for embarking on a marriage, had yielded place to attempts to ascertain the point reached in the major cycle of the cosmos and the appropriate nature of certain actions within that context.

GEOMANCY (*FENG-SHUI*)

Geomancy varies from the two methods of divination described hitherto in two major respects. It is concerned with patterns which already inform the works of nature, and not with those deliberately created by human manipulation; it should therefore be classified as a form of oracle, rather than

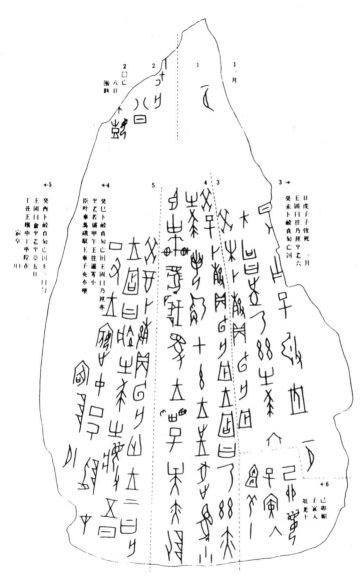

3. Animal's bone, used in divination during the Shang Dynasty; 27.3 cm long. This is one of the more complete and larger examples known, with a comparatively long set of inscriptions. These concern the fortunes of the forthcoming period of ten days, and the subjects in question include: a raid by external enemies (no. 2); the death of the king's son (no. 3); an accident encountered in hunting (no. 4); the connection between a disaster and a dream (no. 5); the use of non-Chinese persons for human sacrifice (no. 6). Reproduced from *Shodō zenshū* volume 1, Plate 2, by courtesy of Heibonsha.

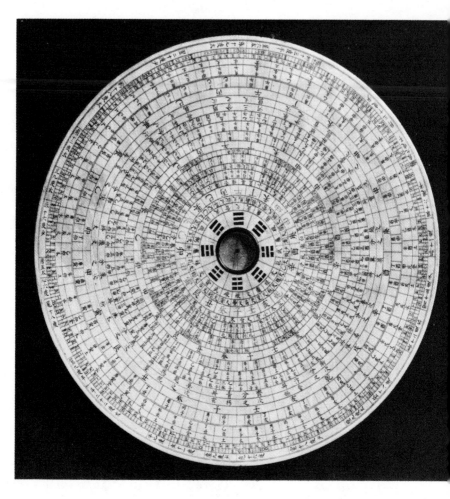

4. Geomantic compass from China, probably eighteenth century; diameter 12 inches. Brought from China by Captain W. Hanwell, R.N., in 1821, and presented to the Cambridge Antiquarian Society in 1822; in the present collection of the Whipple Museum of the History of Science, Cambridge, and reproduced by courtesy of the History and Philosophy of Science Syndicate, Cambridge.

divination, if we follow the distinction that is suggested
above. Secondly, whereas the bones or shells, or the stalks
of the milfoil, could be consulted for a whole variety of
purposes, geomancy was the correct way of answering
particular problems of a specific type. Practised as it is today,
with the help of the magnetic compass, it is the youngest of
the three methods under consideration to reach maturity.

Geomancy is concerned with the selection of particular
sites of land whose inherent qualities are such that they will
be favourable for a defined purpose. That purpose may
range from the establishment of a city, or the erection of a
dwelling house, to the burial of a close relative. Choice of a
favourable site depends on a dual approach, of a type with
which we are already familiar; intuitive and intellectual
elements complement one another.

The intuitive approach is seen in the manner whereby a
master of *feng-shui* comprehends and assesses the properties
of a site that has been suggested for the purpose in mind.
These qualities do not lie open for all to recognise. For while
all men may observe the incidence of hill or river, or the
undulation of the land and its potential consequences, only
the master will be aware of the underlying patterns or
configurations which can exercise a decisive power over the
site and its fortunes. The specialist who is capable of compre-
hending the existence of these qualities may explain them to
others, who do not command his skills, in terms of the
physical features of the land; but the reality with which he
is in contact is of a different order of being.

These inbuilt configurations of the land have sometimes
been associated in the Chinese mind with the concept of the
unseen 'veins of the earth'. Just as the human body includes
veins and arteries as channels that convey a life-giving force,
so too was it conceived that the earth embraced similar lines.
Unlike blood, the life-bringing energy (*ch'i*) of the earth is
not usually to be perceived by the senses; it was thought to
move with greatest ease along winding paths to reach its
destination. A contrary type of force, named *sha*, is destructive and can imperil life; this force can best speed along its
way if its target lies at the end of a straight line. The master
of *feng-shui* can assess, intuitively, how far a site lies open to
such dangers, or in what ways its features are conducive to

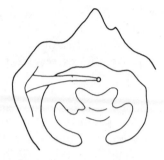

a. Mountain, fed with *ch'i* from side.

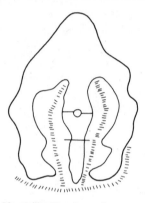

b. Mountain, with extreme tip exposed

to hazard.

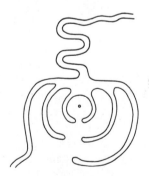

c. Site fed by multiple watercourses.

Figure 4. Typical patterns of geomancy, after Stephan D. R. Feuchtwang, *An Anthropological Analysis of Chinese Geomancy*, Vientiane, 1974, pp. 122, 123, 131; by courtesy of Dr Feuchtwang.

the receipt of *ch'i*. In practice it often occurs that favourable sites are protected by hills so placed that they screen them from baleful forces; and they lie open to the receipt of beneficent influences along flat ground that has no impediment.

Even in this respect, however, an intuitive process became subject to the Chinese love of formalisation and standardisation. The features of the terrain upon which the geomancer would fasten in his explanations were classified in intellectual

Figure 5. Configurations of the earth, from a recent textbook on *feng-shui* (*Ti-li t'ien-chi hui-yüan*, reprinted Taipei, 1970, p. 30).

terms. Sometimes they were described in terms of the symbols of the Five Phases (or Elements), notably the Dragon and the Tiger. In addition, just as texts were produced to assist those who were practising divination with the yarrow stalks, so too a large number of manuals have been published for use in geomancy. These books include diagrams of typical sites; the terrestrial features are classified and described, and their appropriate qualities are laid down in cold print. They demonstrate how an intuitive process has at times been transformed into a didactic tradition.

The other approach to geomancy, which depended on the intellect, came to fruition in the eleventh century; but it may be traced to concepts, principles and instruments that had been evolved for at least a thousand years previously. By contrast with the intuitive approach, which comprehends immediately the qualities of a given site, the intellectual approach combined observation and measurement. Here, the geomancer was concerned with identifying the particular stages reached in the known cycles of change in the heavenly, earthly and human worlds, and with relating those stages to a defined site. He was trying to assess whether the combination of those cycles and the chosen region was such that it would be suitable as a place of habitation for the living or one of repose for the dead.

Material evidence for the antecedents of these practices dates from the second century BC. Fragments have been found of what was probably a manual used in the choice of particular dates that were deemed appropriate for certain activities.[17] There is a marked similarity between the treatment of this aspect of divination, i.e. the selection of fortunate moments in time, with some of the geomantic devices that are set to identify fortunate sites in space. It will be seen that the geomancers' compasses of the Sung period and later were concerned with both types of consideration.

In addition there now exist a total of seven examples, either whole or partial, of instruments which may be regarded as the ancestors of the modern geomantic compass. These instruments consisted of two boards, one square and one circular, which fitted together in such a way that their settings would correspond with the position of the sun in the heavens and that of the operator on earth.[18] From such

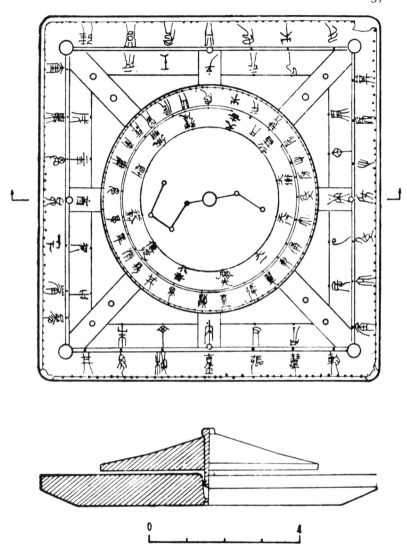

Figure 6. Chinese diviner's board. The circular disc, of heaven, is revolvable in relation to the square disc, of earth. From a tomb in Kansu province, dated not before 8 BC (*Wen wu* 1972 no. 12, p. 15, figure 8).

indications the operator could judge whether a proposed action would be appropriate to the prevailing circumstances of the cosmos, and in what way it would be influenced by the combined rhythms of heaven and earth. The earliest known example of these instruments (*shih*) was found in a tomb which is dated 165 BC. The principles upon which they are thought to provide answers to problems were essentially those which govern the judgements of the modern geomancers' board (see Plate 4).

A number of stages may be traced in the development from these early boards to the evolution of modern devices equipped with a magnetic compass.[19] This refinement was probably first discovered in the eleventh century, at the time when other minds of the Sung age were concerned with problems of metaphysics and the association of the 64 hexagrams with the process of creation. Like their predecessors, the new instruments were intended to display how the coincidence of heavenly, earthly and human cycles would fall upon a given bearing. But the magnetic compass brought a radical change in working methods and in the degree of refinement reached. Once the compass is set, it is possible to read off the positions reached in those cycles along any line or direction that springs from the point of enquiry; and it may then be inferred what influences will be brought to bear upon that point from any direction. It is part of the geomancer's secret to know which directions may safely be excluded from consideration and which ones are dominant.

The dials of these beautiful instruments carry a host of symbols and different series. Universal rhythms are marked out by the eight trigrams, the 64 hexagrams and by the symbols of the Five Phases. There are scientific statements of the rhythms that inform the topographical features of the earth. A second series of circles refers to the chronological circumstances of human birth, as in a horoscope; and a third series denotes the observed and measured rhythms of the heavenly bodies in their orbits. The compass tells the operator which stages are reached in these various cycles along each bearing from the point whereon he stands. In doing so, it shows at which points those cycles can be reconciled or harmonised, as integral parts of the macrocosm. The instrument also illustrates a metaphysical and cosmological process; it shows how the unity of the Supreme Ultimate, symbolised in the Pool of Heaven at the centre, eventually gives rise to the diversity of the 365 1/4 degrees of the circle at the perimeter.

From this information a skilled operator may determine which sites of the earth are likely to be blissful and which baleful, for the particular purpose in mind. For the horoscope of the individual who is concerned may affect decisively the harmony or disharmony of the incoming influences of the cycles of heaven; or it may conflict with the eternal rhythms of the earth. The technique can be reduced to a fine point, at which a geomancer may tell, for example, that a chosen spot will benefit a man whose heart is bent on learning, but harm one who is ambitious solely for worldly gain.

These instruments depend on scientific knowledge and intellectual motives. Their use was combined by Chinese geomancers with the intuitive appreciation of the properties of a site that has been discussed above. Just as the philosophers of the Sung period believed that the random throw of stalks could reveal truth as certainly as their learned theories of time and space, so too did the geomancers who used these instruments believe that there was equal scope for an approach to truth along mystical as well as rational paths.

Attitudes towards geomancy may vary considerably, from those who castigate the practice as superstitious to those who treat its respect for mystical truths with awe. Some may regard it as artificial and fraudulent, others as the spontaneous revelation of truths that otherwise lie hidden and unsung. But little doubt of its efficacy can be entertained by those who have witnessed some of its achievements. Let sceptics visit the valley of tombs of the Ming emperors, north of Peking. They will pass through an area scrupulously isolated by the geomancers of China for a sacred purpose; they will stand in one of the most blessed and numinous sites of the world.

Notes

1 This theory was formulated in perhaps the third century BC. It explained that the continual process of birth, decay and rebirth, as witnessed in the created world, followed a cycle of phases which were controlled respectively by five principal agents. These were symbolised by the five material elements of wood, fire, earth, metal and water.

2 These compendia of rules or conventions for ritual and social behaviour claim to describe the approved procedures of the idealised world of the kings of Chou (traditionally 1122–256 BC). The process of compilation and editorship is subject to question; while the received texts may include some passages that date from the Warring States period (403–221 BC) or earlier, the main significance of the books lies in their reflection of ideas current in the Han period (202 BC–AD 220).

3 This term has been adopted by Professor David N. Keightley in *Sources of Shang History* (University of California Press, Berkeley, Los Angeles, London, 1978). This book is indispensable for the study of the use of bones and shells in divination.

4 The best bibliography for the study of these inscriptions is to be found in Keightley, op. cit. The Chinese Academy of Social Sciences, Peking, is at present preparing the publication of a definitive edition, with facsimiles, of all known inscriptions, examples of which may be inspected in a number of institutions in Europe and North America (e.g. the British Museum, the University Library, Cambridge, and the Royal Ontario Museum, Toronto).

5 See *Shih-chi* chapter 128, part of which dates from *c.* 100 BC, and part from a century later. The meaning of this highly technical treatise has yet to be fully understood. In addition there are many references to the rituals and procedures in works such as the *Chou li*, *I li* and *Li chi* (see note 2 above).

6 See *Li chi, Ch'ü li* (A) (S. Couvreur, *Li Ki*, Ho Kien Fou, 1903, p. 61), and *I li* (SPTK edition 16.1b).

7 See Joseph Needham, 'The cosmology of Early China', in *Ancient Cosmologies* (ed. Carmen Blacker and Michael Loewe, London, 1975), pp. 87–109; and Léon Vandermeersch, 'De la tortue a l'achillée', in *Divination et Rationalité*, ed. J. P. Vernant and others, Paris, 1974, pp. 29–51.

8 See *Shih-chi* 128.6 (Takigawa edition).

9 See *Lun-heng* 14 (Huang Hui edition p. 619) for 300 years; *Shih-chi* 128.6 (Takigawa edition) for 1000 years; and *Huai-nan-tzu* 14.18b (Liu Wen-tien edition) for 3000 years; see also *Huai-nan-tzu* 17.5b.

10 Perhaps the most widely circulated English edition of the book is that of Richard Wilhelm, first published in German; English edition 1951 (*The I Ching or Book of Changes: the Richard Wilhelm*

Translation rendered into English by Cary F. Baynes, foreword by C. G. Jung, London 1951, reprinted 1965 etc.). For a second translation, see J. Blofeld, *The Book of Change*, London, 1965. A valuable introduction to the intellectual background of the book is provided by Hellmut Wilhelm in *Change: Eight lectures on the* 'I ching', London, 1961.

11 See *Shih-chi* 128.10, *Lun-heng* 14 p. 619 and *Lun-heng* 24 p. 997f.

12 For fuller accounts see Cary F. Baynes, *The I Ching or Book of Changes*, London, 1951, vol. 1 p. 392f (1968 edition, p. 721f), and Blofeld, op. cit., p. 59f. In addition several less complex methods have sometimes been used to consult the *I ching*, such as the successive spinning of coins. For a similar means of divination which has been practised outside China, see William A. Lessa, 'The Chinese Trigrams in Micronesia' (*Journal of American Folklore*, vol. 82, No. 326, October to December 1969, pp. 353–362).

13 See J. Legge, *The Chinese Classics* (Hong Kong and London, 1872), vol. V part I p. 141 and part II p. 619.

14 In Wilhelm's translation, those sections of the text that derive from the *t'uan* are headed 'The judgment'; in Blofeld they are entitled 'Text'. Both versions render *yao* as 'lines'. Thanks to the recent discovery of a manuscript copy, it is possible to say that the received version of these parts of the *I ching* is largely identical with a text that was written down *c.* 200 BC.

15 This is not entirely or solely due to the failure of recent scholars to understand the original text. The first European versions were produced by highly distinguished pioneer scholars of the nineteenth century; they tended to reproduce the interpretations provided by their own contemporary Chinese teachers, who were themselves ignorant of the basic meaning. It will readily be accepted that any other course of action by, for example, Dr Legge, would at that time have been arrogant and unjustified. That it may now be possible to improve on these early translations is due to three reasons: (a) the discovery of the bones and shells and their texts, from *c.* 1900; (b) the results of critical linguistic analysis by Karlgren and others, some twenty years later; and (c) the recent discoveries of mantic material of various types and from a later period. Thus, recurrent formulae in the Wilhelm version such as 'perseverance furthers' require reconsideration.

16 I.e., the Five Phases or Elements; the series of ten days of the sun's movements; the twelve divisions of the heavens and of time; the 365 1/4 degrees of the circle; and the 28 divisions in which the Chinese conceived the Zodiac.

17 See some of the 14 fragments of mantic texts from tomb no. 6 Mo-tsui-tzu, Wu-wei, Kansu Province, dated close to the beginning of the Christian era. It is possible that other documents of a similar sort, which still await publication, were found in sites such as Yin-ch'üeh-shan, Lin-i, Shantung; Shui-hu-ti, Yün-meng, Hupei; and Ma-wang-tui, Ch'ang-sha, Hunan.

18   For these instruments, see Michael Loewe, *Ways to Paradise*, London, 1979, p. 75f, 204f, and figures 11, 12.
19   See Needham, *Science and Civilisation in China* volume 4 part I, Cambridge, 1962, p. 204f.

3

Japan

CARMEN BLACKER
Lecturer in Japanese, University of Cambridge

Let us first recall one or two definitions.

By the terms divination and oracles I refer to methods of communication between two worlds or dimensions which are usually divided from each other. We are trying to put questions which we are unable to answer for ourselves to another order of beings whose knowledge transcends the limitations of our own. Our knowledge of time stops short at the present moment. Our knowledge of causes is limited to a few rather crude mechanisms. It is comforting therefore to feel that another order of beings exists, beyond our own natural order and hence 'supernatural', whose knowledge is not subject to these strictures and who can be called upon for advice.

But our questions will have to go out, so to speak, across an ontological gap, from one separate and enclosed world to another. We cannot expect to put them in the ordinary manner in which we bandy questions among ourselves, for they will not necessarily 'reach' the beings on the other side. We must therefore find a special method which will carry us across this divide.

Likewise we cannot expect the answers, if they come at all, simply to resound in the air. We have to discover some sensitive organ through which the supernatural being can leave his imprint in a comprehensible manner. Perhaps there may be even a further layer of mystery. The signs he leaves may have to be interpreted. They are not in plain language, but in a cypher which requires a special faculty to understand.

By the term divination, therefore, I refer to the various methods whereby such questions can be put, and by oracles to the answers vouchsafed by the beings on the other side.

The field afforded for the study of such methods in Japan is a particularly rich one. The Japanese have a long tradition of belief in another world, peopled by superior and usually benevolent divinities, which is accessible to men if they know the proper manner of communicating with it. This other world is by no means hopelessly remote and distant. Given the right time, the right place and the right method, contact can be made with it. It is not surprising therefore to find that a good many different types of divination have made their appearance in Japan throughout the centuries, at all levels of society from the Emperor's Court to the village shrine.

The word for divination in Japanese is *ura* or *uranai*, a term which appears to indicate primarily 'that which is behind, and hence invisible'. The earliest known records indicate the importance placed on divinatory practices. The Chinese history *Wei chih*, which describes the manners and customs of the Japanese people in the 2nd century AD, states that they practised divination by roasting bones. The earliest Japanese chronicles, *Kojiki* and *Nihon Shoki*, compiled in the early 8th century but incorporating orally transmitted material of older date, make frequent mention of divination. The two creator deities Izanagi and Izanami are said to have resorted to divination to discover why they had given birth to malformed children. The early Emperor Suinin likewise resorted to divination to learn the reason why his child was dumb. He discovered that he only had to build a shrine to a certain divinity for the curse to be removed.[1]

From these early times until the present day, the divinatory methods practised in Japan have been legion, too legion for adequate treatment in one chapter. Three processes only will therefore be selected for discussion: the Turtle Shell, *kiboku*, the Oracular Dream, *reimu*, and the utterances of an Inspired Medium, *takusen*.

TURTLE DIVINATION

Divination by turtle was the method used by the official diviners attached to the Emperor's Court for some 1200 years, from the middle 7th century until 1868. It is a method which clearly derives from China. As in the Chinese usage which we saw in the last chapter, the pattern of cracks which results after heat has been applied in a particular manner to the shell, is believed to indicate the answer to the question put. In Japan, however, the process has been somewhat altered to accommodate with the structure of the early Shinto cult. In its essentials it resembles the method which Shinto scholars consider to be older and more purely Japanese, namely *futomani* or divination by the shoulder blade of a deer. Indeed, the examples of divination recorded in the *Kojiki* and *Nihon Shoki* are thought to indicate *futomani*.[2] It was the turtle shell, however, rather than the deer bone which was eventually adopted in the mid 7th century for purposes of the official divining at the Emperor's Court. This preference for the turtle, at first sight odd, probably derives from the magical properties attributed to the creature and to the prestige which attached to the Chinese origin of the process.

Divination for matters of state and for the important ceremonies of the early Shinto cult was carried out by a ministry of religious affairs known as the Jingikan. Its duties were to supervise all matters pertaining to the performance of Shinto rites and ceremonies. Both the regular seasonal festivals, such as the Toshigoi festival held in the second month, and those ceremonies occurring outside the normal calendrical cycle, such as the rites for consecrating a new Emperor, lay within the responsibility of the Jingikan. The rituals which it directed were all of an extreme and minute complexity. Some idea of the exacting nature of the tasks confronting the staff may be gathered from the book of instructions issued to the ministry, the oldest surviving version of which, dating from the 10th century, is known as the *Engishiki*. Here are set out lists of offerings required for the various ceremonies – the exact amount of coloured hemp, thin pongee, barkcloth, salt, dried bonito, abalone or bêche-de-mer – and minute prescriptions for the manner in which the shrine should be decorated for the occasion, even down to the size and number of nails to be used.[3]

Among these exacting responsibilities, divination played an important part. Many of the rites required that a special person be selected to perform a particular sacred task, or a special place discovered where a rite could be enacted or holy food grown. This matter of the right choice of persons or places was crucial, for a wrong choice, resulting in a person not acceptable to the divinities concerned, might well not only nullify the rite, but actually provoke calamity through a *tatari* or curse from the offended deity. Such matters were not therefore left to mere human preference. The divinities themselves were consulted to discover whom they wished to perform the task.

So important were matters of divination indeed, that some 28 persons on the staff of the Jingikan, nearly a third of its total complement, were concerned solely with such duties. All 28 had to belong to the family called Urabe, who were hereditary specialists in divination, and all had to hail from one or other of the three provinces of Izu, Iki and the island of Tsushima. All were strictly graded in accordance with a prescribed hierarchy ranging from the master diviners, *Urabe-chōjō*, at the top down to small boys known as *heza*, who were charged with menial tasks such as kindling fires.

The Jingikan ceased to exist after the Meiji Restoration of 1868, and many of the details of its procedure never seem to have become fully public knowledge. Instructions for the exact method adopted for turtle divination, for example, were confined to handbooks which scarcely found their way outside the ministry compound. Fortunately however the Shinto scholar Ban Nobutomo, some 25 years before the demise of the Jingikan, decided to collect all the documents he could find on the subject and publish as composite an account as he could of the various traditions involved. The result was his lengthy essay *Seibokukō*, 'on correct methods of divination', published in 1844. It is on this work, which affords us invaluable information about the official process of turtle divination, that I have principally relied for the following description.[4]

The first problem confronting the turtle diviner was of course to catch his turtle. But here in fact there seems to have been little difficulty. There must have been a plentiful supply of the shells of the large turtle, *ōgame*, washed up on the beaches of the Japanese islands for it was the duty of three specified seaside districts to supply the number required for the annual needs of the Jingikan. Kii province, for example, had to supply 17, Awa nineteen and Tosa fourteen, some of which were in lieu of ordinary taxes. The total number was therefore fifty, though an extra dozen or so might be required if any extraordinary ceremony had to be performed. One of Ban Nobutomo's texts specifies that no shells must be sent from a living turtle specially killed for the purpose. Only shells washed up on the beach, *ukarekō*, were acceptable.[5]

The texts all make quite clear that turtle divination involves the summoning of a Shinto god, Saniwa-no-kami, who when present will influence the pattern of cracks made on the shell. The summoning of a god always required preliminary religious abstinence by all concerned in the rite. In this case all personnel involved had to avoid eating meat and strong vegetables for seven days, their food had to be cooked on a separate fire, and they must be isolated so as to avoid possible pollution from blood or death.

Having acquired your shell, you next prepared your tools. These comprised:

(1) Certain bamboo stalks, known as *samashidake*, and grown in a corner of the Jingikan compound. They seem to have been used for sprinkling water on the heated portions of the shell to facilitate cracking.

(2) Twigs the thickness of a finger of the kind of cherry tree known as *hahaka*.

(3) A knife, seven inches long, for cutting and paring the bamboo stems.

(4) A chisel, *katahori*, for incising the pattern known as *machi* on the back of the shell.

The procedure then was to cut your turtle shell into a pentagonal form, and with your chisel to incise the figure known as *machi* on the back. You then lit a twig of *hahaka* wood, blew on it to keep it red hot, and inserted the burning brand into the grooves, first down the vertical line and then along the horizontal ones. You went on doing this until there was a loud report, after which cracks of a particular pattern would be seen radiating from the crucial points of the figure. You then with your *samashidake* bamboos sprinkled water on the cracks, which you then, on the outer side of the shell,

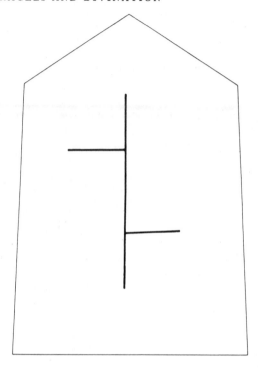

Figure 7. The *machi* figure as incised on the pentagonal shell; after
Ban Nobutomo, p. 472.

blacked in with Indian ink so that they might be more easily
visible.[6]

Let us now look a little more closely at the *machi* figure,
which seems to be a Japanese invention entirely, owing
nothing to any known Chinese practice. Even its name,
machi, remains obscure in meaning and derivation. It
comprises five crucial points from which cracks can radiate,
all of which have their proper names. *Ho* and *to* are the
south and north points, *kami* east, *emi* west and *tame* centre.

The possible directions in which cracks can radiate are
limited usually to three, all of which likewise have names.
Take the north point *to*, for example, A crack to the right,
to-yorime, or a straight crack, *to-uruwashi*, are both *kichi*, good.
A crack to the left, *to-yuruida*, is *kyō*, bad. The same rules
apply to the cracks from *ho*, the south point. With *emi*, on the

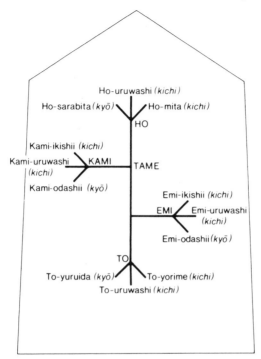

Figure 8. The *machi* figure, adapted from Ban Nobutomo, p. 468.
Note the usage in maps and diagrams whereby the north is placed
at the foot and the south at the top. East accordingly lies to the left,
and west to the right.

west and right, and *kami* on the east and left, cracks upwards
and straight along are *kichi*, good; cracks downwards, *emi-
odashii*, are *kyō*, bad.[7]

The only method of questioning which Ban Nobutomo
records is the cumbersome and time-consuming one of
presenting a list of names, of people or places, until you get a
kichi crack which means 'yes, that person or place is good'.
If for example you wanted an Imperial messenger to go to
the Ise shrine for the Kanname festival, you went through
the names of all the princes of the 5th rank and above, until
a *kichi* crack proclaimed that you had found the right person.

The same process was employed to discover the princess
destined to fulfil the role of *Saigū*, virgin representative of the

Emperor at the **Ise shrine**. Often a mere infant when selected, this unfortunate girl had to pass the rest of her life until the death of the Emperor in a celibate and ritually pure seclusion which amounted to virtual imprisonment in the precincts of the Ise shrine. She too was selected from amongst the eligible princesses by this turtle method.[8]

So too was the place where she was required to pass the first two years of her sacralised existence before setting out on her journey to Ise. This place, known as the Nonomiya or Palace in the fields, was expected to be a lonely spot with a well, a few miles from the Emperor's palace. It too was discovered by the same method of divination, as also was its well.[9]

Though the Jingikan disappeared more than a century ago, and the institution of the *Saigū* died out sometime in the 14th century, the turtle divination is still employed in the course of the important and mysterious rite known as the *Daijōsai*, which represents the climax of the long series of ceremonies by which the Japanese Emperor is consecrated and enthroned. This rite primarily takes the form of a communion meal, in which the Emperor consumes the first rice of the year in company with his ancestral divinities.

The question which the turtle divination is required to answer is: where should this supremely holy rice be grown? The Emperor has to eat the same meal twice, at dead of night in two separate halls known as the Yuki-den and the Suki-den. Two separate fields must therefore be discovered, to be known as the Yuki field and the Suki field.

At the beginning of the present Emperor's reign, the divination for the two fields took place on February 5th, 1928, on a sanded area in the precincts of the palace in Tokyo. Alas, only a few details of the ceremony have been made public. We know that on this sanded area there was a small hut containing a branch of *sakaki* wood hung with paper streamers. This was to act as the vehicle or vessel into which were invoked the two deities petitioned to influence the pattern of cracks. We know that a fire was kindled by rubbing two sticks of *hinoki* wood together, and we know that the turtle shell was cut into a pentagon measuring eight inches at the base and five from top to base. But of what then transpired and how the cracks were interpreted, nothing has been divulged from the confines of the palace. All we know is that the Yuki rice field was decreed to be found in Shiga prefecture, and the Suki rice field in Fukuoka prefecture in northern Kyushu.[10]

It seems clear that the cumbersome yes-no method was not the only technique of turtle divination practised by the Urabe experts in the Jingikan. Of the methods yielding more complex answers to questions, however, little seems to be known. Throughout the medieval period, it appears that any mysterious or untoward occurrence – a violent hailstorm, an epidemic, inexplicable rumbling noises in the palace – were always submitted to the Jingikan so that divination could be made for any ominous significance. The 13th century work *Heike Monogatari*, for example, records that on one occasion three doves appeared and fought together until all were killed. The Court authorities considered this occurrence so strange that they ordered a divination from the Jingikan. The answer was '*omoki on-tsutsushimi*', great caution must be observed, a result which could not have been obtained by the simple yes-no method. No further details of the procedure, alas, are forthcoming.[11]

Before we leave the turtle shell and pass on to the oracular dream, a question suggests itself. The method just described depends basically on an element we can call pattern. So do many other divinatory methods which spring at once to mind. From a *pattern* of cracks, of the broken or unbroken lines of the *I ching*, of newly dissected intestines, of flights of birds in the sky, prophesy is made possible.

I suggest that all these various methods may originally derive from the faculty which we can broadly call dowsing. The term dowsing covers not only the divining of underground water, its depth, volume and direction. With a trained and sensitive dowser, the faculty can be applied to many other things hidden from ordinary human sight.

The trained dowser will always contend that the knowledge of these hidden things lies somewhere in his own mind, in a layer not usually accessible to ordinary consciousness. But to reach this level of knowledge in his own mind, he needs some kind of intermediary instrument or conductor. A forked stick held in his hands will move when he passes over an underground flow. It will likewise move in response to his questions: how deep is the water? Twenty feet? Thirty feet? Fifty feet? And how many gallons an hour? One hundred? Two hundred?

But what moves the stick, he tells you, is no mysterious outside force. It is his own muscles activated by the seeing layer of his mind. His conscious mind is not aware that he is making these movements, but it is not his conscious mind which is involved. And how has he been able to reach this buried layer of his mind? By means of the stick, which acts as a conductor.

The forked stick however is not the only possible form of conductor available to the dowser. He can also make use of a pattern. By looking at a pattern, of cracks or broken lines or birds in the sky, the seer is conducted to a level of his mind which knows the answer and enables him to speak in prophecy.

At this stage, needless to say, no fixed rules govern the procedure, decreeing that a particular pattern always carries one particular meaning. Later on, however, it is probable that someone without the seer's gift will have to take over the process. In the case of a family like the Urabe, for example, gifted people may have been produced for several generations. Eventually, however, someone without the gift must have found himself saddled with the duties. For such ordinary people, the only course is to follow fixed prescriptions, defining a crack to the right as auspicious and one to the left as inauspicious.

I suggest that these rules, in the form in which they have come down to us, are no more than dead, hardened residues left behind by the passing of the gifted seer.

DREAM ORACLES

The oracular dream, solicited by means of a practice which is a clear example of incubation, seems to have survived in Japan well into the 15th century. The pilgrim, harassed by some insoluble problem, journeys to the holy site in the hope of being granted by the divine owner of the place a dream which will point to the solution of his problem.

Many accounts of such dream oracles can be found

scattered throughout medieval Japanese literature. From these we learn that incubation sites were to be found both in Shinto shrines and in Buddhist temples. Among the Shinto sites, the most celebrated were the shrines of Itsukushima, Kamo, Kibune and the god Hachiman at Usa in Kyushu. Among Buddhist temples three in particular, dedicated to the Bodhisattva Kannon, were renowned for their dreams. These were Kiyomizudera in Kyoto, Ishiyamadera near Lake Biwa, and Hasedera, south of Nara.[12]

The procedure for consulting the oracle seems to have been similar irrespective of whether the divinity was a Shinto *kami* or a bodhisattva. You made your journey to the holy site, observing meanwhile the rules of abstinence from meat and strong vegetables, and furnished with a suitable offering for the divinity. You then made a vow, *kigan*, that you would remain in the place for a specified number of days in the hope of being granted a dream. Seven, twenty-one and a hundred seem to have been the favoured numbers. You then exerted yourself during that period, by means of further prayer, offerings and abstinence, to cajole the divinity to vouchsafe you a dream. Every night you slept in the principal hall of the shrine or temple, as near as possible to the inner sanctuary where the divinity dwelt. A dream of the expected type and structure was given to you, often on the last night of your avowed vigil.

An invaluable source of information regarding the incubatory practices of medieval Japan is to be found in the scroll painting known as *Ishiyamadera Engie*. This scroll, commissioned by the Ishiyama temple to commemorate the various miracles wrought there by the Bodhisattva Kannon, includes several scenes depicting dream oracles. It thus affords us a rare glimpse of the conditions experienced by dream pilgrims of the 15th century.[13]

Two scenes may serve as examples. Plate 5 shows the case of the 'wife of Fujiwara Kuniyoshi', a well born and wealthy lady, but unhappy because she has been divorced by her husband. Driven by her misery, she has come into the temple for seven days' *sanrō* or secluded retreat. We see her asleep in the principal hall of the temple, before the sanctuary with its latticed grille where the holy statue is enshrined.

She can clearly afford some elegant comforts. She sleeps

not on the bare boards or thin matting which is the lot of poorer pilgrims, but on a couple of thick mats with ornamental borders. A rich screen surrounds her to keep off draughts and give her some measure of privacy. She is wrapped in a voluminous cloak and attended by two small girls.

She is rewarded by a magnificent vision of Kannon, who has appeared to her sleeping eye clad in floating draperies and standing on lotuses. She is presenting the lady with a magic jewel, *nyoi-hōju* which, in the manner of such dream gifts, was still in the lady's hand when she woke up. The text informs us that she took the jewel home, and that soon afterwards her husband came back to her, begot a son, and that the family lived happily and prosperously ever after.

Plate 6 shows us the 'mother of Michitsuna', another aristocratic but unhappy lady, well known in literature as the writer of the melancholy medieval chronicle *Kagerō Nikki*. She too has made a *sanrō* retreat to the temple in the hope of obtaining a dream which will cure her despair at the neglect of her husband Fujiwara Kaneiye. She too is rewarded by a dream, for to her sleeping eye there has appeared the figure of a Buddhist priest who is pouring water from a basin on her right knee. The meaning of this enigmatic action is not clear, but it seems to have been efficacious. For soon afterwards her husband Kaneiye himself made a pilgrimage to the temple, and there was reunited with the poor lady with all the affection for which she had so much longed.

We see her lying asleep, not in the main hall of the temple but in a rather richly appointed private room. Screens and curtains of state surround her, and she is attended by two girls, wide awake and gossiping.

The scroll shows us elsewhere a scene depicting less wealthy pilgrims, unable to afford the luxuries enjoyed by these ladies. They sleep either on bare boards or on a thin mat, wrapped in anything warm they can muster, and sharing a common pillow in the shape of a log of wood.

Three points suggest themselves with regard to these dream oracles. First, what kind of problems were expected to be solved by oracular dreams? Second, who are the dream figures? And third, how old is the custom of incubation in Japan?

Prominent among the various kinds of trouble which impelled people to seek help from an oracular dream was sickness. The pilgrim is afflicted by an obstinate and apparently incurable malady, and comes to the temple in the hope of a cure. Several instructive examples appear in the 15th century work known as *Hasedera Reigenki*, a collection of stories of the miracles performed by the Kannon of the Hasedera, many of which describe an oracular dream.

A man called Kiyohara Natsuno, for example, was horribly disfigured by leprosy and made the pilgrimage to the Hasedera after all other attempts at cure had failed. After spending seven days in seclusion in the temple, he dreamed that a boy appeared from the inner sanctuary and said, 'Your sickness is very difficult to cure because it is due to karma from a past life. But Kannon has nevertheless commanded me to heal you.' The boy thereupon put out his tongue, which was very long, and licked the man all over his body. When the licking was finished, the man woke up in great astonishment, to find himself clean and cured.[14]

Another man, Ōe no Hirosumi, developed terrible boils all over his back, which burst in five places. No medicine had the slightest effect, so in despair he made the pilgrimage to the Hasedera. He was only in the temple one day and night before dreaming that a boy appeared from behind a curtain and rubbed some red ointment into his back. He woke the next morning to find that the boils had vanished.

Again, the *Hasedera Reigenki* tells how the girl who subsequently became the Empress Takako, consort of the 12th century Emperor Nijō, suffered when a small child from the unfortunate defect of having such a short tongue that she was scarcely able to speak. Her nurse brought her to the Hasedera, where on the seventh night of their vigil both she her nurse experienced an identical dream. Both saw a priest in a dark robe appear from the inner sanctuary and say, 'In a noble and honest face, the tongue should always reach the tip of the nose.' He thereupon put his hand into the girl's mouth, pulled out her tongue and stretched it until it reached the tip of her nose. Both then woke up to find that the girl's tongue was elongated to a normal length and that she was able to speak.[15]

Already from these few examples a consistent pattern may

be discerned. The sufferer sees a figure appear from the holiest part of the shrine, who proceeds to *do* something to the sick part of the body. The sleeper then awakes to find himself cured.

These stories bear a striking resemblance to the cases recorded on the stelae at the shrine of Asklepios at Epidaurus, to which sick people came from far and near in the similar hope of a cure through an incubatory dream. They were required to have the details of their cases – the sickness, the offerings made to the shrine, the dream and the final cure – inscribed on plaques, which were then erected in the precincts to encourage other pilgrims. These stelae, excavated about a century ago, describe a procedure similar to the cases we have noticed in the Hasedera. A woman blind in one eye dreamt that the god Asklepios cut out the injured eyeball and poured a drug into the socket. She awoke cured. A man with incurable lice dreamt that the god stripped him naked and brushed the lice off his body. He too awoke cured. A man with a red brand mark on his forehead dreamt that the god tied a bandage round his head. When he woke up he found that the red mark had been transferred to the bandage and that his forehead was clean.[16]

Just as in the cases recorded at the Hasedera, the dream figure does something to the injured part of the body, which results in a cure when the patient awakes.

A second category of problem believed to be soluble by dreams was an incomprehensible misery or misfortune. A monk unable to learn a particular passage of scripture by heart, a man humiliated by his unaccountably black skin, the two ladies reduced to despair by neglect of their husbands, all sought help through dreams. The dream figure sometimes explains to them the cause of their misfortune before eliminating it. Sometimes he merely performs a mysterious action on the patient which results in his cure when he awakes.

A third category of pilgrim simply wishes to know what fate awaits them in the future. Here the dream figure often shows a picture or emblem which symbolises what the future holds in store. An example may be found in the *Sarashina Nikki*, an 11th century work by an anonymous young girl. She describes how her mother, anxious to know her daughter's future destiny, instructed a priest to go to the Hasedera and to remain there for three days until he had a dream about the girl's future. The mother sent a mirror with the priest as an offering, and told the girl meanwhile to observe the rules of abstinence.

Eventually the priest returned, reporting that he had been successful. A beautiful and noble lady had appeared to him, holding up the mirror in her hand. On one side he could see a figure rolling about on the floor weeping. But on the other was an image of a rich robe trailing under a curtain, and beyond a glimpse of a garden full of blossoming trees and singing birds. 'This will make you happy', the lady had said, and the dream ended.[17]

Who then are the principal figures which appear in these incubatory dreams? They are curiously limited in number. In the Kannon temples for example, no more than three figures are reported as appearing to the sleeping eye of the pilgrims. The noble and beautiful lady, such as appeared to the wife of Fujiwara Kuniyoshi and the priest described in the *Sarashina Nikki*, is clearly a manifestation of the Bodhisattva herself. The other two are taken to be her 'messengers', whom she sends to perform certain tasks on her behalf. These take the form of either a miraculous Boy, sometimes described as golden, or of a Buddhist priest, usually described as old and wearing a dark robe.

In some of the healing dreams recorded in the *Hasedera Reigenki* the figure does his work on the sleeper's body in silence. But some spoken utterance is usual, in plain prose with no enigmatic cypher or symbolism needing interpretation.

In later medieval literature, however, the oracular words in the dream are often delivered in the form of an *uta*, or poem in the classical metre of 31 syllables. Such poetic oracles always seem to be delivered by Shinto gods, such as Hachiman or Kibune. In the *Heike Monogatari*, for example, where a number of miraculous dreams are recorded, the oracular utterance frequently takes poetic form. When Taira Munemori passed a seven night vigil in the Usa Hachiman shrine he was vouchsafed a dream in which he saw the door of the inner shrine burst open, and heard from within an awful and hair-raising voice chanting the 31 syllables of a poem. Terrified though he was, Munemori was able to summon up the wit and courage to murmur a suitable old poem in reply.[18]

Our third point concerns the possible antiquity of the practice of incubation. Saigō Nobutsuna in his interesting book *Kodaijin to Yume* (Ancient Peoples and their Dreams) suggests that the practice may be far older than the introduction of Buddhism, or indeed of any cultural influence from China. In these ancient times, however, by which we should understand the 4th and 5th centuries AD, it was the Emperor alone who exercised this link with the supernatural world. The Emperor was the principal 'dreamer', and incubation was an important part of his religious duties. His palace therefore, always comprised a special hall where such dreams could be solicited, equipped with an incubatory bed known as a *kamudoko*. Saigō cites Chapter 65 of the *Kojiki* in support of his theory. Here it is stated that the Emperor Sūjin, grieving that so many of his subjects had died in a terrible epidemic, lay down upon the *kamudoko* in the hopes of learning through a dream the cause of the sickness. Sure enough, the god Ōmononushi appeared to him, speaking oracular words advising how the calamity might be averted.[19]

Saigō also cites the Yumedono, or hall of dreams, which at the end of the 7th century the celebrated Regent and Buddhist sage Shōtoku Taishi is said to have constructed next to his sleeping chamber. After bathing three times he would enter this hall, and emerge on the following morning to speak of 'things good and bad all over the world'. This Yumedono, Saigō believes, must have been an incubation chamber where contact could be made with the supernatural world. The mysterious *kamudoko* therefore is likely to have been a bed in such a chamber.[20]

One final point suggests itself before we leave the subject of incubatory dreams. We referred earlier to the ancient ceremony of the *Daijōsai*, the climax of the ritual sequence whereby a new Emperor is consecrated, and to the divination by turtle for the two fields in which the rice is to be grown for the Emperor's communion meal. This solemn meal the Emperor eats in two halls of ancient construction known as the Yukiden and the Sukiden, built without a scrap of metal shortly before the ceremony takes place, and dismantled the very next day. Within the inner chambers of these two identical halls are a number of enigmatic objects, the use and function of which have been forgotten. They play no part in the ritual. The Emperor does not touch them. But clearly, in ancient times, they were there for a purpose.

One of these objects is a bed known as the *shinza* or god-seat. It is constructed in three layers, one of which projects outwards to form a shelf on which are placed a fan and a comb. At the foot of the bed lies a pair of slippers. In the *Engishiki* the bed is mentioned, but not a word is said about its meaning or function. Is it a throne, some scholars have speculated? Or does it symbolise a marriage bed? But no one has suggested that it might represent the *kamudoko*. It does not seem impossible that the ritual of consecration might have included an incubatory encounter with an ancestral deity, who would convey to the Emperor advice about his coming reign.[21]

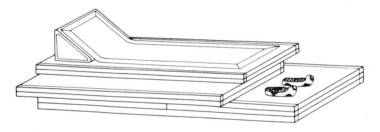

Figure 9. The *shinza*, or god-seat, as used in the *Daijō-sai*; after Holtom, by courtesy of Dr Masanao Sekine and *Monumenta Nipponica*.

Later with the coming of Buddhism, the function of dreaming was no longer confined to the Emperor, but spread to all and sundry. It is interesting to note, however, that the form taken by the incubatory dream is always the same. It is unlike any other type of supernatural dream recorded in Japan, but very like other incubatory dreams recorded in other unconnected parts of the world. Always, as we have seen, a single figure emerges from the inner shrine and speaks directly to the sleeper. Such dreams stand in sharp contrast with other dreams recognised to be supernatural, but which are unsolicited, given to the sleeper without prior warning, and not necessarily in a sacred place.[22]

THE INSPIRED MEDIUM

Now for our third mode of divination, the inspired or possessed medium. Here a supernatural being with a greater range of knowledge than man, is cajoled to leave his own world and take up a temporary abode in the body of a suitable human being. There he is induced to 'borrow' the medium's voice in order to answer questions about the welfare of the community which are beyond the competence of man.

It seems that from an early date special people capable of acting as mediums for supernatural beings were apt to make their appearance in Japanese communities. These specialists were able to achieve at will a state of trance in which their own personality was displaced, allowing the spiritual being to 'possess' them and speak through their mouths. In pre-Buddhist times these people seem usually to have been women, and to have employed various techniques, such as violent dancing, by which they could throw themselves into the required state of trance.

Since the introduction of Buddhism, however, this single function has split into two. The medium, still usually a woman, has become a passive figure whose body the god borrows as the vehicle from which to deliver his oracle. The active task of summoning the deity by spells and magic sounds, putting questions to him once he is lodged in the medium's body, and finally despatching him back to his own world, has been taken over by the male figure of a Buddhist ascetic. The task of performing this mode of divination, and of eliciting the resulting oracle, is therefore divided between these two complementary figures.[23]

This kind of oracle has survived into recent times in two principal contexts. The first was a village festival in which the local tutelary deity was invited to descend among his worshippers. He was feasted and entertained, and finally begged to answer certain questions about the future prospects of the village before returning home.

Second, the same ritual is still found practised on a particular holy mountain where certain deities are believed to have their abode.

The village oracle, *takusen matsuri*, used to be a widespread phenomenon in Japan. Now, alas, scarcely a single example survives in its genuine form. Until the middle 1960s some half dozen instances could still be observed, and it is fortunate that all of them were properly described and recorded before they disappeared.[24]

The basic structure of the rite is as follows. The local guardian divinity, the *ujigami*, is on a particular day in winter invited to prophesy on matters which will affect the village during the coming year. The rice harvest is of foremost importance, and always the god is asked to indicate how the early, middle and late rice crops will turn out. Other crops such as soy beans and millet will then be the subject of enquiry, followed by questions as to fires, drought, flood or sickness.

The medium through whom the god speaks was sometimes a member of an ascetic religious order, but more often was recruited from amongst the ordinary farmers or fishermen of the village, the 'gift' manifesting itself spontaneously and later being consolidated by a regime of traditional austerities.

A village oracle which survived until 1965, and which was carefully recorded by Hori Ichirō before its disappearance, was the *Sakumatsuri*, enacted in the town of Sakata in Yamagata prefecture. Here the medium used to be a member of the ascetic order known as Isse-gyōnin, and the place of the rite was a Buddhist temple called Kaikōji. So violent was the medium's trance that it was customary to bind his feet under him as he sat cross-legged, and to tie a towel round his head so as to blindfold him. He was brought into the required state of trance by a deafening clamour of banging drums, rattling iron rings and loud shouted chanting of the Heart Sutra. The trance was characterised by a violent flailing on the floor with a wand, and by an extraordinary leaping several inches into the air from a cross legged position.[25]

Then the clamour of drums and chanting ceased, and the voice of the official interrogator was heard calling out a series of questions.

'How much early rice can we expect this year? . . . How

much middle rice? . . . How much late rice? . . . How about the beans? . . . Will there be any fires in the village? . . . Any sickness this winter? . . .'

At once, on the heels of the question, without a second's hesitation came the answer from the possessed man as he flung himself up and down. The answer always came in a single word, screamed in a strange voice.

'Seven . . . eight . . . yes . . . no . . . yes. . . .'

The questions were always put in a set fixed order. First came those pertaining to the welfare of the whole village: the rice harvest, the beans, drought, winds, rain, pests. Then followed questions concerning individual households. Professor Hori recorded in 1962 that no less than twenty villages from the surrounding district had converged on the temple, and that each medium was allowed to answer for two villages. He would then retire exhausted, and another man would take his place.

The *matsuri* died out a few years after Professor Hori recorded it because no one could be found any longer to act as medium. The same story goes for the other villages where such rites used to take place. The supply of people gifted with the ability to achieve the necessary trance suddenly dries up. No one comes forward in the village. There is no one in the next village and no one within travelling distance. The rite therefore vanishes.

It survives, however, in another context and place. Instead of inviting the god to visit the village, the village, or certain members of it, travel to the mountain where the god is believed to dwell. In the past there were many such mountains. Now only one is left, Kiso Ontake in Nagano prefecture, where such rites can be seen.

To this mountain every summer great numbers of the pilgrim groups known as *kō* converge, dedicated to the worship of the various divinities inhabiting the mountain. These white clad parties appear from all over Japan, from as far away as Aomori in the north and Kyushu in the south, and make their way to the summit of the mountain by two approved routes. These *kō* sometimes draw their members from one village or one quarter of a city, sometimes from a wider area comprising several communities. The annual climb of the holy mountain is their culminating moment of the year, for there they can make a direct contact with the divinity who has charge over them. This they accomplish through two special officers. The *nakaza*, or 'between-seat', is the medium through whom the divinity is enabled to speak. She is brought into a state of trance by the *maeza* or 'front-seat'. This officer, like the interrogator in the village ritual, summons the deity into the medium's body, questions him and eventually sends him back to his own world. It is usually he who also acts as the *sendatsu* or leader of the party.[26]

In former times no one set foot on the holy ground of the mountain without first undergoing a period of strict preliminary abstinence. All pilgrims had to abstain from meat and strong vegetables, cook their food on a separate pure fire, and perform frequent cold water austerities. Such disciplines have now virtually disappeared. I met only a few people in the course of my four ascents of the mountain who acknowledged having undergone any preliminary abstinence.

At a number of spots on the way to the summit, one is liable to encounter a group of crouching white figures. In their midst, perhaps with his back to a statue, stiffly sits a man with a wand in his hands. Strange gasps and bursts of sound usually come from his mouth, to which the crouching figures reverently respond. Sometimes his voice is loud and resonant. Sometimes only a low muttered gabble is emitted. The wand usually quivers, sometimes swishes to and fro like a flag.

This sight always betokens an *oza* séance, in which one of the divinities of the mountain, *Ontake Daijin* or *Ryūjin*, has been summoned into the body of the party's medium and induced to make oracular utterance. The questions put are similar to those asked at a village *matsuri*. A *kō* from a country village will ask about the coming harvest, and about the storms and pests to be expected in the coming month. They may also ask practical questions about their journey, about the kind of weather to be expected and the best huts in which to stay the night. A city *kō* will ask questions about the prospects of prices and trade. All, however, seemed to have an unquenchable appetite for divine utterances. Several times a day, whenever they came to a suitable spot, they would put their medium into a trance and address more questions to their divinity. Some, not content with several times a day, would spend half the night in séance in the hut where they stayed.

Various methods were employed to entrance the medium. The *maeza* would emit sudden loud shouts of 'E', 'Hyun', or 'Shin', at the same time pointing his hands in the sword mudra at the medium's solar plexus. He would repeat with gabbling force the Heart Sutra, or the spell in nine syllables known as *Kuji*, which creates a gate through which no evil influences may pass.[27] He may also repeat many times the syllables *A-Un*, the first and last letters of the Sanscrit alphabet.

The most impressive trances were to be witnessed at the shrine at the summit, Kengamine. Sometimes several parties at a time could be seen consulting their divinity, ensconced in different parts of the shrine enclosure. The behaviour of the medium in trance varied from cataleptic stiffness to furious violence, shrieking and leaping about among the volcanic crags.

Here then are three kinds of divination and oracle in Japan. In all three methods, diverse though they are, we recognise a means of communicating with a world of spiritual beings whose range of knowledge is greater than our own and who can therefore be petitioned for help and advice. We recognise further that the world view which validated such methods is fast vanishing. Turtle divination is virtually extinct. At the dream oracle sites it is scarcely remembered that incubation was once practiced there. In the villages where the trance oracle used to take place suitable mediums are no longer forthcoming. Even on Mt Ontake the trances have notably diminished during the last few years.

It remains to be seen what substitute will be found for these practices. For the area of life which lies perilously outside human control is still large and mysterious.

5. The incubatory dream in the Ishiyamadera of the wife of Fujiwara Kuniyoshi; from a scroll in the keeping of the Ishiyamadera, and reproduced by courtesy of Kadokawa Shoten, Tokyo, and Ishiyamadera.

6. Dream of the mother of Michitsuna; from a scroll in the keeping of the Ishiyamadera; reproduced by courtesy of Kadokawa Shoten, Tokyo, and Ishiyamadera.

Notes

1　For the *Wei Chih* reference, see Ryūsaku Tsunoda and L. Carrington Goodrich, *Japan in the Chinese Dynastic Histories*, South Pasadena, 1951, p. 12. The *Kojiki* may be read in D. Philippi's translation, Tokyo and Princeton, 1968, and the *Nihon Shoki* in W. G. Aston's *Nihongi*, reprinted London 1956.

　　See also M. Revon's comprehensive article on Japanese Divination in Hastings's *Encyclopedia of Religion and Ethics*, Vol. 4, p. 801–806. M. Revon deals with a number of methods for which no space can be found here. For example *tsuji-ura*, or cross-roads divination, referred to in the poems of the 8th century anthology *Manyōshū*; *hashi-ura*, or bridge divination; *koto-ura*, or harp divination as performed at the Ise shrine to determine the ceremonial purity of the priests taking part in the ceremonies. M. Revon also deals with the question of the ordeal in its divinatory form, mentioning ordeals by hot water and snakes. Sir Ernest Satow's contribution on 'Ancient Japanese Rituals', in *Transactions of the Asiatic Society of Japan*, reprints Vol. 2, December 1927, may also usefully be consulted.

2　A continental origin may also be ascribed to *futomani*. See for example Torii Ryūzō, who found very similar practices still surviving in Mongolia. *Jinruigakujō yori mitaru Jōdai no Bunka*, Tokyo, 1925, p. 68.

　　For the various archeological finds of bones and shells, see *Shūkyōgaku Jiten*, Tokyo, 1973, article *uranai*.

3　See Felicia Bock, *Engi-Shiki: Proceedings of the Engi era*, Vol. 1, chapter 2, Tokyo, 1970; Robert Ellwood, *The Feast of Kingship*, Tokyo, 1973, chapter 3. Note that some of the work of official divination was done at another office, the Ommyōryō.

4　*Seibokukō, Ban Nobutomo Zenshū*, Tokyo, 1907, Vol. 2, pp. 441–557. Examples of the works consulted by Ban are: a 17th century handbook for the practice as carried out in Tsushima province, by Fujiwara Masanobu, master diviner for the district; another for the island of Hachijōjima, and another for the shrine in Izu province to the god Shirahama Daimyōjin. Ban adds that the traditions of the Yoshida family regarding turtle divination have always been kept secret and are hence inaccessible.

5　Ibid., p. 461.

6　Ibid., pp. 448–60. The *hahaka* tree is given classical sanction in chapter 17 of the *Kojiki*.

7　Ibid., pp. 468–76.

8　For the Saigū princess, see Felicia Bock, op. cit., pp. 151–85, and Robert Ellwood, 'The Saigū: Princess and Priestess', *History of Religions*, Vol. 7, No. 1, August 1967.

9　An example of an old Nonomiya may be seen today at Sagano, west of Kyoto.

10　D. C. Holtom, *The Japanese Enthronement Ceremony*, Tokyo, 1972, pp. 74–8, and Ellwood, *The Feast of Kingship*, chapter 1.

11   *Heike Monogatari*, book 1, 'Shishigadani no koto', Utsumi's edition p. 47.

12   For a lucid account of Japanese incubation practices see Saigō Nobutsuna, *Kodaijin to yume*, Tokyo, 1972. Also Kikuchi Ryōichi, *Chūsei Setsuwa no kenkyū*, Tokyo, 1972, pp. 106–22.

13   *Nihon Emakimono Zenshū*, Vol. 22, Tokyo, 1966.

14   *Hasedera Reigenki, Zoku Gunsho Ruijū*, Vol. 799B, p. 233. The date of this work is doubtful, but believed to be about 1435. See Yoshiko Dykstra, 'Tales of the Compassionate Kannon; the *Hasedera Kannon Genki*', in *Monumenta Nipponica*, Vol. 31, No. 2, Summer 1976.

15   Ibid., pp. 235–7.

16   See Mary Hamilton, *Incubation or the cure of disease in pagan temples and Christian churches*, London, 1906, and C. A. Meier, *Ancient Incubation and Modern Psychotherapy*, Evanston, 1967.

17   See Ivan Morris's translation of the *Sarashina Nikki, As I crossed the bridge of dreams*, London, 1971, pp. 78–80.

18   *Heike Monogatari*, Book 8, 'Usa gyōkō no koto', Utsumi's edition p. 444.

19   Saigō, op. cit., pp. 40–1.

20   Ibid., pp. 35–40.

21   D. C. Holtom, op. cit., p. 96–8. Felicia Bock, op. cit., Vol 2, pp. 42, 49. Ellwood, *The Feast of Kingship*, p. 133–4. The reticence of the *Engishiki* as to the objects in the two halls is ascribed by Robert Ellwood, p. 132, to reverence. The first book to offer a full description of the rite was the *Daijō-e gishiki gushaku*, by the 18th century Shinto scholar Kada Azumamaro. This work was suppressed by the Bakufu, but is reprinted, together with Kada's other three works on the ceremony, two of which contain illustrations, in *Kada Azumamaro Zenshū*, Vol. 10. See Ellwood, pp. 121 and 132–3. See also Origuchi Shinobu, 'Daijōsai no hongi', in *Origuchi Shinobu Zenshū*, Vol. 3, p. 174, Tokyo, 1967.

22   See for example Sugahara Akihide, 'Chūsei shotō ni okeru jōkyō ha-aku no henshitsu, *Heike Monogatari* no yume no setsuwa wo tegakari ni', in *Nihon ni okeru shakai to shūkyō*, Tokyo, 1972.

23   For a fuller discussion of the shamanic medium in Japan, see my *The Catalpa Bow*, London, 1975, chapters 1, 6 and 8.

24   Ibid., chapter 13, for a fuller discussion.

25   Hori Ichirō, 'Isse gyōnin to toshi-uranai no kamizuke', in *Shūkyō shūzoku no seikatsu kitei*, Tokyo, 1963.

26   See *The Catalpa Bow* chapter 14. Also Percival Lowell, 'Esoteric Shinto', part 1, *Transactions of the Asiatic Society of Japan*, Vol. 1, 1893, pp. 109–15.

27   The *kuji* is a spell of Taoist, not Buddhist origin, which was adopted by the Shugendo sect and assigned nine mudras to correspond with the nine syllables. See *Mikkyō Daijiten*, Vol. 1, p. 331.

4

The Classical World

J. S. MORRISON
Formerly President of Wolfson College, Cambridge

INTRODUCTION

I shall begin with the Romans, if only because acquaintance
with ancient oracles and divination begins at school, or used
to begin, with Livy, his lists of portents and his accounts of
the taking of auspices by Roman officials, and with Virgil,
his memorable account of Aeneas' meeting with the Sibyll
of Cumae and of Aeneas' calling up of the ghosts of the dead.
If we did our homework well we learnt[1] to distinguish omens
which were given (*oblativa*) e.g. thunder and lightning, the
flight of birds, monstrous births, the sweating of statues, from
omens which were provoked (*impetrativa*) e.g. the appearance
of the liver of sacrificed victims, the behaviour of chickens
when fed. And we were told that a good deal of this practice
derived from the Etruscans. The lip of our somewhat tasteless
cup was sweetened by our teacher with the remark of Cato[2]
that he was surprised if one entrails-inspector (*haruspex*)
meeting another in the street did not smile, and with the
story[3] of Publius Clodius in the first Punic war, who was so
eager to engage the enemy that when the chickens refused
to eat (and the omen was therefore unfavourable) he had
them thrown into the sea: 'if they won't eat, let them drink'.
We laughed, but the Romans knew it as a moral story to
illustrate the dangers of jesting in sacred matters. Clodius
met with disaster and was convicted of treason, while his
colleague, Lucius Junius, who shared his attitude to omens,
commited suicide after losing his fleet in a storm.

The story of Clodius comes from the 3rd century BC, but by the time of Cicero in the 1st century attitudes were different. In 45 and 44 BC, when compulsorily retired from public life, he wrote the books *On the Nature of the Gods* and *On Divination*. In the former the Stoic Balbus, who believed in the gods and, unlike the Epicureans, in their care for men and therefore in divination, laments that 'through the negligence of the leading men (*neglegentia nobilitatis*) the art of augury has been lost. Men no longer believe in the truth of omens, which are now taken only as an outward formality. And so in the greatest affairs of state, such as the present wars which touch the safety of our whole nation, there is no heed of omens. No auspices are taken. . . . Our generals give up their augural office before they begin their campaigns'. In the introduction to the book *On Divination*, Cicero observes that all the philosophers (including Socrates, Plato and Aristotle) believed in divination with the exception of Xenophanes, who was a sort of Unitarian, and Epicurus who believed in the existence of the gods but regarded them as irrelevant to human life, although some philosophers rejected the artificial, and believed only in the natural, forms of divination, i.e. in divination by inspiration and by dreams.

In the remainder of the first book Cicero's brother Quintus defends divination, but in the second book Cicero, with almost the passion of a Lucretius, rejects all forms of divination as superstition, but approves of the retention of the *ius augurum*,[4] in spite of its assumption of a belief in the truth of omens, for reasons of state (*reipublicae causa*). After all, he had held the office of augur himself since 53, and no doubt justified his hypocrisy on grounds such as these. His attitude is a typically Roman one. In this spirit the books of the Sibyll of the neighbouring Greek city of Cumae were early brought to Rome, where they were put under the control of ten officials appointed by the state; and thus were no longer available for use by an irresponsible priesthood to disturb public order, but could be recruited when necessary as a support for government policy; and the Etruscan *haruspices* were similarly controlled.

These books of Cicero effectively sum up the various attitudes of educated Romans at the end of the Republic to artificial and natural divination. Some believed in the latter but not in the former, some in both and some in none. These books also give an idea of the various types of divination practised by state officials and by private persons at this period and earlier. Under the Empire divination was still practised by the college of augurs, but the spread of sophistication, and the growing influence of Christianity, hastened the decline in belief in its truth which Cicero already attests. Cicero's survey also serves to mark out the territory with which this chapter must necessarily deal.

THE ORIGINS OF DIVINATION

We may now turn back from the Roman world of the 1st century BC to the Greek world of the 8th, when Greek religious institutions and Greek society were developing those peculiar characteristics which we wish to examine. The Homeric poems provide the earliest secure evidence for oracles and divination in antiquity. The world of Crete and Mycenae, the Bronze Age, may however provide one clue, which Homer seems to corroborate, for necromancy, the calling up of the ghosts of the dead for consultation. The Haghia Triadha sarcophagus from 14th-century Crete (Plate 7) shows a scene of sacrifice in which a bull's blood is being poured into the earth, and other offerings are being made, while, apparently in answer, a figure rises from the ground in front of a tomb.

With this scene may be compared Odysseus' visit[5] to the river of Ocean at the confines of the world, his libations to the dead and preparation of sacrifice to them and in particular to Teiresias the prophet (*mantis*): 'When I had finished my prayers and invocations I took the sheep and cut their throats over the trench so that the dark blood poured in'. The souls cluster round but Odysseus keeps them off with his sword. 'And the soul of the Theban prophet now came up with a golden rod (*skēptron*) in his hand.' He greets Odysseus and says: 'Step back now from the trench and hold your sword aside, so that I can drink the blood, and prophesy truth to you'. And then Teiresias tells him how he can get home.

In this connexion we may remember that in the *Iliad* at the funeral feast of Patroclus animals are slaughtered and blood poured into the ground around the bier[6] and the ghost of Patroclus comes and stands at the head of Achilles as he lies asleep and tells him what he must do. But the most surprising echo is the 5th-century text from Aristophanes[7] which, possibly because of Socrates' interest in the 'care of the soul', speaks of him as a *psuchagogos*, a necromancer: 'there Peisander came wanting to see the soul which had left him when he was alive' (apparently a reference to his 'losing heart' in battle) 'having a camel-lamb as a sacrificial victim. He cut the throat like Odysseus and withdrew, and then there came up for him from below to the blood of the camel, the bat Chaerophon', who always looked like a ghost. Aristophanes is writing a complicated parody of the necromantic scene in the *Odyssey*, but it seems unlikely that he is not aware of some contemporary practice of spirit-raising, not of course to be attributed to either Socrates or Peisander, behind the parody.

The only 5th-century evidence for the practice, as far as I am aware, is the scene in Aeschylus' *Persae*[8] where the ghost of Darius is raised to give guidance to his queen and to the Persian elders in the face of Xerxes' defeat at Salamis. This is a play about contemporary events. She says to the chorus: 'My friends, with these libations to the dead I bid you chant hymns of good omen. Call upon the spirit of Darius and I will send these honours to be drunk by the earth for the gods below.' 'Lady Queen', they reply, 'do you send libations to the chambers beneath the earth, and we with hymns will ask for kindly guidance of the earth-bound dead'. We are not told what the libations consisted of. They invoke Earth and Hermes, guide of souls (*psuchopompos*) and finally Darius himself, to come. And he appears. The Jena *lekuthos*[9] may be recalled on which Hermes is depicted letting winged souls out of a large jar, resembling Tartarus as described by Hesiod in the *Theogony*.

The ghost of Teiresias is raised in the *Odyssey* by reason of his reputation as a *mantis* in his earthly life, which earned him alone of the dead the right to have full consciousness and retain his prophetic gift. He appears regularly in Attic tragedy where the Theban legends are concerned. In the *Iliad* the *mantis* of the Greek army is Calchas. The opening lines speak of the plague which afflicted the Greek army through Apollo's anger. An assembly is called and Achilles speaks[10]:

> Come let us enquire of some *mantis* or priest (*hiereus*) or interpreter of dreams (*oneiropolos*), for dreams come too from Zeus, who may tell why Phoebus Apollo is so wroth, if he has some complaint about prayer or hecatomb.
> And amongst them stood up Calchas son of Thestor, far the best of bird-augurers, who knew what is and what is to come and what has been before, and led the Achaean ships to Ilium through his mantic art which Phoebus Apollo gave him.

Calchas, like Teiresias, is a *mantis* and is here distinguished from a *hiereus* (who sacrificed and interpreted the omens of sacrifice) and an *oneiropolos*. All these, it should be noted, could be expected to provide an answer, by their various means, to Achilles' question. Calchas' way was bird-augury, interpreting the behaviour and cries of birds. The *mantis* is listed in the *Odyssey*[11] among the common craftsmen (*demioergoi*) who were always welcome at a prince's table. The others are: the carpenter, the singer, the doctor and the herald. The *prophētai domōn* of Aeschylus' *Agamemnon*,[12] the interpreters of omens attached to the palace, who speak darkly about Helen's departure, are presumably such retained *manteis*. In the second play in the trilogy, the *Choephoroi*,[13] retained dream interpreters are also mentioned.

It is interesting that the *mantis* is not merely a forecaster of future events, his sphere of knowledge embraces the past and present as well, he tells the truth as opposed to the appearance of things. He knows, in the *Iliad*, why Apollo is angry. Furthermore 'he led the Achaean ships to Troy'. His mantic art would tell him the right time to set out and the right time to seek harbour, it would also tell him the right course to sail. None of this would come to him through bird-augury. He must have had the practical skill of the navigator. So Helenus, on the Trojan side, who is like Calchas 'the best of bird-augurers'[14] also 'hears the voice of the immortal gods' i.e. like Calchas he possesses intuitive knowledge of the truth. While Calchas is also a navigator, Helenus is also a fighter.

In the *Odyssey*,[15] a bird omen occurs in the palace of

Menelaus to whom Helen is now restored. Helen herself declares that she will interpret it: 'Listen to me. I will be *mantis* as the immortal gods cast it in my mind, and as I think it will be accomplished'. So Phemius, the singer attached to Odysseus' palace, is not a trained bard, one who has served an apprenticeship with another bard. 'I am self-taught', he says, 'Zeus has put into my heart the many and various paths of song'.[16]

In addition to the three categories of divination mentioned by Achilles, augury by *mantis*, sacrifice by an *hiereus*, and dream interpretation by an *oneiropolos*, there is a fourth: second sight. Theoclymenus, a descendant of the legendary seer Melampus, whom Telemachus falls in with on his travels and brings back to Ithaca with him, claims mantic powers[17] and interprets a bird omen. When he sits down to dine with the suitors,[18] he suddenly cries out:

> Unhappy men, what is it that ails you? There is a shroud of night drawn over you from head to foot, a wailing bursts forth, and your cheeks are wet with tears. Blood drips from the walls and roof beams. The porch and the courtyard too are full of ghosts, trooping down to the blackness of the pit. The sun has vanished from the sky and a cursed mist has spread over the earth.

Theoclymenus seems to be less of a professional *mantis* than Calchas, perhaps by reason of his rootlessness, although he came of a mantic family. His gift of second sight seems to be exercised involuntarily, as Cassandra's was. Cassandra, as she appears in Aeschylus' *Agamemnon*, is an obvious parallel to Theoclymenus. Priam's daughter, given mantic powers but denied credibility by Apollo, is brought back to Argos by Agamemnon as his concubine. He returns in uneasy triumph, and goes into the palace, as the audience know, to his death. She is left outside, and Aeschylus gives, in a scene of 300 lines,[19] a detailed study of mantic possession which is one of the most moving and terrifying passages in Greek tragedy, and which it is difficult to believe was not taken somehow from the life. She senses correctly the murderous history of the Atreidae, the palace a charnel house that drips with children's blood. She sees and describes in minute detail the murder of Agamemnon which is taking place inside the palace; and she foretells her own death.

Calchas knows what is, what is to come and what was before. This description of mantic power exhibits a very important point of contact between the province of the *mantis* and that other great area of revelation in Greek thought, *sophia*, which in its early stages is both poetry and philosophy.

The proem to Hesiod's *Theogony*[20] begins with the Muses of Helicon, the daughters of Zeus, who in both the *Iliad* and the *Odyssey*[21] are the inspirers of poets. Here is Hesiod's description of his initiation into the poetic art.

> One day they taught Hesiod glorious song. . . . (They told him). 'We know how to speak many false things which are like the truth, and we know when we wish to speak true things.' So spake the ready-voiced daughters of great Zeus, and they plucked and gave me a rod (*skeptron*), a shoot of sturdy laurel, a thing to admire, and breathed into me a divine voice, to celebrate things which shall be and things which were before.

The Muses, like Apollo, are the offspring of Zeus. Like Apollo they grant the laurel as the symbol of their power of inspired speech. They speak[22] what is, what is to come and what was before. They are 'ready-voiced' (*artiepēs*), an epithet which Pindar[23] attaches also to Apollo. We can see how very similar, almost identical, is the range of ideas of poetry and prophecy. A fragment of Pindar runs[24]: 'Prophesy, Muse, and I will declare it forth'. As Teiresias has a *skeptron* to symbolise his gift of prophecy and the Pythia at Delphi (p. 99 below) gives responses with a sprig of laurel in her hand, so the poet has a *skeptron* of laurel to symbolise his gift. All three speak the word of Zeus, and it is probable that the *skeptron* which was passed from speaker to speaker in a political assembly and from guest to guest in a drinking party to give him the ear of the gathering had a similar significance.

Another poet, two centuries later, describes his initiation into *sophia* in the proem to his work. Parmenides[25] describes how he goes down to the underworld in a chariot, a supernatural mode of conveyance which Pindar also claims.[26] Here he meets a goddess who greets him kindly: 'Welcome, my son, you who come to our abode with immortal charioteers at the reins' (the daughters of Phoebus Apollo). ... 'It is needful that you learn all matters – both the un-shakeable heart of well-rounded truth and the opinions of men that lack true belief.' Parmenides' goddess-mentor thus gives the same sort of message as Hesiod's muse-initiators; the poet must learn to speak the revealed truth as well as men's opinions which are by comparison falsehood.

Pindar describes the initiation of Iamus, the founder of the family of prophets belonging to Zeus' oracle at Olympia, as follows[27]: 'Now when he had come unto the fruit of sweet Hebe golden crowned' (i.e. was grown up) 'going down into the midst of Alpheus by night beneath the open sky he called upon mighty Poseidon his grandsire, and upon the bow-bearing guardian of Delos divine' (i.e. Apollo) 'asking for his own self the grace to rear some people. And with quick response (*artiepēs*) the voice of his father sought and answered him, 'Come up my son and follow hither my guiding voice to a place which all men shall resort unto.' So they came to the steep rock of high Cronium' (at Olympia) 'where he endowed him with a gift of prophecy two-fold, first, that from that day he should hear the speech that knows not falsehood, and further . . . he bade him set up his oracle on the crown of the altar of Zeus.'

Thus Iamus is to have two distinct gifts: he is to have an intuitive knowledge of the truth, in Homer's words about Helenus he is to 'hear the voice of the gods', and secondly he is to have oracular powers. Epimenides of Crete[28] who was not a poet or philosopher but a kind of religious consultant in matters of purification, claimed to have slept for many years in a cave and there to have had revealed to him 'truth and justice'. Plato[29] says that Epimenides came to Athens 'ten years before the Persian wars at the bidding of Apollo's oracle and made such sacrifices as the god prescribed'. Aristotle[30] seems to put him at the beginning of the 6th century. In any case he seems to have been concerned with the ritual cleansing of the city.

This claim of a Greek *sophos*, whether a poet like Hesiod or Parmenides, or a prophet like Iamus or Epimenides, to have a supernatural contact with a source of revealed truth as the basis of his activity finds its most sophisticated expression later in Plato's philosophy. The ordinary man, Plato says, sees only a dream-image, a *phantasma* or *eikōn* of the truth. *Phaedrus*[31]: 'So dull are the organs of sense with which men approach these likenesses that hardly a few can see that kind in the likeness of which they are made'. The originals, on the other hand, are clear and bright and seen only by philosophers, who recognise them as the truths which they have glimpsed as souls in a discarnate state.

The point need not be further pursued. Francis Cornford made it in *Principium Sapientiae*.[32] He dwelt upon the aspect of the philosopher as the conscious inheritor of a past in which the exceptional wisdom of the *sophos* had been attributed to divine inspiration and expressed in poetry. He regarded the seer, the poet and the philosopher as originally identical, a shaman-like figure, and in the course of Greek intellectual history gradually differentiating into the separate figures of *mantis*, *poietes* and *sophistes-philosophos*, who in the archaic and classical periods appear as consciously distinct, yet as exhibiting still the marks of their common origin, in particular in their common awareness of the inspirational source of their knowledge.

Apollo appears to be the divine reflection of this shaman-like figure. In Homer he plays the lyre at Zeus' table while the Muses sing.[33] He grants the gift of prophecy, and he is the healer as well as the sender of pestilence. At the beginning of the 5th century, Pindar sums up this deified personality in the 5th Pythian[34]: 'He distributes to men and women healing even of heavy sickness. He brought the lyre, and grants the Muse to whomsoever he will, leading into the heart good order that is without strife; and he attends the prophetic shrine.' The political function of the *sophos* as producing good order and harmony in society is deeply interesting, and has a distinguished future, again culminating in Plato, but this cannot be pursued here.

I hope I have been able to illustrate, necessarily rather briefly, how the art of the *mantis* fits into the general picture of archaic Greek *sophia* and how Apollo, as the mouthpiece of Zeus and a divine shaman-figure, comes to be connected with it as part of a very varied field of activity.

THE MAIN ORACLE CENTRES IN GREECE

We can now turn to consider the main centres in Greece where the word of Zeus was given, in various ways, to human enquirers.

(i) The oracle at Dodona is regarded by ancient writers[35] as the first prophetic centre. Excavation has shown that the cult there goes back to the 8th century. At a dramatic moment in the *Iliad*,[36] Achilles agrees to commit the Myrmidons to battle under Patroclus, and prays to Zeus: 'Lord of Dodona, dwelling afar, ruling over hard-wintered Dodona; and around dwell the Selloi, your interpreters (*hupophētai*) of unwashen feet, sleeping on the ground'. Dodona is in NW Greece near modern Jannina, in an area accessible from Achilles' Thessalian home over the Pindus range. In the *Odyssey*[37] Odysseus in the disguise of a Cretan traveller concocts the story that he (the Cretan traveller) had heard news of Odysseus who had 'gone to Dodona to listen to the counsel of Zeus from his high-foliaged oak, how he should return to Ithaca, openly or secretly'. Oaks in Greece were recognised as belonging to Zeus,[38] and we may compare the oak of Jupiter on the Capitol at Rome and the sacred oaks of northern Europe. The *Odyssey* passage suggests a stage when the oak itself was regarded as giving an answer to questioners, mediated through the *hupophētai*.

The two taboos which they observe, 'unwashen feet and sleeping on the ground', both probably indicate closeness to earth, which is always regarded as a source of prophecy, as we shall see in the case of Delphi. In connection with the former it is interesting that Theoclymenus' ancestor Melampus, the legendary seer, has a name which means 'black foot'. Homer does not say how the oak was thought to give its message, but later writers[39] speak of a piece of the oak at Dodona which was built into the stempost of the Argo, and was able to speak. The Argonaut legend comes from neighbouring Thessaly. Mopsus, one of the two Argonaut *manteis*, is said to have come from Titaressus near Dodona and to have understood the prophesying of birds by Apollo's teaching.[40] This clue suggests that birds spoke from the tree and that their cries were interpreted. But Aeschylus[41] did not take this way out. Prometheus is speaking to wandering

Io: 'When you came to the Molossian plains and round about steep-ridged Dodona where are the oracles and seat of Thesprotian Zeus, and, unbelievable miracle, talking oaks, by which clearly and with no riddles you were addressed as she who would be the famous spouse of Zeus'.

There is, however, an enigmatic fragment of Hesiod[42] which seems likely to refer to birds as the oracle-givers. 'There is a certain Dodona built as a town at the farthest bound. It Zeus has loved and [wished it] to be his oracle centre for mankind.' Then there is a gap. 'And they dwelt in the stock of the oak where those who live on earth fetch all their prophecies.' Sophocles[43] tells the story of the prophecy concerning Heracles: 'as the ancient oak of Dodona had once spoken by the mouth of the two Peleiads' (Doves). The Peleiads might be actual doves, or, more likely, priestesses impersonating doves. In the same play Heracles refers to the old prophecy: 'which I wrote down in the grove of the Selloi, dwellers on the hills whose couch is on the ground. They were given by my father's oak of many tongues'.

In a fragment,[44] Sophocles certainly speaks of prophetic priestesses of Dodona, and Herodotus[45] in a long passage gives the results of his first-hand investigations of the oracles of Zeus at Siwa in Egypt and at Dodona. By his time there are certainly prophetesses as well as men of Dodona (?= Selloi) attached to the sanctuary at Dodona. There is an oak, but nothing about taking omens from it or about doves.

Excavation of the site has produced a great many folded lead strips from the end of the 6th century to 250 BC containing enquiries which could be answered (as the enquiry of Odysseus could have been) by a simple 'yes' or 'no'. One must suppose that the enquiry was made in this form and that originally the rustling of the oak-leaves, later the noise of doves, and later still the utterances of two priestesses (the Peleiads) were interpreted by the Selloi. By the end of the 5th century, in the words of a fragment of Euripides[46] 'at the holy seat of Dodona beside the sacred oak women convey the will of Zeus to all Greeks who desire it'. Plato says[47] that the prophetesses at Dodona become mad, and we may therefore infer in spite of Herodotus' silence on the matter that the prophetesses gave some sort of inspired utterance which required interpretation. Practice at Dodona seems to have ultimately conformed to what we shall see was the practice at Delphi.

Finally there is the story of the Spartan consultation 'about victory' before the battle of Leuctra in 371 BC,[48] which attests a different but possibly parallel method of divination.

> When the Spartan envoys had duly placed the vessel in which were the lots, a monkey, which the king of the Molossi (the local ruler) kept as a pet, overturned the actual lots and all the other things prepared for the sortition, and scattered them this way and that. Then the priestess who was in charge of the oracle is said to have told the Spartans that they ought not to be thinking of victory but of saving themselves.

We shall see that at Delphi too there was divination by lot as well as by inspired utterance.

(ii) Delphi is the most famous of the Greek oracular centres and a great deal has been written about it. Here we may draw attention only to those features which are relevant to the general picture of Greek divination which I have been trying to draw.

Dodona, though reputed the oldest oracle, does not show traces of cult before the eighth century, but at Delphi the shrine of Athena Pronaia near the cleft of Castalia shows continuity of worship from pre-Hellenic times. The *Hymn to Apollo* speaks of the first ministers (*orgeones*) of Apollo there being Cretan[49]: and this origin seems to be confirmed by the furniture of the oracular chamber. The *omphalos* (a betyl stone), the tree from which in the *Hymn* Apollo is said to speak while his servants announce his utterances, and the eagles[50] described by Pindar are all paralleled in Cretan cult. Only the tripod is new. The earth goddess, the occupant of the prophetic seat before the arrival of Apollo, or her surrogate the snake the Python, which Apollo slays,[51] may be the old snake goddess of Crete and possibly the original goddess worshipped in the temple of Athena Pronaia. Athena, on the acropolis at Athens, has a familiar snake. The taking-over by Apollo, whether peaceably as in Aeschylus or violently as in the *Hymn* and in Euripides, must indicate the sort of break with tradition which the shaman-figure of Apollo necessarily made, coming ultimately (possibly via Delos) from Asia Minor where Apolline oracles are numerous, e.g. Patara and Branchidae.

The statement in the *Hymn* that Apollo first prophesied 'from the laurel'[52] suggests an early stage parallel with the speaking oaks of Dodona. That it is Apollo speaking the will of Zeus is made quite clear[53]: the Pythia speaks of Apollo: 'for Zeus has framed a mind inspired with mantic skill within him and has seated him as the fourth *mantis* (after Earth, Themis and Phoebe) on this throne, and Loxias (= Apollo) is the mouthpiece of his father Zeus'. Yet as a god Apollo cannot be physically present, so he speaks 'possessing' the Pythian priestess. 'So I', the Pythia says 'take my seat upon the throne and if there is any Greek here let him come after drawing lots as is customary, for I speak prophecy as the god instructs.'

The Pythia, a woman past the age of child-bearing,[54] goes down[55] into the *adyton* or inner sanctuary and sits on the tripod[56] as Apollo is said to have done when he first occupied the shrine,[57] while the inquirer who has paid the fee (the *pelanos*, see below) remains in the outer room, the *oikos* or *megaron*[58] into which he is also described as going down.[59] The enquirer then sacrifices a goat which is declared acceptable if it shivers on being douched with water.[60] The enquiry is probably written.[61] The Pythia then utters in a state of possession, and the utterance is interpreted and put into hexameter verse by the *prophētēs*.[62]

These responses were, apparently, originally only given on the seventh day of one month in the spring,[63] but subsequently[64] 'the god occupied a mortal body once every month' with the exception of the three winter months when the god was absent. In the years of the oracle's popularity, two Pythias were employed on these response days with one in reserve.[65] There was an alternative mode of response here as at Dodona, i.e. by lot, an answer 'yes' or 'no' to a question framed suitably. This might possibly take place on other days of the month. A remarkable vase-painting (Plate 8) shows the Pythia seated on a tripod and thoughtfully gazing at a flat dish which she holds in her left hand while she grasps a sprig of laurel in the other. In front of her but separated by a column, which may indicate the division between the *megaron* and the *adyton*, there is a man standing, presumably the enquirer. We must suppose that the dish contains the lots (black and white beans), one of which she will pick up with her right hand, thus indicating an answer 'yes' or 'no'. It seems that the word for any kind of oracular answer, *anaireisthai*, to pick up, derives from this procedure.

Enquirers could be individuals or cities. Two remarkable inscriptions survive laying down the tariff for public and private enquiries for two Greek cities, Phaselis and Sciathos. The Phaselis inscription is dated 420 BC. The Phaselians will pay the *pelanos* to the Delphians according to the following tariff: for matters of state 7 dr. 2 obols, for private enquiries 4 obols. There were six obols to the drachma and a drachma was a day's pay for an Athenian oarsman in the 4th century. The Sciathus inscription is fifty years later: 'if anyone presents himself for consultation by two beans the fee for a state enquiry shall be one Aeginetan stater (=2 Athenian dr.) and for a private enquiry the equivalent of one obol. The remarkable difference in fees may be because the Phaselis tariff was for an inspired response, while the Sciathus enquiry was for a response by lot. Or it may represent the difference in prosperity between the two cities. One thing at any rate is clear *aneu chalchou Phoibos ou manteustai*: no fee, no consultation.

There are many other problems. For example, scholars have been determined to place the Pythia in an underground chamber or cave, but no signs whatever of a cave have been found. The Romans, indeed the Greeks of the late 4th century, became convinced that the priestess' possession was to be explained by vapours rising from a fissure in the rock,[66] but geologists have been definite that the limestone rocks of Delphi could have produced no such vapours, nor has a cleft been found. There is also the puzzling occupation of the temple in the winter months by Dionysus, and the presence of his tomb in the *adyton*. But these matters are not to be discussed here.

7. Necromancy, by sacrifice and offering; after a painting on the Haghia Triadha Sarcophagus, 14th century Crete (after Parabeni, *Mon. Ant.* XIV Pl. 1–3).

8. The Pythia; Attic red-figure vase of about 440 BC, in the *Staatliche Museen*, Berlin, DDR.

DIVINATION IN ATHENS IN THE
5th AND 4th CENTURIES

Some attention has been given to the mantic art in archaic
Greece and to the two most famous oracular centres, Dodona
and Delphi. It remains to see the impact of these institutions
on the life of Athens in the 5th and 4th centuries which is
tolerably well illustrated for us by surviving literature and
inscriptions.

Three names repeatedly occur here in connection with
religious matters: *mantis*, with which we are familiar,
chrésmologos an oracle expert, and *exēgētēs*, an expounder either
of oracles or of ritual prescriptions.

An irreverent, but enlightening, treatment of a *chresmologos*
is to be found in Aristophanes *Birds*.[67] The new bird-city has
been founded and a succession of people turns up wanting to
take advantage of the business opportunities offered. The
Athenian founder, Peisthetairus, is on the point of sacrificing
a goat when the *chresmologos* appears.

Chr. Don't start the goat.

P. Who are you?

Chr. Who am I? a chresmologist.

P. Chresmologist be damned.

Chr. My dear sir, you mustn't despise religion. There happens to be an oracle of Bakis which fits Bird City to a T.

P. Then why didn't you tell me about it *before* I founded
this city [the normal time for oracle consultation]?

Chr. Heaven prevented me.

P. Well, I suppose there is no harm in hearing the verses.

Chr. (*Chants*) Nay but if once grey crows and wolves shall
be banded together Out in the boundary space
between Corinth and Sicyon dwelling.

P. But what have the Corinthians to do with me?

Chr. In the riddle Bakis meant the air. (*Chants*) First to
Pandora offer a white-fleeced ram for a victim. Next
who first shall arrive my verses prophetic expounding
... to him give a clean cloak and new shoes.

P. The shoes are there too?

Chr. Take the book and look it up. (Chants) And give a
cup and fill his hand with tripe.

P.   "Give tripe" 's there too?

Chr.   Take the book and look it up. (Chants) And if, divine youth, you do as I bid, you will be an eagle in the clouds; but if you don't do this, you won't be a dove or an eagle or a woodpecker.

P.   This is in it too?

Chr.   Take the book and look it up.

P.   But the oracle's not like that at all, not the one I copied out from Apollo. That one goes like this: (chants) But when a buffoon comes along without an invitation, and pesters the sacrificers and wants some tripe, then you beat him.

Chr.   But that's ridiculous.

P.   Take the book and look it up. And don't spare the eagle in the clouds, whether he be Lampon or the great Diopeithes.

Chr.   (dumbfounded) Is this all there?

P.   Take the book and look it up. Shoo, off with you.

What were these books of oracles which the *chresmologoi* possessed and expounded? Bakis' oracle-book was a famous one as we shall see. But there were others under the names of Musaeus and Orpheus. Onomacritus was the first *chresmologos* we hear much about at Athens although Lysistratos[68] may have been earlier. Herodotus[69] speaks of him aiding the sons of the tyrant Peisistratus when they were in exile in Persia. He says: 'Onomacritus, an Athenian *chresmologos* who had edited the oracles of Musaeus, beset Xerxes with his prophecies'. He adds that Onomacritus had been banished from Athens by Hipparchus, Peisistratus' son, 'because Lasus of Hermione had caught him in the act of inserting among the sayings of Musaeus a prophecy that the islands near Lemnos were to vanish into the sea' (presumably a *vaticinium post eventum* to bolster Musaeus' credibility). Aristotle said that Onomacritus forged Orphic poems.[70] Herodotus[71] also speaks of an unnamed collection of prophecies which fell into the Spartan king Cleomenes' hands when he occupied the Athenian acropolis after expelling the Peisistratids. 'The sons of Peisistratus owned them, but left them in the temple when they were driven out, and Cleomenes picked them up as they lay there'.

They may of course have been the Musaeus collection.
Herodotus gives an account[72] of the Athenian consultation
of the oracle at Delphi before the battle of Salamis and of the
interpretation given by the *chresmologoi*. It is interesting that
Themistocles challenges their interpretation. Like Calchas
and Helenus as bird-augurers, so the Athenian *chresmologoi*
did not have absolute authority of interpretation, an amateur
could try his hand as well. Herodotus speaks of the oracles of
Bakis in connection with the battle of Artemisium,[73] and this
book turns up later, with the oracles of Musaeus, in connection with Salamis.[74] The oracles of Bakis also appear in the
Knights of Aristophanes[75] where Cleon has his own collection
which Demosthenes urges Nicias to steal, and he does.[76] The
characters are Demos, representing the Athenian people,
Cleon the present demagogue-favourite, and the Sausage-
seller who is competing for Demos' attention.[77]

Demos   Let me see, whoever do these oracles belong to?
Cleon   Mine are Bakis'.
Demos   And your's?
SS.   Glanis', Bakis' elder brother.
Demos   What are they about?
Cleon   Athens, Pylos, you, me, every damn thing.
Demos   And your's? what are they about?
SS.   Athens, soup, Spartans, fresh mackerel, bad measure
          in the market, you, me, every damn thing.
Demos   Well, then, why not read them to me, *and* the one
          about *me*, the famous one I love so much, that I
          shall become an eagle in the sky.

And so on. It transpires that a number of the oracles were
given by Apollo, so it is reasonable to suppose that they are
all genuine or supposititious Delphic oracles assembled by
Bakis, Musaeus etc (Glanis looks like an invention). And it
appears from Aristophanes that they were, or at any rate
some of them were, political forecasts, the ancient equivalent
of the Gallup poll.

At the outbreak of the Peloponnesian war, Thucydides
says[78] 'the *chresmologoi* chanted oracles of all kinds and they
listened to them as each man was inclined' (again very like
the Gallup polls). Thucydides also records[79] that when the

news of the disaster at Syracuse hit Athens 'besides being severe on the politicians who had joined in promoting the expedition, the Athenians were angry also with the *chresmologoi* and *manteis* and any one who in any way by divination had raised their hopes of taking Sicily'. Thucydides doesn't say much about this earlier, but Plutarch[80] fills the gap with the information that Alcibiades, to counter the opposition of the *hiereis* (sacrificial priests) to the expedition, gained the support of other *manteis* and produced ancient *logia* (a word used by Herodotus for *chresmoi*) to the effect that Athens would get great glory from Sicily. 'And *theopropoi*' i.e. official enquirers 'came to him from Ammon with an oracle saying that the Athenians would capture all the Syracusans'. Plutarch[81] also says that when an eclipse of the moon took place just as Nicias was about to make his last attack against Syracuse, he had no skilled *mantis* at hand since Stilbides, who had accompanied the expedition and kept Nicias' superstitious fears in check, had died a short time before.

Stilbides was a reputable *mantis* who appears in Aristophanes[82] and elsewhere in Old Comedy. His name (Brightson) is similar to that of another well-known *mantis* at Athens at this time, Lampon (=Shiner) and the coincidence suggests that there were mantic families who named their sons with the profession in mind. Truth is bright and clear. Lampon appears in the well known story told by Plutarch[83] about Pericles asking Lampon and Anaxagoras to give competitive explanations of the portent of the one-horned ram. Lampon declared that it foretold Pericles' *monarchia*, while Anaxagoras dissected the animal and demonstrated the pathological cause of the phenomenon. Lampon was also the butt of comedy from the 40s onwards as gluttonous (Cratinus) and a slippery customer.[84] When the international colony of Thurii was founded in 440, Lampon is said to have been sent as *exegetes* for the foundation of the city, i.e. presumably to look after the religious aspects of the foundation. In 418 a long inscription[85] recording a decree of the Athenian assembly about the payment of first-fruits to Eleusis contains a rider proposed by Lampon.

The *chresmoi* we have noticed hitherto have been mainly political. There was another kind. Plato in the *Laws*[86] says that the religious rituals of the new state should be prescribed by *chresmoi* from Apollo at Delphi, Ammon at Siwa and Zeus at Dodona, and in the *Republic*[87] he says less precisely, but certainly meaning the same thing, that the religious observances of the state are to be left to Apollo alone. Earlier in the *Republic*[88] he mentions ritual prescriptions concerning the after-life being contained in the books of Musaeus and Orpheus, so that we can attribute such material also to the books of Musaeus and Orpheus which Onomacritus is said to have meddled with.

To return to the *manteis*. Besides Stilbides and Lampon, we hear of others. Herodotus[89] says that before the battle of Plataea in 479 'Teisamenos was the man who performed the sacrifice for the Greeks, for he accompanied the army as a *mantis*'. Here he performs the duty of a *hiereus*. One Telenikos, a *mantis*, appears in the casualty list[90] for the tribe Erechtheis in 459/8 BC. Hierocles, a *hiereus* who has a scene devoted to him in the *Peace* of Aristophanes[91] appears in an inscription of 446/5 BC[92] as bidden to accompany three men chosen by the Athenian Council from among their number to carry out the sacrifices required by the *chresmoi* about Euboea. To get it done quickly, the generals are to help and provide the money. Hierocles appears to have been given the right of dining at the public expense in the *prytaneion*. A fifth name in this connection is Diopeithes who, according to Plutarch, as a religious leader proposed a bill to prosecute atheists and teachers of meteorology. We have seen that Aristophanes calls him 'great'[93] where the scholiast says he was a *chresmologos* and orator, the latter no doubt because of the bill he proposed. Aristophanes, *Knights*, also calls him a greedy beggar, while other comic writers (Ameipsias, Telecleides, Phrynichus) call him crazy. That he was nevertheless a reputable person is suggested by the well-attested fact[94] that he was called in to decide a dispute between the Spartan kings after the end of the Peloponnesian war.

The position of these people, *manteis*, *chresmologoi*, *hiereis* at Athens seems to have been unofficial, unestablished. Yet at the same time they were highly respected and played important semi-official roles. Aristotle[95] says that they assisted the *hieropoioi*, who were annually appointed officers, in sacrifices offered by the state. They were the experts while the *hieropoioi* were the amateurs. Cicero[96] seems to be about right when

he says: *Athenienses manteis omnibus semper consiliis adhibuerunt.*
'The Athenians brought in *manteis* in all their deliberations'.

Aristophanes' criticism of the *manteis* focusses on their
claim to foretell the future, their meddling in public affairs
and their maintenance at public expense; also on their self-
interested greed. But these attacks are mild and trivial
compared with what we find in tragedy. Sophocles presents
Jocasta in the *Oedipus Tyrannus*[97] as condemning all forms of
mantiké – but look what happened to her. Sophocles is
certainly not putting his own views here, but he is likely to
be reflecting contemporary criticisms. A more balanced view
is given by the chorus in the same play[98]: 'Zeus and Apollo
are wise and know mortal affairs, but there is no certainty
that a *mantis* carries more weight than I'. Here the chorus
expresses what we have noticed as a persistent anti-
clericalism in these matters. When Oedipus thinks that
Teiresias is plotting against him, he says some harsh things[99]:
'this scheming mullah, this tricky beggar, whose seeing is in
profit and in prophecy is blind'. And Creon makes similar
remarks about him in the *Antigone*[100]: 'the whole tribe of
manteis is money-grubbing'. And no doubt they, too, echo
contemporary attitudes.

But it is Euripides who really goes to town on the subject
of *mantike*, though in one place he shows some sympathy for
the poor *mantis*. Like Sophocles, he expresses the view that
Apollo's oracles are firm and that it is the prophecy of mortals
that is to be rejected.[101]

The messenger in the *Helen*[102] is more specific:

I perceived how seers' craft is rotten and full of falsehood. Nothing is sound in burnt offerings nor in the cries
of birds. It is folly to suppose that birds help humankind.
Calchas neither spoke nor indicated to the army when he
saw his friends dying for a phantom, nor did Helenus, but
the city was sacked in vain. You may say that he did not
because the god did not wish it. Why then do we have
manteis at all? We should ask good things directly from the
gods with sacrifices, and leave *manteis* alone. For this
invention was a snare and a delusion. No one gets wealth
by burnt offerings unless he works as well. The best *mantis*
is brains and good judgment.

This is an echo from Antiphon[103]: 'prophecy is the guess of an intelligent man'. Elsewhere Euripides repeats Aristophanes' criticism that *manteis* are all wickedly ambitious and greedy. In the *Bacchae*,[104] Pentheus says that Teiresias is only keen on Dionysus because of the opportunity for extra fees a new deity would create.

In the *Phoenissae*, however, Euripides allows Teiresias to put his side of the picture[105]: 'whoever practices the science of burnt offerings is a fool, since if he happens to indicate things hostile he is disliked by his clients. But if he speaks what is false out of pity for his clients, he wrongs the gods. Apollo alone, who fears no one, should declare prophecy to men'. The defence seems to add up to much the same conclusion as the criticism. It is interesting that for all his attacks on Apollo on other counts, Euripides does not challenge him on this. The Apolline oracle seems to have been above criticism.

Plato, writing in the 4th century, reveals another side of *mantike*[106]: 'beggarly *manteis* knock on the doors of the rich and persuade them that they have power from the gods by sacrifices and incantations to make restitution by means of pleasurable feasts for any injustice committed by a man and his forbears'. That there must have been very real fear of avenging spirits is shown not only by tragedy, in particular Aeschylus, where we might be tempted to dismiss it as archaism, but also by the speeches of Antiphon where we meet sentences like the following[107]: 'If we the avengers of the dead prosecute the innocent out of malice, we shall, since we are not avenging the dead, be haunted by terrible spirits of vengeance, the suppliant souls of the dead. The dead man deprived of the gifts of god naturally leaves behind him as god's punishment the hostility of avenging spirits'. And there are plenty of other such passages. The attitude of mind revealed in them may account for the appearance of people called *exégétai* in 4th-century literature. They seem to be recognised consultants in matters of religious law and custom, particularly in cases of expiation. Four examples can be given: (1) In Plato's *Euthyphro*[108] Euthyphro's father has a slave who murdered a fellow slave on Naxos. So he tied him up and threw him into a ditch and sent a man to Athens to enquire from the *exegetes* what should be done (the fact that the man, not unexpectedly, died is another story).

(2) In Isaeus[109] there is the question of payment for the funeral of a grandparent. The speaker made an inquiry of an *exegetes* and, following his instructions, paid a ninth share.

(3) In a speech attributed, probably wrongly, to Demosthenes,[110] the speaker is involved in the death of a nurse in his house as the result of a violent burglary.

> As soon then as she was dead I went to the *exegetai* to discover what I should do in the matter and I explained to them the whole occurrence. . . . When the *exegetai* heard my story they asked me whether they should expound the sacred law to me or should give me advice. I said, both; and they continued: we will expound the law and give you advice on what is expedient. First carry the spear on the bier and make a declaration at the tomb asking if there is any next of kin of the woman, and then watch over the tomb for three days . . . do not accuse anyone by name but only those who have done the deed and committed the murder, and secondly do not bring a case to the king archon. . . .

(4) Finally there is the case of the superstitious man in Theophrastus[111]: 'And if a mouse eats the corn-bag he goes to the *exegetes* and inquires what he must do: and, if the *exegetes* gives him the answer 'give the bag to the cobbler to mend' he doesn't pay attention to this advice but goes away and makes an expiatory sacrifice'.

Another province of the *exegetai* was *Diosémiai* i.e. rain, thunder, lightning, eclipses, earthquakes. These were reasons for interrupting public business, the assembly,[112] the law-courts,[113] elections and the start of military expeditions.[114] It was apparently the *exegetai* who were consulted and who, like umpires in a cricket match, decided whether or not to interrupt play.

Who were these *exegetai*? In his life of *Theseus*,[115] Plutarch says that Theseus made the Eupatridai, the traditional noble families of Athens, *exegetai hosiōn kai hierōn*, expounders of holy and sacred things. There is late 5th century evidence[116] that the Eumolpidai, the traditional aristocratic family of Eleusis, exercised the function of *exegesis* there. We know also from later inscriptions[117] that there were at Athens '*exegetai* from the Eupatridai'. We may remember that at Rome the obsolescence of divination was ascribed to the neglect of it by the *nobiles*. However, a decree of 440/433 BC[118] proposed by Pericles, in laying down the categories of people who were entitled to dine at public expense in the *prytaneion*, includes 'the *exegetai* whom Apollo chose to expound the customary rules (*ta nomima*) and those whom he shall choose in the future'. This decree seems to indicate with sufficient clarity that the 'expounders chosen by Apollo', who are called in later inscriptions *puthochrestoi* and are distinct from the 'exegetai from the Eupatridai', were in fact officially recognised at Athens. It is these then who expounded to individuals the Apolline code of practice in respect of blood-guilt and took decisions in respect of *diosemiai*.

Finally, and briefly, there is the interpretation of dreams, the third of the categories of enlightenment in Achilles' question with which we started. Greeks always believed that the soul, or part of the soul, was somehow freed from the inhibition of the body during sleep and could indicate truth of the present, past or, particularly, future, by means of dreams. Pindar[119] speaks of an image of life (*aiōnos eidōlon*) 'which alone is from the gods. It sleeps when the limbs are active, but to men asleep in many dreams it gives presage of a decision of things pleasant and things severe'. And Aristotle's view is much the same[120]: 'when the soul is by itself in dreaming, then it achieves its own nature and presages and foretells the future'. So men were generally believed to foretell the future when on the point of death,[121] their soul similarly on the point of liberation. Plato's view[122] was different: the seer who has the visions (in sleep) is not employing the divine and immortal part but the irrational and appetitive, which receives warnings and admonitions in these symbolic images from the reason and requires the aid of reason's waking reflection to interpret them.

In either case dreams need interpretation by experts, *oneiropoloi* as they are called in Homer and in Herodotus.[123] Dreams come from earth, as Aeschylus and Euripides[124] say, and earth must be propitiated. Sacrifice must be made to the spirits below who avert evil.[125] In tragedy there are a number of such scenes of propitiation,[126] and there is a parody of one in Aristophanes *Frogs*.[127] In the prologue to Aristophanes'

Wasps,[128] the two slaves swap dreams and practise some do-it-yourself, cheap interpretation. The most vividly dramatic of these scenes in tragedy is in Aeschylus *Choephoroi*,[129] when Electra and the chorus come out of the palace bearing propitiatory offerings for Clytemnestra's evil dreams. The chorus speaks: (Headlam's translation)

> A cry was heard, it pierced the night, prophetic terror breathing wrath to come, hair-raising panic swiftly scattering slumber, heavy haunting shriek of fear; it rang out loud and shrill, where the women's chambers are. And then the prophets taught of god, after they had read the dream, cried out the message. 'Dead men in the earth are wroth with those that murdered them. Now to placate such ills implacable – O hear Earth, Mother – fearful she sent me, godless woman.'

And they go on their way to placate the nether powers with libations.

Here the dream does not foretell the future. It does what Calchas did in the *Iliad*, it reveals the truth about a situation. We should, I think, be wrong if we supposed that belief in such revelatory power in dreams was not part of the consciousness of 5th-century Athenians, just as belief in vengeful spirits of the dead certainly was. Interpreters of dreams were common in Athens, and Antiphon himself wrote a book on 'the Interpretation of Dreams', which seems to have shown that the meaning of a dream might be the opposite of the obvious one. His purpose may have been to discredit all interpretation.

We are used to thinking of Athens in the 5th and 4th century as the abode of reason and enlightenment. In some sense it was, but there was another side to the picture which this chapter has tried to show. In the *Prometheus Vinctus*, Aeschylus puts into the mouth of his hero an account of the arts of civilisation which he claims to have brought to mankind. Sandwiched in between medicine and mining, we find a description of the arts of divination which may serve as a concluding summary[130] although it also reminds us that there were branches of the mantic art which we have been unable to touch:

And many ways of prophecy I put in order, and first interpreted what must come of dreams in waking hours, and the obscure import of wayside signs and voices I defined, and taught them to discern the various flights of taloned birds, which of them favourable and which of ill foreboding, and the ways of life by each pursued, their mating seasons, their hatreds and their loves for one another; the entrails too, of what texture and hue they must appear to please the sight of heaven; the dappled figure of the gall and liver, the thigh-bone wrapt in fat and the long chine I burnt and led man to the riddling art of divination; and augury by fire, for long in darkness hid, I brought to light.

All these beliefs and practices must belong to the civilisation of Periclean Athens. It seems that it was not only Livy's boring old Romans who were riddled with superstition, but the exciting enlightened Greeks as well.

Notes

1   W. E. Heitland, *The Roman Republic*, Cambridge, 1909, I, pp. 22–3.
2   Cicero *de div.* II, 24.
3   Valerius Maximus II, iv, 3.
4   Cicero *de div.* II, 35, 75.
5   *Od.*, 11, 13f.
6   *Il.*, 23, 30–4, 65.
7   *Birds*, 1553f.
8   *Persae*, 619f.
9   M. P. Nilsson, *Geschichte der Griechische Religion*, Munich, 1941, I, Tafel 33, 3.
10 *Il.*, 1.43f., 62f.
11 *Od.* 17, 382f and 19, 135.
12 *Agamemnon*, 409.
13 *Choephoroi*, 37.
14 *Il.*, 6, 76 and 7, 53.
15 *Od.*, 15, 160f., and 172.
16 *Od.*, 22, 347–8.
17 *Od.*, 17, 154.
18 *Od.*, 20, 351f.
19 *Agamemnon*, 1035–1330.

20 *Theogony* 1–115.
21 *Il.*, 2, 485; *Od.*, 1, 1; 8, 73; 8, 481; 17, 518f.
22 Hesiod *Theogony* 38.
23 *Ol.*, vi, 61f.
24 Frg., 137 Bowra.
25 Diels-Kranz, 27 B 1.
26 *Ol.* ix, 81; *Isth.* ii, 2 and viii, 68.
27 *Ol.*, vi, 57–76.
28 Maximus of Tyre 10 and 38: Diels-Kranz 3 B 1.
29 *Laws*, I, 642d.
30 *Ath. Pol.* I.1 (Shortly before Solon's archonship).
31 *Phaedrus*, 250b.
32 Published posthumously; Cambridge 1952.
33 *Il.*, 1, 603.
34 *Pyth.* v, 63–8.
35 *Phaedrus*, 275b.
36 *Il.*, 16, 234.
37 *Od.*, 14, 327 and 19, 296.
38 *Il.*, 5, 693 and 7, 60; Aristoph., *Clouds*, 402.
39 Aesch. frg. 20 and Ap. Rhod., I, 526–7.
40 Ap. Rhod. I, 65–6.
41 *P.V.*, 829.
42 134 Rz, 240 Merk. West.
43 *Trach.*, 155f.
44 Frg. 456 Jebb-Pearson.
45 II, 52f.
46 *Melanippe Desmotis*, Page *Greek Literary Papyri* London 1942. I, 112, 11–13.
47 *Phaedrus*, 275b.
48 Callisthenes *FGrH* 124, 22 a and b; Cicero, *de Div.*, 1, 34 and 76, and 2, 32 and 69.
49 Hom. *Hymns* III 388.
50 *Pyth.* iv, 4.
51 Hom. *Hymns* III 394; Eur. I.T. 1247f.
52 Hom. *Hymns* III 396.
53 Aesch. *Eum.* 17.
54 Diodorus 16, 26, 6.
55 Aesch. *Eum.* 38; Plut. *Mor.* 397a.
56 Eur. *Ion* 91.
57 Eur. *I.T.* 976, 1247; Soph. Frg. 1044 Jebb-Pearson.
58 *Herodotus* VII, 140.
59 *Herodotus* V, 92e.
60 Plut. *Mor.* 435b, 437a.
61 Sch. Aristoph. *Plutus*, 39.
62 Herodotus I, 48 and VII, 142.
63 Plut. *Mor.* 292d-e.
64 Plut. *Mor.* 398a-b.
65 Plut. *Mor.* 414b.
66 Diodorus 16, 261–4.

67 *Birds*, 959f.
68 Herodotus VIII, 96.
69 Herodotus VII, 6.
70 Aristotle Frg. 7 Ross.
71 Herodotus V, 90, 2.
72 Herodotus VII, 140f.
73 Herodotus VIII, 20, 2.
74 Herodotus VIII, 77 and 96.
75 123–4.
76 115f.
77 1002f.
78 II, 21, 3.
79 VIII, 1.
80 *Nicias*, 13.
81 *Nicias*, 23.
82 *Peace*, 1032.
83 *Pericles*, 6.
84 Aristophanes, *Birds*, 521.
85 IG I^2 76, Tod 74.
86 *Laws* V 738 b-e.
87 427b.
88 364 d-e.
89 Herodotus IX 33.
90 *IG* I^2 929, Tod 26, 128–9.
91 1043f.
92 *IG* I^2 39, Tod 42, 65f.
93 *Birds*, 988.
94 Xen. *Hell.* III, 3, 3; Plut. *Ages.* 3, *Lysander* 22 etc.
95 *Ath. Pol.* 54, 6.
96 *de div.* 1, 95.
97 707f.
98 499f.
99 387–8.
100 1055.
101 *El.* 399–400.
102 744–57.
103 Diels-Kranz 87 A 9.
104 255–7.
105 954f.
106 *Rep.* 364b.
107 IV, 1 (4).
108 *Euthyphro* 4 b-e.
109 8, 39.
110 Demosthenes 47, 68.
111 16, 6.
112 Aristoph. *Ach.* 169f, *Eccl.* 790f; Thuc. V, 45, 4.
113 Pollux 8, 124
114 Aristoph. *Clouds*, 577f.
115 Plutarch *Theseus* 25.

116   *IG* 1² 76, Tod 74.
117   Jacoby *Atthis*, Oxford, 1949 p. 10 No. 11 (late 1st century BC).
118   *IG* 1² 77: Jacoby *ib.* p. 8 No. 1.
119   Frg. 116 Bowra.
120   Aristotle Frg. 12a Ross.
121   Plat. *Apol.* 39c, *Phaedo* 85b.
122   *Tim.* 71a–72b.
123   e.g. V 56.
124   *Suppl.*, 899–902; *I.T.* 1261–62.
125   Xen. *Symp.* iv, 33.
126   Soph., *El.* 406f., 644.
127   *Frogs*, 1331–40.
128   9f.
129   *Choephoroi*, 33f.
130   484–99.

5

The Germanic World

HILDA ELLIS DAVIDSON
Vice-President of Lucy Cavendish College, Cambridge

There is an Icelandic proverb quoted in the saga of Grettir the Strong which reads: *Spá er spaks geta.*[1] This has caused some difficulty to translaters, and has been rendered: 'The guess of the wise is truth', but this statement needs qualification and conceals the real meaning of the Icelandic. *Spá* here is a noun meaning prophecy or revelation; it is also found as a verb: to prophesy. The speaker is addressing a man with special gifts of second sight, and he declares that 'Prophecy is the wise man's guess', or, if you like, 'The wise man's guess reveals hidden truth'. Behind this use of the word *spá* – which can be recognised in the Scots dialect word *spaewife* – there is a rich tradition which continued into Christian times in the Scandinavian North, and indeed has not wholly vanished.

When the severe volcanic eruption took place on Heimaey in the Westman Islands in 1975, authorities and people were taken by surprise, and the population moved out by the fishing fleet in the middle of the night, only just in time. Yet I heard that the newspapers were full of letters from those who afterwards claimed to have had foreknowledge of the catastrophe in dreams, and the ability to 'dream true' is still taken very seriously in modern irreligious Iceland. In medieval Icelandic literature we find, together with a strong sense of the power of fate, the assumption that events to come

can be revealed by those possessing certain powers, and that
the future, and indeed the past also and what may be hidden
in the present, may be uncovered in various ways. Sometimes
this depends on certain skills and techniques, and sometimes
the knowledge comes unbidden in the form of dreams,
visions, omens and portents. I shall be dealing here mainly
with the first of these two categories, but it is impossible to
keep them completely apart.

It was also held in pre-Christian times among the Germanic
and Scandinavian peoples that it was possible to enquire of
the gods in various ways to discover their will, and to receive
a specific answer, so that it may be claimed that oracles as
well as divination were used by them; I am accepting here
the definitions given in the OED, which defines divination
as 'the foretelling of future events or discovery of what is
hidden or obscure by supernatural or magical means', and
oracle as 'the instrumentality, agency or medium by which
a god was supposed to speak or make known his will'.

Iceland in the Viking Age was a meeting place for two
rich cultures, the North Germanic, brought by Scandinavian
settlers, and the Celtic, since many of these had spent years
in the British Isles before coming to Iceland, and had Scottish
or Irish kindred or dependents. Of the Celtic heritage I am
not qualified to speak, but both Celts and Germans clearly
set great store on divination, which was a major factor in
their religion before they were converted to Christianity. For
knowledge of this as practised by Germanic peoples on the
continent, before the Viking Age, we rely mainly on information from Latin writers. Both Julius Caesar and Tacitus were
much impressed by the faith which the Germans placed in
auguries.

CONSULTATION OF LOTS

Tacitus was writing at the end of the first century after
Christ, and for the Germans he makes it clear that divination
was of importance both in tribal and family life. It is
not very likely that he himself visited Germany,[2] but
his informants and sources seem to have been good, and as
our knowledge of the early Germans increases, so does

confidence in Tacitus as a reliable source. In a section on
auguries in the tenth chapter of his *Germania*, he tells us how
they practised the drawing of lots when they needed to make
a decision[3]:

> Their procedure in casting lots is always the same. They
> cut off a branch of a nut-bearing (i.e. fruitful) tree[4] and
> slice it into strips; these they mark with different signs and
> throw them completely at random on to a white cloth.
> Then the priest of the state, if the consultation is a public
> one, or the father of the family if it is private, offers a
> prayer to the gods, and looking up at the sky picks up three
> strips, one at a time, and reads their meaning from the signs
> previously scored on them. If the lots forbid an enterprise,
> there is no deliberation that day on the matter in question;
> if they allow it, confirmation by the taking of auspices is
> required.

It seems reasonable to assume, although we cannot be sure,
that the signs made on these small slips of wood were of a
similar type to the runic symbols which we know were in
use by the end of the third century, and which continued to
be used by Germanic and Scandinavian peoples long after
they became Christian. Runes were used to inscribe names,
phrases, memorial inscriptions, and what seem to be spells
on wood, stone, bone and metal, and would be particularly
well suited for the kind of consultation which Tacitus
describes, since each sign had its own name and represented
something definite: for instance in Old Germanic, U was the
aurochs, the giant ox; in Old English, M was man, G was
gifu, a gift, R was *rad*, a journey; in Norwegian, Th was *þurs*,
a giant, and so on.[5] If three signs of this type were picked out,
the augurer could decide on the nature of the link between
them and its bearing on the question asked, and give an
answer accordingly. Simpler forms of consultation were no
doubt also used, as for instance among the Slavs to the south
of the Baltic, in the late Viking Age, who are said to have
used lots coloured black on one side and white on the other,
presumably giving a simple yes or no.[6] The importance of
the number three, which continues to be emphasised in later
accounts of the drawing of lots, is apparent also in the

division of the runic *futhorc*, or alphabet, into three rows, a
rule retained even when extra signs were added, or when, as
in the Viking Age in Scandinavia, the signs were reduced in
number.

The drawing of lots in this way was used to decide which
victims should be selected for sacrifice. Julius Caesar in the
first century before Christ knew of such a custom, as his
friend Gaius Valerius Procillus narrowly escaped death when
on an embassy to the German leader Ariovistus.[7] The Roman
was treated as a prisoner of war, and lots were cast three
times (in his presence, Caesar tells us) to decide whether or
not he should be put to death at once by burning, but they
came out in such a way each time that the execution was
postponed; later he was released by his own men when they
came upon a party of Germans retreating with their prisoners.

Alcuin's *Life of St. Willibrord*, written in the eighth century,
describes a similar incident, after the saint had committed
sacrilege in the eyes of the pagans on the island of Heligoland
by baptizing converts in a holy spring and killing sacred
cattle.[8] The king, convinced that the gods would be angered
by such behaviour, cast lots three times a day for three days,
in order to decide which man in the company should be put
to death, but each time Willibrord was spared, although
another man was executed. The same idea of lots used to
select a victim, according to the will of the gods, is found in
the story of King Vikar, a ruler in Norway; the source of
this is of twelfth-century date, but likely to be based on earlier
Viking Age traditions.[9] The king had promised a human
sacrifice to Odin in return for a favourable wind, and lots
were drawn to find out who should die. The man marked
out for death proved to be the king himself, and it was
decided to stage a mock sacrifice; but Odin would not be
cheated, and through the agency of the old warrior Starkad,
Vikar met his end by hanging and stabbing in the approved
manner.

We do not know exactly how this kind of selection was
organised; possibly, as on occasions in the sagas when lots
were consulted over more frivolous matters, each man was
represented by a piece of wood bearing his own mark[10];
perhaps in some cases the lots made it clear how many
captives should die. In a letter of Sidonius, Bishop of

Clermont in the fifth century, he expresses his disapproval of the habit of Saxon pirates of killing one man in every ten from among their prisoners after a successful expedition, before embarking for home[11]: '. . . performing a rite which is all the more tragic for being due to superstition, and distributing to the collected band of doomed men the iniquity of death by the equity of the lot.'

Again, lots were used to determine whether it was the will of the gods to engage in battle. Caesar stated that among the Germans on such occasions the rite was entrusted to the older women, the *matres familiae*, and that the people took such decisions so seriously that they refused to go to war if the gods opposed it, however favourable their position might be. Ariovistus gave up one attack on the Romans because the *matres* declared after consultation of the lots that nothing should be done until the moon was full.[12] In the Viking Age there is a significant passage from the ninth-century *Life of Ansgar*, the Archbishop of Hamburg-Bremen, written by his successor Rimbert not long after the events described, which shows that lots were still being used as a means of reaching decisions on military matters.[13] In the mid-ninth century, a Swedish king Anund was exiled from his kingdom and asked the Danes for help, offering in return to support them with his fleet of eleven ships in a raid on the market town of Birka in east Sweden. They found Birka unprotected with only the *praefectus* Herigar in charge, and he and the townspeople took refuge in Sigtuna. Herigar met Anund and agreed to pay 100 lbs in silver as a ransom. The money was duly handed over, but the Danes remained unsatisfied, feeling that they could get more by plundering the rich town. Herigar was a Christian, and he now told the pagan townspeople to appeal to the Christian God for help. Meanwhile Anund had proposed to the Danes that they should casts lots to discover if it were indeed the will of the gods to destroy this town, a place in which great and powerful deities had been worshipped. Rimbert continues:

As his words were in accord with their custom they could not refuse to adopt the suggestion. Accordingly they sought to discover the will of the gods by casting lots and they ascertained that it would be impossible to accomplish their

purpose without endangering their own welfare and that
God would not permit this place to be ravaged by them.
They asked further where they should go in order to
obtain money for themselves so that they might not have
to return home without having gained that for which they
had hoped. They ascertained by the casting of the lot that
they ought to go to a certain town which was situated at
a distance on the borders of the lands belonging to the
Slavonians. The Danes then, believing that this order had
come to them from heaven, retired from this place and
hastened to go by a direct route to that town.

Thus the lots were cast not only to find out if a prospective
attack would succeed, but also to determine what the next
move was to be. Herigar's appeal to the pagan Swedes to
turn to the Christian God may well have been wishful
thinking on the writer's part, but there seems no reason for
him to have invented the consultation of the lots, which he
claims was a familiar practice among the Danes. The
assumption is that the gods determined the way the lots fell,
and Tacitus stated that among the Germans the practice was
preceded by prayer. There is no doubt as to the close
association between runes and revealed wisdom, and runes
and the gods, particularly the god Odin. In *Hávamál* 138, a
Norse mythological poem of the Viking Age, Odin declares
that he is hanged on a tree as a sacrifice ('myself given to
myself', as he expresses it), and remains there for nine nights
without food or drink, pierced by a spear. The poem
continues:

> I peered downwards,
> I took up the runes,
> lifted them screaming,
> then I fell back.

The interpretation of this passage is by no means easy, but
a possible inference could be that the god of death and
inspiration is here performing the ritual of consulting the
runes – perhaps establishing it – while hanging as a sacrifice.
Thus two rites associated with divination, the casting of
lots and the obtaining of secret knowledge by means of a

costly sacrifice, would be combined. Some terms surviving in Old Icelandic may possibly be associated with this custom: Dérolez[14] suggested that *blotspan* (literally, 'sacrificial slip of wood') is another name for the lot on which a sign was inscribed, and that the term *hlautteinn* (literally 'sacrificial-blood twig') is not, as is suggested in *Eyrbyggja Saga*, a rod for sprinkling the blood from the sacrifice round the temple, but again the piece of wood which serves as a lot. Association with blood and sacrifice in this way might be explained if the runes were reddened with blood, as they are said sometimes to be when used in magical practices, to give them potency.

The word *þulr*, the meaning of which is generally given as poet, orator or sage (cf. *þylja*, to chant, murmur) is of relevance here. It occurs three times in the same poem, *Hávamál*, which is concerned with Odin, the High One; once in *Vafþruðnismál*, applied to the wise giant with whom Odin has a contest in knowledge, and once in *Fafnismál*, applied to Regin the smith, a supernatural figure.[15] In one of the *Hávamál* passages there is a reference to '. . . runes and inter-preted signs, signs of great power and great strength, those which the mighty Thul painted and the High Power carved, and which the Utterer of the powers engraved.' Then comes a series of questions to the hearer. Can he cut and paint runes? Can he test and inquire? Can he make sacrifices and send forth? These suggest a close connection with divination practices. In another passage we are told: 'It is time to chant at the seat of the Thul, at the Well of Urd. I beheld and was silent; I beheld and pondered; I listened to the speech of men. I heard deliberations concerning runes, nor were they silent as to their meaning in the hall of the High One.'

It is not clear whether we are to assume that the Great Thul is Odin himself, sitting in a special seat and deciding how the runes shall fall (we shall return later to the seat of the seeress). Alternatively, we may here have a technical term associated with enquiry and divination which has here been transferred into the world of the gods. In either case it is clear that Odin is connected with runes and that these are seen as the means of obtaining secret knowledge. In *Beowulf* 1160 the man called Unferth has a similar title, *þyle*; he sits near the king and acts as a spokesman, interviewing Beowulf on his arrival, and engaging in a verbal attack on him, belittling his exploits. It is evidently his responsibility to know all about the visitor and his career, although there is no indication here that he has practised special rites to obtain his knowledge. However, if in *Hávamál* the Great Thul sits beside the Well of Urd, the emphasis must be on the gaining of secret information, for this is the well into which Odin looks when he wishes to know what is to befall, paying for the privilege with one of his eyes. If *þulr* is taken to mean sage or seer, the connection with poetry and oratory will follow naturally, since the seer will chant his revelations in poetic form, and Odin is associated with all these different functions. In the use of lots, then, it seems that we have a continuous tradition which went on from Roman times into the Viking Age, and was closely linked in Scandinavia with the god Odin.

HORSE AUGURY

The other official method of divination mentioned by Tacitus as used by the Germans was the consultation of horses sacred to the gods. White horses were kept in the sacred groves, and when men wished to know the will of the gods, they observed the behaviour of these horses when yoked to a special chariot. The nobles and priests, Tacitus declares in a striking phrase in *Germania* 10, are merely servants of the gods, but the horses are in their confidence. In an article on the rock-carvings of the Bronze Age in Sweden, Bertil Almgren refers to the tradition of the Unseen God, emphasising the powerful symbolism of the empty wagon, the riderless horse, and the unmanned ship.[16] Tacitus' description of the wagon of Nerthus, whom he identifies with Terra Mater, Mother Earth, is well known; her wagon was apparently left empty, or contained only a symbol of the deity, until the priest in some unspecified way recognised the presence of the goddess within and knew that it was time to set out on the yearly procession round the region.

One story from the Icelandic *Flateyjarbók*, late though this is, provides a possible clue as to how the divine presence was manifested.[17] Here there is a reference to the god Lytir, thought to be one of the Vanir, the fertility deities, perhaps equivalent to Freyr. King Erik of Uppsala had two wagons driven to a certain place, where he sacrificed to the god, and left one wagon there all night. In the morning he went back to see if the god had come, 'according to custom', but there was no sign. He left the wagon a second night without result, and then made a fresh sacrifice. After the third night, he found that the god had at last entered the wagon, and we are told that it was now so heavy that as they drove it back to Uppsala the beasts drawing it fell dead before they reached the king's hall. The wagon was brought into the hall, and Erik welcomed the god, drained a horn in his honour and put questions to him, which the god answered, although we are not told in what manner the answers came. It is perhaps worth mentioning that two finely made and decorated little wagons of wood have survived from the Iron Age in Denmark, preserved in the peat, while from the Viking Age we have the elaborately carved little wagon from the Oseberg ship burial.[18] These may be surviving examples of the sacred wagons of Vanir deities, such as were once used in divination ceremonies.

A different kind of horse augury without use of a wagon was known to the Wends, the pagan Slav people on the south Baltic coast, who were near neighbours and bitter enemies of the Danes in the twelfth century.[19] At Ancona on the island of Rügen the temple of the god Svantevit stood until it was destroyed by the Danish king Valdemar I in 1169, as described by Saxo in Book XIV of his history. Here there was a white horse sacred to the god, which none but the priest might ride, and elsewhere there is mention of a black horse belonging to the god Triglav at Stettin, and of another sacred horse at Rethra. When it was desired to know the god's will, spears were laid on the ground; there are references to two crossed spears at Rethra, three pairs at Ancona, and nine laid out in a row at Stettin; the horse was led to the spears and watched to see whether his hooves touched them, and whether he put forward his right or left foot to step over them. Consultation of lots sometimes preceded this ceremony.[20] It has been suggested that such forms of divination were due to Germanic influence, but it is always difficult in such cases to be sure which way the influence has gone. For instance the horse Freyfaxi in

Hrafnkels Saga, which his owner shared with the god Freyr, and which no one was allowed to ride, may have been suggested to the saga-writer from his knowledge of these sacred horses of the Slavs.[21]

AUGURY BY DUEL

The third type of augury mentioned by Tacitus in *Germania* 10 is the duel between two men before a battle. This he says was seen as a method of forecasting the issue of serious wars: 'They contrive somehow to secure a captive from the nation with which they are at war and match him against a champion of their own, each being armed with his national weapons. The victory of one or the other is thought to forecast the issue of the war.'

Some doubt has been thrown by commentators on the reliability of Tacitus here,[22] but such a practice was fully in keeping with the Germanic attitude towards luck in battle; the victor would be the man possessing greater luck and power, and therefore his people could rely on divine favour. Certainly the organised duel between two champions from opposing sides is well established in later sources. We have, for instance, a challenge given by one leader to another in Paul the Deacon's history of the Lombards, in the eighth century[23]: 'What need is there that so great a multitude perish? Let us go, he and I, to single combat, and may that one of us to whom God may have willed to give the victory have and possess all these people safe and entire.'

The official duel was also recognised as a means of settling a dispute within the community, and is referred to in the laws of various Germanic peoples from the sixth century onwards, and practised in Norway and Iceland before the Conversion.[24] It was not an equivalent of the Christian trial by combat, where God was called upon to vindicate the innocence of an accused person, but rather a means of finding out once more which of the two had luck on his side, and was therefore likely to possess the favour of the divine powers who represented order against chaos.[25]

BIRD AUGURY

The Germans are also said to predict the future through the behaviour and flight of birds, although Tacitus does not suggest that this was organised into an elaborate system. The practice seems to have continued, although not in any formal way, into the Viking Age. Above all it was the crow and the birds of Odin, eagle and raven, which were observed by travellers and warriors on the look-out for omens. Ravens before battle were hailed as a sign of victory; it is a good sign to meet a dark raven on the road, we are told in the poem *Reginsmál* (stanza 20). One of the first men to arrive in Iceland, Floki Vilgerðarson (known as Floki of the Ravens) took three ravens with him when he sailed·from Norway, and loosed them one by one when he wished to know what course to follow; the third guided him in the direction of Iceland.[26]

The suggestion has been made that this story is based on actual practice by seafarers, since a powerful bird like the raven would be likely to fly towards land if it could[27]; but in any case the tradition of turning to the raven and other birds for guidance is well established in Icelandic poems and sagas. Odin himself in *Grímnismál* 20 is said to send two ravens round the world each day to bring him tidings; similarly Dag, an early king of Sweden, is said in *Ynglinga Saga* 18 to have understood the speech of birds and to have had a sparrow which flew through many lands and brought him tidings. Sigurd the Volsung obtained inspiration from a taste of the dragon's roasted heart, and the first result of this was that he gained understanding of the speech of birds and received counsel from two nuthatches on the tree above him, who warned him against the treachery of Regin the Smith. These two birds evidently played a part in the story of the young hero at a relatively early date, before the surviving literary versions were written, since they are shown on tenth-century carvings depicting the exploits of Sigurd the dragon-slayer.[28]

Among the various skills taught to the young king in the poem *Rígsþula*, such as the management of weapons, horsemanship and knowledge of runes, is mentioned the ability to understand birds, and at the point where the poem breaks off, he is being counselled by a crow to go out and win renown in the eastern regions. Similarly the valkyrie in the ninth-century poem *Hrafnsmál* is said to be wise and to understand the speech of birds, and in the poem she converses with a raven. On many occasions the gods themselves take on bird form, particularly the shapes of hawk and eagle,[29] and such episodes, together with the emphasis on the importance of the counsel of birds, could have grown out of the practice of divination by observation of birds in an earlier period. A connection is implied by the use of the verb *galdra* for chanting of spells and incantations, since this is also used for the cry of a bird. The evidence of both art and archaeology suggests that the concept of the wandering soul in bird form was familiar in the North at an early date,[30] so that another reason for turning to the cries or movements of birds as a means of guidance could be because this was at one time believed to be a method of holding communication with the dead.

INTUITIVE AUGURY: SEERESSES

These are the main systems of augury which, according to Tacitus, were practised by the Germans. When, however, the first Scandinavians came out to Iceland in the late ninth century, they seem to have used methods of a different kind, associated with the natural features of the new landscape, and of an intuitive rather than deductive type. Thorstein Rednose, for instance, said to possess great powers of foreknowledge,[31] used to be consulted every year as to which sheep should be singled out for killing in the autumn. He could make a wise decision, because he knew which animals were doomed to die in any case, and so his flocks prospered. Thorstein is not said to have worshipped the gods, but he made offerings to a waterfall near his farm, throwing gifts of food into it. At the end of his life, when he was asked as usual which animals should be killed, he replied: 'Slaughter what sheep you choose; it may be that I am doomed, or the whole flock, or perhaps all of us together', and that night he died, and the sheep plunged into the waterfall, and all perished.

Another settler, Lodmund the Old, sought guidance as to

where to settle by throwing the high-seat pillars from his home in Norway into the sea as his ship approached Iceland.[32] However it was three years before he discovered that they had come ashore in the south of the island, and in the meantime he had built himself a house in eastern Iceland. Immediately he learned of this, he prepared to move, loaded up his ship, and then lay down in it and forbade anyone to speak his name. There was a great crash, as a landslide came down on the spot where his house stood, and after this he made a solemn pronouncement, a kind of curse: no ship should survive the voyage which sailed out to sea from that place. The point of the story seems to be that Lodmund realised that he had unwittingly failed to follow the destiny indicated by the arrival of his high-seat pillars, and knew this must render him liable to bad luck; he evaded the effects of this by bringing down a landslide on the house, and transferring the ill fortune to any ship which later sailed from the place where he first settled. Such a search for guidance, linked with waterfalls, mountains and the sea, resembles methods of consultation used by the Lapps in the relatively recent past, when they desired to know whether or not to proceed on a journey or hunting expedition, according to whether they had the goodwill of the local spirits of the land.[33] We hear of no organised divination ceremonies held by these early Icelandic settlers, and Thorstein and Lodmund seem to be working for themselves and their households only. Their intuitive foresight, however, has much in common with the inspiration of the seeress, an important figure in Germanic tradition from early times.

Tacitus emphasises more than once the importance of certain women among the Germans who acted as seeresses, with special gifts which caused them to be consulted by their tribes. In his *Histories* he refers to Veleda, a maiden of the tribe of the Bructeri in the Rhineland, who 'enjoyed extensive authority according to the ancient German custom which regards many women as endowed with prophetic powers, and, as the superstition grows, attributes divinity to them.'[34] This is confirmed by a passage from *Germania* 8: 'They believe that there resides in women an element of holiness and a gift of prophecy. In the reign of the Emperor Vespasian we saw Veleda long honoured by many Germans as a divinity; and even earlier they showed a similar reverence for Aurinia and a number of others.'

It is clear from the *Histories*[35] that Veleda was consulted by her people on matters of policy, and she was chosen as one of the arbiters when an agreement was made with the people of Cologne. However the embassy sent by the towns-people was not allowed direct access to the seeress, who remained on a high tower; 'one of her relatives chosen for the purpose', we are told, 'carried to her the questions and brought back the answers, as if he were the messenger of a god'. Veleda predicted what was to come and her enormous popularity among the Germans was said to be due to her foretelling of the German successes and the destruction of the legions in the revolt of AD 69. If the Romans wanted to come to terms with the Bructeri, it had to be done through Veleda, and the Roman general Cerialis had secret communications with her and her relatives, urging her to cease to encourage revolt against the Romans.[36] She was brought to Rome after the fighting of 77–8, and Statius refers to 'the prayers of captive Veleda',[37] but whether she was removed to prevent trouble, or whether she herself sought asylum outside Germany, is not known.

Considerable interest was aroused in the 1940s by the discovery of an incomplete Greek inscription on a marble fragment in the temple of Ardea in Rome; one interpretation of this was that it was a satiric poem in the form of an oracle about Veleda, alluding to the maiden worshipped by the drinkers of the Rhine waters, the seeress who no longer needed to be provided for, since she was now occupied in snuffing out lamps in the temple.[38] However there is no general agreement about this interpretation and we do not know whether Veleda was ever at Ardea or not. Tacitus mentions other seeresses, one of whom was called Aurinia, while other writers refer to Ganna, a priestess of the Semnones honoured by Domitian, and to an unnamed wise woman of the Chatti.[39] The name Veleda is from *veles*, 'seer', a word related to the Irish *file*, poet, and the names borne by such women may have been special ones given to them in their professional capacity. Mention of Veleda's relatives raises the question of whether she resided with her family or whether these people were members of some kind of community, but unfortunately our information about them is all too scanty.

The idea of a seeress consulted for guidance is still emphasised much later in Old Norse literature. The name used for such women varies; sometimes *spákona* is used, meaning a woman with prophetic gifts, and there is a masculine equivalent *spámaðr*; these terms, however, may be loosely employed for people with knowledge of magic or spells. A more precise term for a woman practising divination is *vǫlva*, usually translated 'seeress', and for this there is no masculine form. The *vǫlva* might visit houses and make predictions concerning children or young people, or be visited by those wishing to consult her, but her characteristic function was to conduct a ceremony to which people of the neighbourhood were invited, at the end of which she first replied to questions concerning the future of the community, and then gave answers to individual questions put by those present concerning their personal problems. In describing such ceremonies, the saga-tellers of the thirteenth century or later are presumably dealing with what by this time was a literary tradition, but the considerable amount of material surviving suggests that the concept was an important one in pre-Christian times. We have also poems represented as the revelations of a *vǫlva* concerning the remote past or the future of gods and men.

The divination rite in which the *vǫlva* took part was known as *seiðr*, and sometimes she is called a *seiðkona*. The derivation of the word *seiðr* is not known, but there is some reason to connect it with song or singing, as Strömbäck suggests in a valuable study published in 1935, where he has collected all references to *seiðr* in the literature and analysed them.[40] In spite of some confusion in the accounts, certain features stand out clearly. The *vǫlva* sat upon a seat raised high above the ground; this is called a *seiðhjallr* (*seiðr*-platform), and occasionally more than one person is said to get on to it at a time, but the important point about it appears to be that the *vǫlva* sits on it, and from this exalted seat can 'see' what is normally hidden from men's eyes. It is interesting to recall the seat of the Great Thul in this connection, and the special seat of the god Odin, from which he was able to view all worlds. It has been suggested by Kiil that we have an illustration of such a platform on the ninth-century tapestry from the Oseberg ship-burial in Norway.[41]

The *vǫlva* on her seat was sometimes surrounded by a number of singers, a kind of choir, who chanted the incantation required. In one of the relatively early accounts of the visit of a *vǫlva* to a farm in northern Norway, in *Ǫrvar-Odds Saga* 2, she was accompanied by a choir of fifteen youths and fifteen maidens, 'a great band of singers, because there had to be much singing of songs when she was there'. In the fullest account of such a ceremony in *Eiríks Saga rauða* 4, the *vǫlva* asked that one particular song called *Varðlokkur* should be sung, but no one in the little Greenland community where the ceremony took place knew this song, until it was discovered that a young girl on a visit from Iceland had been taught it by her nurse in childhood. She was a Christian and very reluctant to take part, but was finally persuaded to sing the song so that the ceremony could continue. The name of the spell is related to the Scots dialect word *warlock*, wizard, and the meaning is thought to relate to the power to shut in or enclose.[42] This might be interpreted in two ways; first, the song could attract and hold the helping spirits who enabled the *vǫlva* to obtain her knowledge, and this seems the implication made by the saga-teller:

> The *spákona* thanked her for the song, and said that many spirits had come there, and thought the song fair to hear, 'those which before would have turned away from us and given us no hearing; but now there are many matters open to my sight which before were hidden both from me and from others'.

Alternatively, it could mean that the song had the power to arouse the *vǫlva* from her state of trance and summon back her wandering spirit to be enclosed in her body; although there is no indication of this in the saga, there are parallels in descriptions of shamanistic ceremonies in northern Europe and Siberia, and Strömbäck quotes an example among the Lapps of a maiden singing a song to attract back the shaman's spirit. After the song had been sung, the *vǫlva* was able to tell those present how long the famine afflicting them would continue, which had been the primary object in holding the ceremony, and also to reply to individual questions put to her, while in particular she rewarded the girl Gudrid for her help by telling her what her future was to be.

It is implied in a number of accounts that the *vǫlva* obtained her knowledge while in a state of trance; she is said to gape, to fall down as though dead, to be roused with difficulty, to be utterly exhausted when the ceremony is over, and so on.[43] In the more detailed descriptions, there are resemblances to performances of shamans among the Eskimo, Lapps, Finno-Ugric and Turko-Tatar peoples of more recent times.[44] In the saga of Erik the Red, the *vǫlva*'s costume is described in detail; it consisted of a blue cloak decorated with stones and with straps or hangings, a hood, gloves of catskin lined with white fur, calfskin boots with the hairy side outwards, glass beads, a skin pouch full of charms, and a staff bound in brass with a knob at the end; this has close similarities with many shamanistic costumes in north-eastern Europe and Siberia. The main differences, however, are that dancing and drumming, generally used by shamans in these areas to induce a state of ecstasy, play no part in the Norse accounts of *seiðr*; moreover the *vǫlva* does not conduct these ceremonies for the purpose of healing, as is customary for shamans among the Lapps and other peoples. *Seiðr* as depicted in the sagas is essentially a divination ceremony, although occasionally said to be used for hostile purposes to affect the minds of others.[45]

The 'little *vǫlva*', as she is called in the saga of Erik the Red, is said to be the last survivor of nine sisters, and to have practised her skills in the Icelandic colony of Greenland. It hardly seems likely, however, that so elaborate a ritual could have gone on in the new settlement, founded by Icelanders in the last years of the tenth century and speedily converted to Christianity. It is possible that the saga-teller wished to include some divination and prophecies about the future of his heroine Gudrid, whose descendants were distinguished members of the Icelandic church, and that he chose to embellish his description with details from a written account of some ceremony witnessed elsewhere, perhaps in Norway or further east.

The minute details included, such as the special meal prepared for the *vǫlva* before the ceremony, consisting of goats milk porridge and the hearts of all living creatures procurable, which she ate with a brass spoon and a knife with a handle of walrus ivory, broken at the point, seems to rule out the possibility that here we have vague memories of pagan ritual from a much earlier period. It is even doubtful whether a ceremony of this kind would ever have taken place in Iceland. The many references in the sagas to seeresses visiting different farms and predicting the future imply that such practices were certainly known there, but perhaps a distinction should be made between wise women who visited homes in this way and the workers of *seiðr*, conducting elaborate ceremonies from a high seat; the latter may have functioned in Scandinavia only. Certainly the memory of such rites has influenced the sagas, and renewed interest may have been aroused by descriptions of shamanistic ceremonies brought back by travellers to eastern Europe in the late Viking Age.

The poems about seeresses must also be taken into account, *Vǫluspá* is one of the most impressive mythological poems which survives, generally assumed to have been composed in Iceland about the end of the tenth century.[46] This poem is presented as the utterance of a *vǫlva* replying to questions about the creation in the beginning of time, and the end of all things when gods, men and monsters alike perish at Ragnarok. She tells how earth and sky were formed out of chaos, and the first man and woman created out of driftwood on the shore; she recounts how the gods established themselves in Asgard, and lived in contentment around the World Tree, naming created things, making tools and fine treasures, building halls, and sitting in counsel to establish the laws which governed the worlds. But at last calamity came upon them, with greed, oath-breaking and treachery, and war broke out between the different races of the gods. Omens and portents preceded the end, Balder was slain, and the monsters which the gods had held secure broke loose to join the frost-giants in an attack on Asgard. In the final battle both gods and monsters perished, and raging fire and over-whelming seas engulfed the earth. Finally the seeress sees a vision of a new world rising purified from the waves, and a new age beginning, when the sons of the gods rule in the place of their fathers. This powerful imaginative poem shows the conception of a seeress as one who has the power to look backwards and forward in time; she can recall what has passed, and see in a vision what is to come; her opening words, when she calls for silence, imply that she is addressing the gods, and it appears to be Odin who is compelling her to speak.

We do not know whether this is a daringly original conception of a poet aware of the teachings of Christianity and at the same time versed in the ancient lore of the northern gods, or whether the poem belongs to an established tradition. A second poem known as the *Shorter Vǫluspá* survives in a fragmentary state, but this may well be an imitation of the longer one. In another poem, *Baldrs Draumar*, Odin is described as travelling the road down to the underworld, to discover the reason for the ominous dreams which trouble Balder; he reaches the grave of a dead *vǫlva*, and calls on her to arise. In her reply she stresses the extreme deadness of her condition, after lying long in the earth beneath rain and snow, but he calls on her to answer, and reluctantly she tells of Balder's approaching death. In this case the wisdom of the seeress is obtained from the world of the dead, and it seems that the practice of necromancy, arousing the dead to gain hidden knowledge from them, has here been linked with that of the *vǫlva* descending in spirit to the underworld to attain wisdom. The revelations of *Vǫluspá* are said to be gained from knowledge of the depths beneath the worlds, among the roots of the World Tree uniting the realms of gods and men; it is imagery which appears to be based on an established tradition of divination of considerable depth and richness, going far beyond literary imitations of foreign material. Yet it may be noted that the *vǫlva* is not shown as revealing the will of the gods, like the early German seeresses, or speaking as their mouthpiece, as an oracle; it is the gods themselves, as well as men, who wait upon her, and seek to know what is hidden from them by a greater power still, that of Fate.

Strömbäck believed that there was Lapp influence behind the ceremony of *seiðr*, but it may be noted that it is always the seeress who dominates it, whereas shamans among the Lapps in the earliest accounts appear usually to have been men. The sagas have instances of Lapp men consulted by

Norwegians; for instance, in *Vatnsdœla Saga* 12 Ingimund consults three Lapps, offering to pay them in butter and tin if they will get him news of a little token of Freyr which he has lost, and discover if it is in Iceland. The three retire into a hut for three days, and then tell him that they have with much labour journeyed to Iceland and seen the place where the token is hidden, showing where Ingimund's home is to be. Similar powers of divination are sometimes possessed by Icelanders, as in the case of Lodmund the Old, mentioned earlier, who lay down in his ship and forbade anyone to speak his name. We have another significant parallel in the account of how the Icelanders decided to adopt Christianity in the year 1000.[47] The pagan Lawspeaker was given the responsibility of making the decision, and he withdrew to his booth and lay down under his cloak, keeping silent for a day and a night. Then he gave his answer: it was essential for Iceland to have one law and therefore one faith, and so they should observe Christianity as the official religion. This was accepted, although those who wished to observe the old rites were permitted to do so privately. Like Veleda in the Rhineland, the Lawspeaker sought for a revelation which he could pass on to his people concerning the course which they should follow at this critical moment of their history, and they accepted the counsel which he gave.

This kind of wisdom, not surprisingly, was held in high honour. There is a story of Thordis *spákona*, said to be wise and foresighted, and therefore consulted on important matters.[48] The people of the district, according to *Vatnsdœla Saga* 44 asked her to appoint the award in a lawsuit between Gudmund the Mighty, a successful and arrogant man, and another man called Thorkell, and at first Gudmund refused to accept her decision. She then told Thorkell to wear her hood and to take a special staff which she gave him, and to strike Gudmund on the cheek with it; after this, Gudmund's memory failed him suddenly at a crucial point in the proceedings, and he lost the case. While one cannot assume that this is a reliable historical tradition, it shows that it was thought reasonable to consult a *spákona* in a matter of this kind, and dangerous to ignore her ruling.

In a story of the same Gudmund in *Ljosvetninga Saga* 11, he himself is said to have consulted a wise woman concerning his future, desiring to know whether vengeance would be taken on him for having killed a man. She met him on the shore, and appeared dressed as a man, with a helmet on her head and an axe in her hand. She waded into the sea and thrust the axe into the waves, acting very violently, but no change took place, and she returned to Gudmund and said: 'I do not think that anyone will wreak vengeance on you, and you may sit peacefully at home in honour.' Then he asked her whether one of his sons might be attacked in a vengeance attempt; she went back into the sea, and this time as she struck the water there was a loud crash, and it became stained as if with blood; one of his sons, she told him, would have a narrow escape from death. 'But I will not undergo this great strain again', she went on, 'for it has been of no small cost to me, and neither threats nor fair words will be of any avail'. This emphasis on the painful nature of the search after hidden knowledge is frequently found in the literature. The account of the consultation of the sea in this story is of some interest; it might be based on a misunderstanding of some account of a dream or trance, which the story-teller has turned into action in the real world, but on the other hand the use of the sea as an augury is in keeping with other practices in the sagas, such as the throwing of the high-seat pillars overboard to guide settlers to the place where the gods wished them to make their homes.[49]

In the majority of these accounts it is not clear how the men and women who could foresee the future gained their knowledge, and there is no direct indication that they are revealing the will of the gods. However, the consultation of gods and goddesses is mentioned more than once. We know that Odin was closely associated with the revelations of runes, and that the high-seat pillars were connected with the god Thor. In a detailed account in *Eyrbyggja Saga* 4 of the arrival of one of Thor's devoted worshippers in Iceland, he is said first to have 'enquired' of his friend Thor what he should do: should he make his peace with the king, or leave the country and seek some new destiny for himself? 'The result of his enquiry', we are told, 'directed him to Iceland.' Here the word used for enquiry is *frett*, which appears to have been a technical term; it may be linked with the Scots dialect word *frete* (freyte, freit, frett, freet), the meaning of which, according to Craigie's *Dictionary of the Older Scottish Tongue* is: 'a superstition, belief or observance, especially a belief in omens, anything regarded as an omen or foreboding'. When Thorolf, in the saga account, was drawing near Iceland, he threw out the high-seat pillars which he had brought from the temple of the god Thor in Norway, and on one of which a figure of Thor was carved. The pillars moved rapidly towards land, and guided him into Broadfirth, where he found them at the foot of a headland afterwards called Thor's Ness. Here we have something akin to the movement of the wagon drawn by sacred horses in Germany, but instead of a horse the agent is the sea, over which, as god of sky and storm, Thor had special power.

Freyr and Freyja, the Vanir deities, must also have been associated with divination. In *Vatnsdœla Saga*, in the story of the lost silver token of Freyr already referred to, this object (which might conceivably have been some kind of lot, with Freyr's image or sign upon it), replaces the pillars in other tales; it leads its owner to the site in Iceland which the god has chosen for him. The account here is confused, since Ingimund had to consult the Lapps, as we saw earlier, to find out where the token had gone. In *Viga-Glums Saga* (9;19;26), a man offers an ox to Freyr, with a prayer that his enemy may be driven off his land, and the ox bellows and falls down dead as a sign that the offering has been accepted, and that Freyr will grant his request. Glum, the victim of Freyr's decision, is told of it in one of the few dreams in the sagas in which a god appears in person to the dreamer. He sees Freyr sitting on a chair on the seashore, looking angry, and is told by his dead forbears that they have in vain besought the god to change his mind concerning Glum and the land. The death of the ox might well have been an imitation of some classical source, where the behaviour of the victim to be sacrificed formed part of the augury, but the implication is that this kind of enquiry was associated with Freyr's cult.

In the poem *Hyndluljóð*, Freyja herself acts like a *vǫlva*, journeying to the underworld to seek information for her protégé Ottar; she takes him with her, disguised as her golden boar, and forces a hostile giantess to reveal to him the information which he desires concerning his ancestry.

The boar was one of the symbols of the Vanir, and the Swedes, who worshipped Freyr at Uppsala as the founder of their royal dynasty, had in the sixth century huge boar helmets, some of which seem from pictures of this period to be almost boar masks. I think it possible that the king himself may have put on such a mask when he consulted the god, whose name Freyr (meaning Lord) he himself bore, and thus became Freyr's mouthpiece. There is indeed some reason to believe that the ceremony of *seiðr* was closely connected with the Vanir, and with Freyja in particular. Their cult was linked with the burial mound, and with dead ancestors in the underworld, and divination may well have been practised in their cult centres in Norway and Sweden; it is perhaps significant that Snorri Sturluson, writing in the thirteenth century, declared in *Ynglinga Saga* 4 that it was Freyja who taught *seiðr* to the gods.

We find also that there is a well-established tradition in the literature that the *dísir*, supernatural women who act as protectors and bring luck, appear in dreams to the men whom they support, to warn or give counsel. They are associated with the ancestors, and it seems reasonable to assume that they were originally the goddesses of fertility, whose worship formed part of the Vanir cult. The importance of the dream as a warning or portent of things to come is much emphasised both in the poetry and the prose literature; its use in the sagas is complicated by the fact that popular Greek and Latin dream-books had been translated into Icelandic by the time that they were written, but there was certainly a strong native tradition of dream symbolism previously existing in Scandinavia.[50]

One significant aspect of dreams in Icelandic literature is the assumption that they can be deliberately induced. There is a strange episode in *Hálfdanar Saga svarta* in *Heimskringla*, in which the king consults a wise man, Thorleif *spaki*, as to why he never dreams. He is told to sleep in a pigsty if he desires dreams, and Nora Chadwick interpreted this as a figurative expression for a burial mound; a pigsty could have been a rendering of such a poetic expression as 'the dwelling of the boar', which could be a reference to Freyr inside his mound.[51] There are a number of instances in the sagas where men sleep on a mound and have communication with the dead occupant by means of a dream; in one case a shepherd who slept on a mound was taught a verse by the dead man to recite in his honour, and he, like Caedmon after his meeting with an angel in Bede's story, was able to repeat the verse after he awoke, and so began his career as a poet.[52] In another tale, a man deliberately chose to sleep on a mound in which a number of men were buried; he learned in his **dream** that a piece of gold taken from one of these would give the power of speech to anyone on whose tongue it was laid, and in this way a dumb woman was cured.[53]

There are few instances, however, of a god communicating direct with a sleeper; it is as though the dead, always closely associated with Freyr, have replaced the god as the old beliefs were forgotten. As presented in the sagas, this way of gaining knowledge is represented rather as a kind of necromancy, arousing the dead in order to gain help from them, and this was condemned as unlawful in Christian times. There was a special term for it: *útiseta* (the act of sitting outside), and it is said of a second Thorleif, descendant of the Thorleif *spaki* who gave advice to King Halfdan, that 'he had the custom, a frequent practice among men of old, of sitting outside for long periods on a burial mound by his farm'[54]; while in *Mariu Saga*[55] it is said that if a man sits outside on a freshly-flayed ox-hide in a secluded spot in the forest, when he wishes to know the outcome of a battle, drawing nine squares around the skin, the devil will finally bring him the answer to his question. This particular passage is almost certainly based on some Latin legend, but shows the use of the term 'sitting outside', while there is good evidence for the use of the ox-skin in this way in Celtic tradition. The account links up also with an extraordinary example of the calling up of the dead in *Færeyinga Saga* 40, where Thrand, a man who is something of a wizard, sets up a structure of some kind inside a hall, with nine squares placed out from it in all directions; he then sits silently by the fire until at last three dead men come in in turn and walk up to the fire, and those watching can tell from their appearance how each has died.

There is no opportunity here, however, to follow up the subject of communication with the dead, or the wider one of the concept of Fate among the Germanic and Scandinavian peoples, which goes far beyond the scope of this chapter. Nor have I dealt here with the extensive subject of omens, of great importance in Norse literature. But even in this brief survey I hope to have made it clear that the practice of divination was well established in Germanic tradition, and continued to be of importance in Scandinavia during the Viking Age, with much rich symbolism and elaborate ritual associated with it. It has left a mark on the surviving literature, although in many cases the writers may not fully have understood what they were describing, and it has imparted deeper significance into many tales and poems, in spite of the wide gaps in our understanding. Prophecy may indeed be the wise man's guess, but it was clearly much more than this to those aware of the ancient traditions of gaining hidden knowledge, those who had not yet lost the sense of continual communication going on between man and the supernatural world.

Notes

1   *Grettis Saga* 31; said by Bardi to his foster-father Thorarin the Wise, who had just guessed, without being told, that Bardi's new ally is Grettir the Strong, and warned him that Grettir is an unlucky man.

2   R. Syme, *Tacitus*, 1958, p. 126f argues against the suggestion that Tacitus could have been legate of Gallia Belgica in the period 89–93. One of the chief sources of Tacitus in his *Germania* is believed to be the lost *Bella Germaniae* of the elder Pliny, which would go back about 40 years before the time of Tacitus himself (see Syme, op. cit., p. 127, and D. R. Dudley, *The World of Tacitus*, London, 1968, p. 220f).

3   The translation used here is that of Mattingly and Handford, Penguin Bks. (revised ed., Harmondsworth, 1970).

4   Presumably some tree bearing nuts, such as oak, beech or hazel; fertile trees were regarded as lucky by the Romans, unless their fruit was black (J. G. C. Anderson, *De Origine et Situ Germanorum*, Oxford, 1938, p. 78).

5   R. W. V. Elliot, *Runes, an Introduction*, Manchester, 1959, p. 45f.

6   Saxo Grammaticus XIV, 564 (Holder's edition, Strassbourg, 1886).

7   Julius Caesar, *Gallic War* I, 47.

8   Alcuin, Life of St. Willibrord (trans. C. H. Talbot, *The Anglo-Saxon Missionaries in Germany*, London, 1954, p. 10).

9   The story of Starkad and Vikar is told by Saxo Grammaticus (VI,

p. 184 (Holder); trans. Fisher and Davidson, Cambridge, 1979, pp. 171–2), and in the later *Gautreks Saga.*

10   This was how the lots were arranged when Harald Hardradi cheated the Greek general and won first choice of lodgings for his men, as told by Snorri Sturluson in *Heimskringla (Har. S. Sigurð.* 4).

11   Sidonius, *Epistles* VIII, 6, 15 (trans. Loeb ed.).

12   Julius Caesar, *Gallic War* I, 50.

13   Rimbertus, *Vita Anskarii* 19; (trans. C. H. Robinson, *Anskar, the Apostle of the North*, London, 1921, p. 65f).

14   R. Dérolez, 'La Divination chez les Germains', *La Divination* ed. A. Caquot and M. Leibovici, Paris, 1968, I, p. 297.

15   *Hávamál*, stanzas 80, 111, 134; *Vafþruðnismál* 9, *Fafnismál* 34. All these poems are in the *Poetic Edda*, and are included in the *Codex Regius.*

16   B. Almgren, 'Den osynliga Godomen', *Proxima Thule* (Svenska Arkeol. Samfundet, Stockholm, 1962), p. 53f.

17   *Flateyjarbók* (Christiania, 1860) I, 467, p. 579.

18   H. R. E. Davidson, *Gods and Myths of Northern Europe* (Penguin Bks., Harmondsworth, 1964), p. 95; *Pagan Scandinavia*, London, 1967, p. 73, 116f.

19   F. Vyncke, 'La Divination chez les Slaves', *La Divination* (as cited in note 14) I, p. 312f.

20   Saxo Grammaticus XIV, p. 564 (Holder); cf. Thietmar of Merse-bourg VI, 24.

21   It is now generally accepted, as a result of the work done by Nordal, that *Hrafnkels Saga* is a work of fiction, and not likely to be based on genuine traditions of the pre-Christian period.

22   Anderson (see note 4 above), p. 82.

23   Paul the Deacon V, 41 (trans. W. D. Foulke, New York, 1907, p. 248).

24   H. R. E. Davidson, *The Sword in Anglo-Saxon England*, Oxford, 1962, p. 193f.

25   V. Grønbech, *The Culture of the Teutons*, London, 1931, II, p. 19.

26   *Landnámabók (Íslenzk Fornrit* I, Reykjavik, 1968) S 5, p. 36. It is interesting to note the variant in *Hauksbók:* 'he worshipped three ravens, the ones which were to show him his course'.

27   W. Lange, 'Flokis Raben', *Studien z.europaischen Vor- und Fruhge-schichte* (Festschrift f. H. Jankuhn, ed. Claus etc., Neumünster, 1968), pp. 354–58.

28   For example, on the Halton Cross in Lancashire and the Ramsund stone from Sweden (see Ellis, in *Antiquity* 1942, p. 220f, and Lang, *Yorkshire Arch. Journ.* 48, 1976, p. 83f).

29   Examples may be found in the *Prose Edda:* Odin takes on eagle shape when escaping with the magic mead, and Loki the shape of a hawk in the story of the stealing of Idunn and her apples.

30   P. Gelling and H. R. E. Davidson, *The Chariot of the Sun*, London, 1969, p. 174f.

31   *Landnámabók* (as cited in note 26) H 355; S 313; p. 358.

32   ibid. S 289; H 250; p. 303f.

33 R. Karsten, *The Religion of the Samek*, Leiden, 1935, p. 12f.

34 *Histories* IV, 61 (translation Loeb ed.).

35 ibid. IV, 65.

36 ibid. V, 24.

37 Statius, *Silvae* I, iv, 89: 'Time allows not to recount the armies of the North and rebellious Rhine and the prayers of captive Veleda' (Loeb ed.).

38 J. Keil, 'Ein Spottgedicht. . . .' *Anzeiger d. Osterreichischen Akad, Wiss.* (phil. hist. Klasse) 84 (1947) pp. 185–90. I am grateful to Miss E. D. Rawson for this reference.

39 See Veleda in Paulys' *Reallencyclopädie der classichen Altertumswissenschaft*. Ganna is mentioned by Cassio Dio, 67, 5, and Aurinia in *Germania* 8; some scholars emend the latter name to Abruna, but Anderson (see note 4) thinks it may be a Celtic name. For the wise woman of the Chatti, see Suet. Vitellius 14, 5.

40 Dag Strömbäck, *Sejd*, (Textstudier i nordisk Religionshistoria, Lund, 1935) p. 119f.

41 V. Kiil, 'Hliðskjalf og seiðhjallr', *Arkiv f. Nordisk Filologi* 75 (1960) pp. 84–112.

42 Strömbäck (as cited in note 38), p. 124.

43 N. K. Chadwick, 'Dreams in early European Literature', *Celtic Studies: Essays in memory of Angus Matheson*, ed. J. Carney, D. Greene, London, 1968, p. 39); cf. Strömbäck p. 153f.

44 H. R. E. Davidson, *The Viking Road to Byzantium*, London, 1976, p. 287.

45 H. R. E. Davidson, 'Hostile Magic in the Icelandic Sagas', *The Witch Figure* (ed. V. Newall, London, 1973) p. 34.

46 A detailed study of the text of the poem by S. Nordal (Reykjavik, 1923, revised 1952) has been translated into English by B. S. Benedikz and J. McKinnell (Durham and St. Andrews Medieval Texts 1, 1978).

47 *Íslendingabók* 7. For discussion of this passage, see D. Strömbäck, *The Conversion of Iceland* (Viking Society, London, 1975, p. 15f).

48 Thordis is also mentioned in *Biskupa Saga I, Heiðarvíga Saga* and various folktales.

49 cf. Vyncke (see note 19) pp. 316–17, for a Slav parallel.

50 G. Turville-Petre, 'Dream Symbols in Old Icelandic Literature', *Festschrift Walter Baetke*, Weimar, 1966, p. 349f.

51 N. Chadwick (see note 43 above) p. 41.

52 Flateyjarbók (see note 17) I, 174, pp. 214–5.

53 ibid. I, 206, p. 254.

54 *Hallfreða Saga* 6.

55 *Mariu Saga* ed. C. R. Unger 1871) pp. 147–8, cf. Strömbäck (see note 38) p. 129.

6

The Babylonians and Hittites

O. R. GURNEY
Emeritus Professor of Assyriology, University of Oxford

In a world where the deities who control events are capricious and unpredictable, one of man's greatest needs is a means of communication that will enable him to learn the fate the gods hold in store or him. He can address them in prayer; he can do his best to please them by sacrifice, music and incense; he can even exert pressure on them by magic. But how can they respond? How can they communicate with him, even if they should wish to do so?

In the ancient world divine communication was thought to be imparted in two ways, direct and indirect: directly by revelation or inspiration, indirectly by signs. The Romans called them *divinatio naturalis* and *divinatio artificiosa*,[1] but in modern times other terms are usually substituted: intuitive or inspired on the one hand, inductive or deductive on the other.[2] However, the term 'divination' itself seems more appropriate to the indirect or deductive method than to direct revelation. I propose therefore to reserve for the latter the term 'oracle' and to avoid this term in referring to what the Romans called *omina impetrativa*, omens deliberately provoked for answering an enquiry.[3]

A concise and convenient summary of the methods for learning the will of the gods is contained in a Hittite prayer:

Either let me see it in a dream, or let it be discovered by divination, or let a 'divinely inspired man' [variant 'an *ensi* priestess'] declare it, or let all the priests find out by incubation whatever I demand of them.[4]

Direct revelation must always have been a comparatively rare phenomenon. It was certainly so in the ancient Near East. To the individual immediately concerned – in our sources usually the King – it might be given in the form of a dream. The earliest recorded instance is that of Eannatum, the Sumerian ruler of Lagash, *c.* 2450 BC, who relates that as he lay sleeping his god, Ningirsu, 'stood at his head' and announced that in the coming struggle with the neighbouring city of Umma the King of Kish would remain neutral.[5] This phrase 'to stand at the head' is a recurrent term in such theophanies and suggests that the apparition was thought to enter through the sleeper's head.[6] The same god, Ningirsu, appeared twice to Gudea, the well-known ruler of the same city some three centuries later, instructing him to build his temple. In the first dream he was not recognized; in the second, however, he 'stood at the dreamer's head', promising a sign for the commencement of the work.[7]

Between 2000 and 1000 BC the Hittite king, Hattusilis III, and his formidable queen, Puduhepa, stand out as particularly addicted to dreams as a channel of communication. This king records four manifestations of the goddess Shaushka, two to himself, one to the queen and one to certain Hittite nobles, while the goddess Hebat and the god Gurwashu are recorded as appearing to the queen.[8] He also records a dream experienced by his father, Mursilis, in which the apparition was not the goddess herself but the young prince, Muwatalli, sent as a messenger by her.[9]

The only other records of dream-theophanies are from the much later reigns of Assurbanipal of Assyria (668–627 BC) and the last king of Babylonia, Nabonidus (555–539 BC). The manifestation of Ishtar to Assurbanipal is perhaps rather to be considered as a form of oracle.[10] Nabonidus, however, had a dream-vision of the gods Marduk and Sin ordering him to restore the temple at Harran, an experience harking back to the classical dream of Gudea. Here again the gods

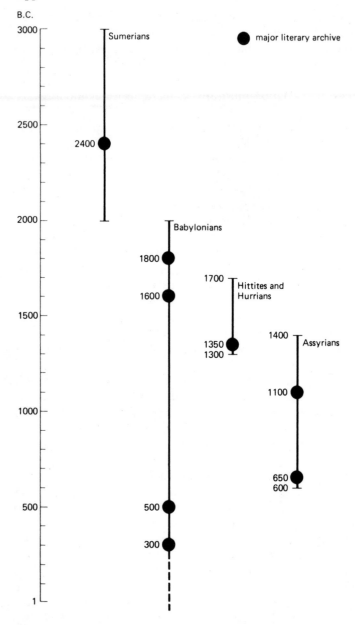

Figure 10. Time chart showing the major finds of cuneiform texts.

were seen 'standing over' the sleeper, exactly as Patroclus in the Iliad 'stood over the head' of the sleeping Achilles.[11]

Direct communication through a medium is attested mainly at two widely separated periods and places: in the eighteenth century, mainly at Mari on the middle Euphrates, and in Sargonid Assyria (seventh century). In the long intervening span of time there is the passing reference in the Hittite prayer just quoted to revelation through the 'divinely inspired man' or the ensi priestess, or by incubation; but there are no relevant examples.

At Mari the evidence consists of some 28 letters to the king from provincial governors reporting pronouncements by various individuals claiming to convey divine messages for the king's ear.[12] In nine instances the message is said to have been imparted by the god in a dream either to a priest or to a person with no particular qualification. But in the majority the medium is either a *muhhû*, fem. *muhhûtu*, or an *āpilu*, fem. *āpiltû*. There are *muhhu* and *āpilû* of the gods Dagan, Shamash and Adad, which suggests that they may have been professionals attached to temples. These are true prophets, uttering their message with authority in the first person, with or without the introductory formula familiar from the Old Testament 'Thus speaks the god . . .', and there is no reference in their case to a dream. The *muhhû*, who survived in later literature in the form *mahhû* as the type of a raving madman, was an ecstatic, claiming divine possession.[13] Nothing precise is known of the *āpilu*, whose name means literally 'answerer'.[14]

The late Sargonid evidence consists of a small corpus of oracles delivered by the goddess Ishtar of Arbela to the Assyrian kings Esarhaddon and Assurbanipal.[15] Arbela seems to have been the nearest approach in ancient Mesopotamia to the great Hellenic oracle-centres like Delphi or Dodona. The oracles generally begin with the injunction 'Be not afraid!', and the formula 'I am Ishtar of Arbela' is frequently repeated. The actual speaker of the words is always identified by name and occasionally by profession. Three are men of Arbela, three women of Arbela, there is a man and a woman from Assur and women from Kalhu and an otherwise unknown place Darahuyya. One man is called a *raggimu*, one woman a *raggintu*, literally 'shouter'. The only other profession is that of a woman called 'king's *šelûtu*' of which nothing is known. These persons evidently performed a function similar to that of the Old Babylonian *muhhû* and *āpilu*, terms no longer in current use. But whereas the messages of the earlier prophets have come down to us in the paraphrase of local governors, the Assyrian reports speak to us directly in the words of the oracle. They are couched in a characteristically vivid style; for example: 'Like a winged bird I coo over you, I wheel and circle round you; like a good little dog I run about in your palace',[16] or 'Did I not break the wing of that wind that blew against you? I will flay your enemies. They will roll about at your feet like apples in June.'[17] Assurbanipal seems to have received just such an oracle, beginning 'Be not afraid!' when he went to Arbela to pray to the goddess for help against the Elamites.[18] And in this case he relates that a *šabrû* priest lay down simultaneously and had a dream of Ishtar in her full war panoply appearing to Assurbanipal and delivering to him a message of reassurance. One suspects that the oracle heard by the king and the vision seen by the priest reflect one and the same carefully staged performance in the darkness of the temple.

In this context it must also be mentioned that not only the gods but the spirits of the dead could be consulted. This practice is attested only in a rather obscure and mutilated Neo-Assyrian letter apparently reporting that the spirit of a dead queen was called up to bless the instalment of the crown prince,[19] but the necromancer, *mušēlû eṭemmi* or the female *ša'iltu*, appears alongside other diviners in lexical texts and in an Old Assyrian letter. There is a suggestion that necromancy may have been a clandestine practice regarded officially with disapproval.[20]

Oracles, however, and ecstatic utterances, as well as necromancy, played a comparatively small part in this civilization. Its hallmark, rather, was divination by indirect methods. The gods were believed to communicate with men by a language of signs, which might be spontaneous (*omina oblativa*) or provoked (*omina impetrativa*). In a prescientific age it is natural to take strange and unpredictable occurrences, outside the regular course of nature, as portents, warnings of divine displeasure. Such superstitions are worldwide. In ancient Mesopotamia they led to the development of a class of experts claiming special knowledge for the interpretation of omens and prodigies and professing special techniques for provoking them as occasion required. Their professional name was *barû*, from the root *barû* 'to see', here in the sense 'to examine, inspect'. Their science enjoyed enormous prestige and was believed to derive from the semi-mythical antediluvian king of Sippar, Enmeduranki, who received it directly from the gods Shamash and Adad and was regarded as the *barû*'s professional ancestor.[21]

Kings, hoping to obtain the blessing of the gods before some important enterprise and unable to wait for the appearance of a spontaneous 'sign' (*ittum*), would call in the *barû* and demand an impetrated response (*têrtum*). The favour of the gods would first be sought by sacrifice, and when the animals – normally sheep – were opened up it would soon have been observed that the entrails were apt to exhibit an extraordinary degree of variability. What more natural than to suppose that here, concealed within the animal just dedicated to them, the gods were 'writing' their message in the form of a code?[22] However that may be, the science of 'extispicy' or 'haruspicy', divination by inspection of the entrails (*exta*), is attested in the south of Mesopotamia from the dawn of history.

The evidence at the beginning is slight but unmistakable. The expression *máš-šu-gíd* for the diviner, literally 'the one who stretches his hand into the sacrificial animal' (later *máš-šu-gíd-gíd*) occurs already in the pre-Sargonic lists of professions from Fara and Abu Salabikh.[23] From the time of the pre-Sargonic king Ur-nanshe (grandfather of the above-mentioned Eannatum) priests were 'nominated by the sacrificial animal' (*máš-pà*), which can only refer to an act of extispicy.[24] The existence of the practice at least from the period of the dynasty of Akkad is further confirmed by the 'historical omens'.[25] A clay model of a liver bears the words: 'Omen of Naram-Sin who captured the town of Apishal'. Another has 'This is the liver concerning King Sin-iddinam on whom in the temple of Shamash in the month Elunum a ladder(?) fell.'[26] Later such models were replaced by descriptions and followed by interpretations such as 'This is a liver-omen of Sargon who marched to Marhasi and Ishtar made a light appear for him when he was running into darkness(?)'; and a later version of the first-quoted omen runs 'it is a liver-omen of the ruler of Apishal whom Naram-Sin captured by breaching (the wall).' It is generally believed today that such omens derive from an actual coincidence of a particular conformation of the liver with a particular historical event, which was recorded and filed away for future reference.[27] We learn from them colourful details, such as that Sin-iddinam was crushed by a ladder, or that Amar-Suen died from 'the bite of a shoe', probably an infected foot.

The first actual documents of the *barû*'s craft come from the Old Babylonian period, or rather just before that period (*c.* 1900 BC), in the shape of 32 liver models found at Mari. These are all of the 'historical' type just mentioned.[28] Slightly later are models of livers, lungs and intestines showing single features and made for purposes of instruction. Now too begins the process of codification. The Sumerians and Babylonians were indefatigable makers of lists, whether of legal formulae, of 'things' classified in various ways, or of the decisions of the law courts, the listing of which produced what we call the ancient 'law codes'. Omens were listed in a similar way, as conditional clauses, the protasis describing the omen as observed, the apodosis its interpretation. In this way the *barû* acquired his basic handbooks for reference. One already ran to at least a series of 17 tablets.[29] In succeeding centuries these handbooks proliferated, until by the 7th century BC and later the series *barûtu* had at least 55 tablets, with a vast number of excerpts, commentaries and compendia of all kinds. They may be illustrated by a few examples:

If there is a cross drawn on the 'strong point' of the liver, an important person will kill his lord.
If there are two 'roads' on the liver, a traveller will reach his goal.
If the lung is red on right and left, there will be a conflagration.
If on the right of the liver there are two 'fingers', it is the omen 'Who is king? Who is not king?', i.e. of rival pretenders.

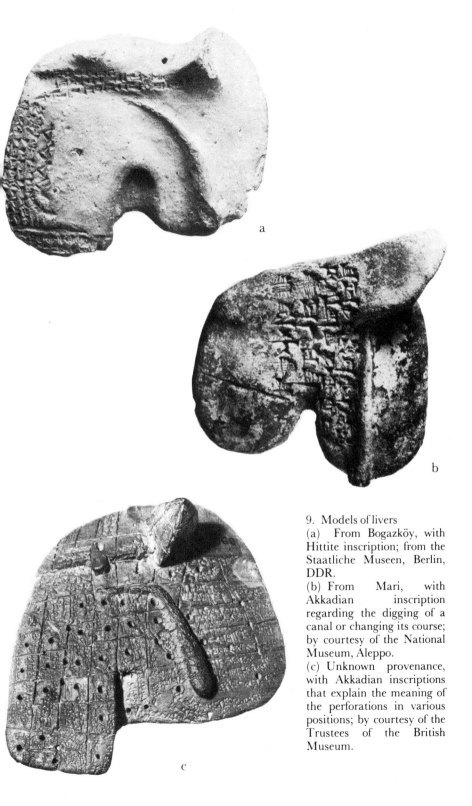

9. Models of livers
(a)   From Bogazköy, with Hittite inscription; from the Staatliche Museen, Berlin, DDR.
(b) From Mari, with Akkadian inscription regarding the digging of a canal or changing its course; by courtesy of the National Museum, Aleppo.
(c) Unknown provenance, with Akkadian inscriptions that explain the meaning of the perforations in various positions; by courtesy of the Trustees of the British Museum.

10. Hypsoma of moon in Taurus; astrological tablet showing the moon in the constellation Taurus, with the Pleiades to the left; by courtesy of the late Professor E. Weidner and the Vorderasiatisches Museum, Staatliche Museen, Berlin, DDR.

Beginning in this period also we have a number of reports
of single acts of inspection which illuminate the *barû*'s
technique.[30] The question to be answered would be posed
at the beginning in detail. For example: 'Is it a fact in regard
to the army of my lord, which he has sent to meet Hammurapi,
that Hammurapi will not capture it, will not defeat it or
cause it to be defeated, will not delay it either with hostile
or friendly intent? As they have set out in good fettle from
the gate of Mari, will they return by the same gate safe and
sound?'[31] The *barû* would then examine the viscera, reporting
on them in a more or less regular order: first the liver, with
the parts taken in a counter-clockwise direction, beginning
with a feature on the left lobe and ending with the caudate
lobe or pyramidal process, called the 'finger'; then a selection
of other organs, the lungs, the breastbone (*kaskasu*), the
stomach, the vertebrae (*kunukku*), an organ called *šubtu* or
šuptu, the spleen (*ṭulīmu*), the pancreas (probably *takaltu*),
the heart, the kidneys and the intestines.[32] In most cases
there would be a countercheck (*piqittu*), presumably by
examining a second victim.[33] The findings would be reported
in detail and the result summarized at the end. The report
just quoted ends: 'My lord need have no fear for his army.'
In other instances this is reduced to a phrase 'the omen is
favourable' or the like. So important had these enquiries
become that the king would often take a *barû* with him on a
campaign, so that inspections could be performed in the
field, as we learn from the Mari letters. The procedure
remained essentially the same for the next thousand years,
though the form of reporting changed slightly. Many reports
omit the question. Were these perhaps used in conjunction
with the so-called *tamîtu* texts, which pose questions in great
detail, either about a campaign or about some personal
problem, but contain nothing else by way of answer?[34]

From the reign of the Assyrian king Esarhaddon (680–669
BC) there have survived a group of prayers addressed to
Shamash,[35] such as the following:

Shamash, great lord, what I ask, answer me with a sure
affirmation. Whereas Bartatua, king of the Scyths, has
sent a messenger to Esarhaddon, king of Assyria, about
a princess, if Esarhaddon, king of Assyria, sends him a

princess as wife, will Bartatua, king of the Scyths, speak
true and faithful words of friendship in sincerity, keep
the oaths of Esarhaddon, king of Assyria, and do all
that is good for him? Is this ordained by the mouth of thy
great divinity?[36]

Here follow the findings of the inspection and its countercheck, quoted straight from the handbooks (protases only);
but no result is given at the end. The tablet may have been
sent for interpretation to a higher authority. An 'extispicy
report' would then be drawn up by him, containing a copy
of the findings and sometimes the question as well, and the
result added in summary form, e.g. 'there are 5 bad signs,
none good; it is bad.'[37] Unfortunately, however, the surviving
'extispicy reports' of this type all come from the reign of the
next king, Assurbanipal, so it cannot be proved that the two
types are mutually complementary. A century later Nabonidus was still conducting enquiries on matters such as the
installation of his daughter as priestess at Ur, with the
traditional *piqittu* to check the results.[38]

Towards the end of the Old Babylonian period, probably
during the 17th century, the science of haruspicy moved out
westward to the countries of the Levant. Model livers,
inscribed and uninscribed, have been found at Ugarit (15),
Megiddo (3), Hazor (5) and Ibla (1), and lungs at Ugarit
and Alalakh (1 each).[39] This territory had now been over-
run by the Hurrians and for about two centuries the science
seems to have undergone a process of adaptation to its new
environment. Finally about 1400 it was transmitted to
Hattusas, the Hittite capital, and was received with a
completely Hurrian terminology for the ominous parts. There
36 model livers have come to light, of the instructional type;
the omens inscribed on them are for the most part in
Akkadian, though in three cases the apodoses are in Hittite.
These and fragments of handbooks which have also survived
– a few translated into Hittite, but for the most part in the
original Akkadian – use the traditional logograms for the
exta, but in one case at least a scribe has added a docket
showing that the logogram for the part he was describing
was read by him as a Hurrian word.[40]

The great contribution of the Hittites was in the elaboration of the method of consultation. From the 14th and 13th centuries we have innumerable lengthy reports which reveal this development in great detail and variety. The Hittites evidently saw that to put a complex question to the oracle was impractical, since in the event of a negative answer it would be necessary to start afresh. Their enquiries were therefore broken up into separate items and they would not pass on to the next till the one in hand had been established by a positive answer. In this way a complex situation could be built up. The system is very sophisticated and the reports run to enormous length.[41]

In these enquiries haruspicy is usually mixed with other forms of divination to be described presently, the different methods being employed as a countercheck. As far as haruspicy is concerned, the technique of reporting is reduced to a kind of acrophonic shorthand, the Hurrian names of the ominous parts being cited by their initial sign only, with only minor departures from the traditional Akkadian order.[42] Here too the animal examined by the *barû* was normally a sheep, but it is a peculiarity of Hittite haruspicy that the so-called 'cave-bird' was apparently subjected to a similar examination, either as a countercheck on the inspection of the sheep or as an independent method of divination.[43] The 'cave bird' is thought to have been a kind of partridge, the *tadorna*.[44] This is not to deny that birds, including the cave-bird, were occasionally also sacrificed in Mesopotamia and 'examined' by the *barû* for purposes of divination; but the references are rare, and the signs studied there seem to have been superficial. There is no evidence that the entrails were inspected.[45]

Some of these enquiries must have been extremely expensive. Even in Mesopotamia divination by the sheep was explicitly recognized as the prerogative of the rich man.[46] But in Hittite, as we can see from a complete example, such as *KUB* XXII no. 70,[47] one of these multiple enquiries might entail as many as 34 inspections of the entrails, presumably of sheep, and 20 of cave birds, each, one may suppose, requiring a fresh victim. Small wonder that extispicy was an art reserved for royalty and affairs of state. Consultations were instituted before a major undertaking, such as a military campaign; but the majority of these enquiries set out to establish the cause of some national misfortune: first, which god is angry, then which of many alternatives is the cause of his anger.[48]

As an adjunct to haruspicy the practice developed of observing also the movements of the victim before and at the moment of sacrifice. This is already attested in Old Babylonian times. For example, 'If the sheep lashes its tail from right to left, you will overcome your enemy. If it lashes its tail from left to right, your enemy will overcome you.'[49]

The repertory of the *barû* included at least two other methods for impetrating omens: lecanomancy and libanomancy; and to these we should perhaps add ornithomancy or augury.

Lecanomancy – divination by means of a bowl or dish – was primarily a technique of pouring oil into water or alternatively water into oil. The oil would form a variety of shapes on the surface of the water and from these the prediction would be derived. The same or similar results could be achieved with flour instead of oil – so-called aleuromancy. There are 6 tablets of oil omens, all in Akkadian: 3 of the Old Babylonian period, 1 middle Assyrian, 2 from Hattusas;[50] and 1 tablet of flour omens.[51] Examples are as follows:

If the oil divides into two; for a campaign, the two camps will advance against each other; for treating a sick man, he will die.

If from the middle of the oil two drops come out, one big, the other small; the man's wife will bear a son; for a sick man, he will recover.[52]

If the flour, in the east, takes the shape of a lion's face: the man is in the grip of a ghost of one who lies in the open country; the sun will consign it (the ghost) to the wind and he will get well.

Libanomancy (or kapnomancy), divination by smoke, was the practice of throwing cedar shavings on the incense burner and observing the direction and the configurations taken by the smoke.[53] It is attested in two Old Babylonian tablets only, for example:

If the smoke bunches toward the east and disperses toward the thighs of the *barû*, you will prevail over your enemy.[54]

If the smoke moves to the right, not the left, you will prevail
over your enemy. If it moves to the left, not to the right,
your enemy will prevail over you.[55]

The oil and smoke techniques, like haruspicy, were part of
the tradition allegedly handed down to the profession by
Enmeduranki of Sippar and are frequently mentioned in the
ritual instructions for the *barû* priest found in the late
Assyrian library of Assurbanipal. They would be the poor
man's substitute for the costly procedure of haruspicy. The
only historical reference to them, however, is in the inscription of the early Kassite king Agum-kakrime, who records
that he consulted the god Shamash by the oil technique
before setting out to recover the stolen statues of Marduk and
Ṣarpanitum from the middle Euphrates.

An entirely different form of lecanomancy practised by the
Hittites will presently be described.

'Birds' are also mentioned as part of the *barû*'s concern,
but from these brief references it is not clear what exactly is
meant.[56] As already noted, the diviner sometimes sacrificed
birds and took omens from signs observed on them, such as
spots of different colours, 'hollows' or holes (*šilu*), splits and
cracks, presumably in the skin when the bird had been
plucked, or from movements and sounds made by them, as
in the case of the sheep.[57] But this is not augury. Omens from
the movements of birds are included in great numbers in the
collection of fortuitous omens called from its first line 'If a
city is set on a hill', a whole section of which is devoted to the
behaviour of animals; and there is an Old Babylonian forerunner in which omens are taken from the actions of herons,
eagles and falcons among others.[58] The practitioner who
interpreted such omens is called *dāgil iṣṣūri* 'the bird watcher'
in a Late Assyrian text. Was the *barû* concerned earlier with
such matters?[59] Did he himself keep birds and release them,
so producing *omina impetrativa*? One tablet at least suggests
that he may have done so. It lists a number of ways of
consulting the *barû* that a man should avoid.[60] Among these
are:

If it is by a cave bird: Shamash will be hostile to
him.

If it is by cave birds in flocks, he will be abandoned in the
  desert.
If it is by a dove: ditto.

'Cave birds in flocks' can hardly be a reference to sacrificial
divination, and presumably therefore all these allusions
concern observations of birds in flight. Another late Assyrian
text suggests that poultry were kept for this purpose[61]:

> In order that so-and-so may carry out his undertaking with
> success, let either a *kudurrānu* bird or a 'broad-wing' or an
> *arabānu* bird run (*lasāmu*) from my right side toward my
> left.

The *kudurrānu* is a crested bird, equated in a lexical text with
the cock (*tarlugallu*). The act of divination (*nēpešti bārîm*) for
which six birds were consigned, according to an Old
Babylonian document, to the diviners, would most probably
have been a divinatory experiment of this kind.[62] The
only textual reference to 'releasing' birds for divination
occurs in the statue of Idrimi from Alalakh, *c.* 1500 BC; but
an unusual verb (*uzakki*) is used, which leaves the exact
meaning in doubt.[63] The movements of poultry would
indeed be a form of impetrated omen. But this type of
divination was evidently unusual in Mesopotamia.

By contrast, among the Hittites ornithomancy was
developed to a fine art, and numerous reports of enquiries
show that it was the second of their three main methods of
divination, a true forerunner of the Roman *auspicium*.[64]
Unfortunately much of the terminology remains obscure.
No less than 27 species of bird are mentioned; as many as 11
in a single text (*KUB* XVIII 12). These reports start with
the 'sighting' of a bird (Akkadian *nīmur*, Hittite *aumen*,
ušgawen 'we saw') and continue with observations of its
movements within a certain field, comparable to the Roman
templum, usually associated with a river. These were clearly
wild birds, the riverside being chosen as the most likely
locality for sightings. In these circumstances it is perhaps not
surprising that a long enquiry may take 3 days. As an
example of this type of report we may quote the following:

An *alliya* bird came back up from behind the river flying low; and it settled in a poplar tree; and while we watched it, another *alliya* bird attacked it from the vicinity and came up from behind the river from the good side, and it went *pariyawan* TAR-*wan* (meaning unknown), but it did not go beyond the river. But the *alliya* bird that was on the poplar rose up and came back *gulzassa* (meaning unknown); and from behind the river it came back up from the good (side) and came across the river and went *pariyawan* TAR-*wan*. Then an eagle came up from in front of the river from the good (side) and went back to(?) the river and went to this side of the good (side). Then a 'broad-wing' came ... up from the river and went *pariyawan* TAR-*wan*.[65]

In these enquiries the practitioner is not the *barú* but a specialist called the 'bird-watcher' or 'bird-operator', who is always mentioned by name. Occasionally such men appear to have possessed birds, since they are said to offer them to a god. Perhaps such birds may have been captured or trapped. Captive eagles are occasionally mentioned in the texts.[66]

The earliest reference to a consultation of the birds in a Hittite text is in the Annals of Mursilis II, *c.* 1330 BC. The absence of earlier occurrences suggests that the technique may not have originated in Anatolia but that it may have been imported from Syria.[67]

The third major type of divination, and in practice the commonest, among the Hittites has the 'logographic' name KIN, probably to be read in Hittite *aniyaz*, vaguely 'the performance'.[68] For this there is an example in Old Hittite (*c.* 1600 BC), and it is probably of native Anatolian origin. There is certainly no parallel in Mesopotamia. It appears to operate with entities having symbolic names, some positive, some negative, such as (on the one hand) the King, the Sun-god, the men of Hatti, the throne, the army, life, peace, blessing, (on the other) the enemy, sin, sickness, fever, anger, peril. There are over 150 such terms. The procedure shows a very regular pattern, but it is only recently that some sense has been made of it. One symbol is said to 'take' a group of several symbols and to give them to or put them in another symbol. If the agent is a god, he is first said to 'arise' (the same verb as is used of the bird rising from the tree). For example:

> The goddess Hannahanna arose, took peace, the country's prosperity and the god Zababa, and they were deposited to the right of the Men of Hatti.
> The Men of Hatti took favour, muscle and bone (i.e. physical strength), the king's campaign and peace, and (they were given) to the gods.
> The enemy took battle and the whole soul, and they were given back to the enemy. (Result:) Favourable.[69]

In some instances a wall is crossed: 'The enemy took favour and the country's prosperity, crossed the wall, and they were given to the Men of Hatti.' (Result not declared.)[70]

It seems that this was some sort of board game, operating with a defined field, divided in two by a symbolic 'wall'. One is reminded of the field of observation of the bird watcher, traversed by a river and a road, which the birds cross. The active agent apparently moves of its own volition: it could be an animal. If the field of activity had a number of points of access, denoted by various symbolic names, one can imagine that the agent might be given its name according to its point of entry, pick up on the way a number of tokens of some sort, and leave by another exit, either depositing the tokens or taking them with it. The positive or negative character of each item would be noted and the result calculated accordingly.

The specialist in this form of divination was 'The Old Woman', the well-attested practitioner of magical rituals.

That this explanation is not far from the truth is supported by a comparison with the Hittite form of lecanomancy exemplified by a few texts of the 13th century. Here the field of activity is a basin or tank (Hittite *aldanni*) and the active agent is nominally a 'snake' (MUS), possibly an eel: 'We "touched(?)" a "snake of the head" for(?) the Weather-god; it took a turn round the tank; it hid itself for(?) the god of horses in the difficulty(?). Sickness came; it hid itself at the Good Moon. The former snake went down from the Weapon to the Palace; it hid itself at the Year.'[71] Here the symbolism is even more obscure, but the general purport is obviously similar: an animal is moving around in a confined space. This method seems to be modelled on the KIN; even some of the symbols, such as Year, Long years, Life, and the Future, are the same. The Old Woman is again the practitioner.

We return now to Mesopotamia and turn to unsolicited omens or *omina oblativa*. Under this heading fall, first and foremost, dreams. We have already considered oracular dreams or theophanies in which a god manifests himself to a sleeper in recognizable form and delivers a direct message, and we have noted that there are seven instances from Mari in which a message is imparted through a medium. We are here concerned with the ordinary type of dream which does not contain a direct message, the so-called 'symbolic' dream.[72]

Only one of the Mari dreams is of this kind. A woman reports that she entered the temple of Belet-ekallim but found the goddess was not there; the statues which were normally in front of her were also missing. She declares that this is a warning of revolt.[73]

The interpretation of symbolic dreams was properly the business, not of the *barû*, but of a specialist called in Sumerian *ensi*, in Akkadian *šā'ilu*, fem. *šā'iltu* 'the asker', usually, it seems, a woman.[74] The *ensi* is found in passing references in pre-Sargonic inscriptions, but the earliest example of an interpreted dream is the first dream of Gudea. Ningirsu appeared to this ruler in the guise of a gigantic man, crowned like a god, winged like the storm-bird, flanked by lions. He was not recognized and Gudea took the dream for interpretation to the goddess Nanshe, who was reputed to be the *ensi* of the gods and was able to identify the persons in the dream and the message they wished to communicate.

Detailed dreams are used with dramatic effect in epics and myths. Gilgamesh took his dreams to his mother Ninsun, who was 'wise in everything'. Dumuzi sought the help of his sister, Geshtinanna, whom he calls 'my scribe who understands tablets', which suggests that the interpretation of dreams was already an art requiring the study of a written tradition. However, a lexical entry equating the 'interpreter of dreams' with 'one who lies at a person's head' seems to indicate that another method was to lie beside the sleeper in the hope of intercepting or sharing the dream as it entered his head.[75] Gudea's third dream seems to have been of this kind.

The earliest example of a dream incorporated in a compendium of omens is in an Old Babylonian tablet which includes a typical nightmare: 'If a man while he sleeps (dreams that) the town repeatedly falls upon him and he groans and no-one hears him, the spirits of luck and good fortune are attached to his body.' (Similarly if some-one does hear him, bad luck is attached to his body.)[76]

Finally the dream omens were collected into a canonical series named after Zaqīqu (Ziqīqu), the god of dreams, in at least 11 tablets, and containing such omens as 'If someone gives him a seal (in his dream), he will have a son. If someone gives him an unperforated seal, he will have a deaf son'.

The title *šā'ilu*, *šā'iltu*, which appears as the equivalent of *ensi* from Old Babylonian times, means literally 'the asker', apparently in the sense 'one who asks the god (for an interpretation)'. The title has its counterpart in the *āpilu* 'answerer' already mentioned as the prophet at Mari speaking directly with the voice of the deity. These persons, though mainly concerned with the interpretation of dreams, had other activities as well. We have already met the female *šā'iltu* in the role of necromancer, 'asking' or consulting the dead. An allusion to the male *šā'ilu* as failing to enlighten the sufferer by his *maššakku*, apparently a word for incense, seems to indicate that he was a competitor with the *barû* in the practice of libanomancy. Other scattered evidence suggests that the *šā'iltu* was particularly consulted by women and that her social standing was not very high. The occasional references to the ensi in Hittite texts leave her exact function in doubt.[77] In the early reference quoted at the beginning of this chapter she replaces the 'divinely inspired man' of parallel passages as a channel of divine revelation.

By means of incubation, dreams can become a form of impetrated omen; but in ancient Mesopotamia, unlike the techniques hitherto discussed, incubation seems to have been practised only by the interested party himself, not by the professional diviner. The *ensis* and *šā'ilus* were not themselves dreamers but the interpreters of the dreams of others. Examples of incubation, widely separated in time, are the second dream of Gudea and a dream of Nabonidus, both provoked by prayer and sacrifice. The *šabrû* priest already mentioned, who experienced the vision of Ishtar addressing Assurbanipal, is perhaps an exception, though it is not said that his dream was deliberately solicited. The only clear reference to incubation by priests as a method of divination is in the Hittite prayer quoted at the beginning of the chapter; and it is perhaps significant that the Hittite version of the 'Cuthaean Legend of Naram-Sin' represents that king as obtaining an oracle by incubation, where the Akkadian version has him consulting the *barû* priests by means of haruspicy.[78]

The Babylonians divided casual omens broadly into two classes, celestial and terrestrial, and in the late Assyrian libraries the celestial omens were collected in the large series called, from its mythological proem, 'When Anu and Enlil', of which there were at least 70 tablets.[79] Only a quarter of this material is strictly 'astrological', concerned with the stars and planets, especially the planet Venus (the goddess Ishtar). The other three sections deal with solar, lunar and meteorological phenomena, the spheres of activity of the gods Shamash, Sin and Adad. The series seems to have been compiled, like most of the canonical works, towards the end of the second millennium; but there are forerunners from the Old Babylonian period, including the famous 'Venus tablets of Ammizaduga', incorporated in the Assyrian compendium. The Hittite archives also contained examples of all classes which must go back through a Hurrian intermediary to Old Babylonian originals, some being translated into Hittite. 'Historical' apodoses referring to kings of the dynasty of Akkad should take the science of celestial observation back to that early period; but most of these are suspect, owing to the use of the word *amût* 'liver' for 'omen', and may have entered the series by a literary transfer from the handbooks of haruspicy. An apparent exception is the omen which has provided historians with details of the downfall of the Third Dynasty of Ur: 'If the yoke star rises with its face towards the west and looks at the face of heaven and there is no wind blowing, there will be a famine and the reign will be disastrous, as when Ibi-Sin king of Ur went in fetters to Anshan.[80] Even here, however, a variant has 'omen' of Ibi-Sin, using the suspect word *amūt*.

The sections on the sun and moon are largely concerned with eclipses, with prognostications depending on the time of year and other details. Examples of other types are as follows:

If in the days of the moon's invisibility the god does not promptly disappear from the sky, there will be a drought in the land. (This comes from an Old Babylonian forerunner.)[81]

If the moon is surrounded by a halo and Jupiter stands in it, the king of Akkad will be imprisoned.

If the sun rises in a cloudbank, the king will become angry and take up arms.

For an example of a planetary omen we may cite:

If Mars rises (heliacally) with colour variations and its light is yellowish, in that year the king of Elam will die.

And for meteorological omens:

If Adad roars in Sivan [May/June]: revolt in the land. (Referring of course to thunder.)

If it rains in Ulul [Aug./Sept.] on the 8th day: widespread loss of life.

If Adad in the middle of the day rains wheat, there will be a flood (presumably referring to hail).

For obvious reasons, the prognostications of the celestial omens are all of a 'public' nature.

The only clear evidence that the Sumerians already practised astrology comes from the cylinder of Gudea (*c.* 2143–2124 BC). In his first dream this ruler saw the goddess Nisaba studying 'a tablet of the star (or stars) of heaven', which was interpreted to mean that she was proclaiming 'the pure star for the building of the temple'. In what way the star was thought to give such a sign is not explained. From

Mari, of the time of Hammurapi (*c.* 1780 BC), there is a letter from the *barû* Asqudum, which is very revealing. The diviner reports an eclipse of the moon; he knows that this is a bad omen, but no more, proceeds to check the findings by haruspicy, and declares that after all the outlook is favourable.[82] Evidently at this time haruspicy was the only reliable form of divination.

A similar situation is recorded in the reign of the Hittite king Mursilis II, *c.* 1330 BC. When setting out on a campaign, this king observed an unspecified solar 'sign'. Obviously fearing that it foretold a disaster to the army, he consulted the diviner and was informed that it concerned, not himself, but the queen.[83] The verb here is that normally used for referring a matter to any of the three standard divination techniques, but the word for the diviner, which would have revealed which technique was used, is unfortunately lost.

It seems that it was not till much later that astrology rose to prominence as a rival to haruspicy. That it eventually did so is seen in some 600 reports on ominous events sent in to the Assyrian king Esarhaddon (680–669 BC) from scholars posted in widely distributed centres throughout the empire. The great majority of these are astrological in character and are often in response to an enquiry from the king as to the meaning of an ominous event. Like the extispicy reports, they quote the relevant omens from the handbook, here complete with the prediction, and a conclusion is drawn regarding the general significance of the omen for the king, but never in relation to a particular matter of policy. Astrology could not be used, as extispicy was, to answer specific questions. The officials who write these reports are not *barû* priests but scholars with various professional designations. One is called 'scribe of "When Anu and Enlil" '. A special title which does not occur elsewhere is 'Chief of the team of ten'.[84]

Horoscopic astrology, the 12 signs of the zodiac, and the doctrine of the *hypsomata* were a still later development. The earliest horoscope (now in Oxford) dates from 410 BC.[85] Two astrological manuals show drawings of the *hypsomata*, or positions of greatest astrological influence: the moon in Taurus, Jupiter in Cancer, Mercury in Virgo. They date from the Seleucid period (after 300 BC). The texts attached to these drawings have by now reached the refinement of dividing each sign of the zodiac into twelve 'microzodiacs' of 2½ days each.[86] This sophisticated astrology, for which the 'Chaldeans' were renowned in the Roman world, was only developed after the fall of Babylon to the Persians in 539 BC.

Terrestrial omens were for the most part collected together in the enormous compendium in 107 tablets entitled 'If a city is set on a hill'. However, a special series was set apart for a particular form of portent that was regarded as having the direst consequences for the community: the birth of a monstrosity.[87] Such occurrences must have been considered portentous from prehistoric times, but the earliest evidence comes from the Old Babylonian period in the shape of a two-column tablet with 127 omens, such as: 'If a monstrosity has a normal head but has another on the right, a successful enemy attack will destroy your country.'[88] A well organised compilation like this seems to presuppose an already existing written tradition of which nothing has survived. Fragments of the same type and translations into Hittite have been found at Hattusas. They include the following: 'If a monstrosity has no right ear, the enemy will attack the king's country. If it has no left ear, the king will attack the enemy's country.'

Such omens were finally assembled in a series of 24 tablets entitled 'If a monstrosity', of which the first four refer to human births, twelve to general anomalies, and eight to specific animals. The scribes evidently filled out artificially a single observation to a 'scientific' whole in order to give the appearance of exhaustive coverage. For instance, the birth of a calf with its mouth on its back actually occurred, as reported in an Old Babylonian letter. The relevant section of the canonical series is not well preserved, but in that dealing with ears we find not only 'If the ears are on its back', but on its neck, below its neck, on its right rib-cage, on its left rib-cage, on its diaphragm, on its buttocks, on its hooves. There are no less than 89 variations on the theme 'If an ewe gives birth to a lion', followed by similar references to other animals. Presumably, if these are not pure figments of the imagination, they must be taken to refer to fanciful resemblances.

That the series was much used is shown by a number of

reports. Among the numerous such reports from the reign of Esarhaddon, nine are concerned with anomalous births. They consist mostly of nothing but excerpted omens, which show the nature of the reported malformation. One is a hermaphrodite, another a lamb with a single horn, another Siamese twins and quadruplets, another a piglet with eight feet and two tails. There does not appear to be any evidence that the officials reporting these anomalies belonged to the *barû* profession. They write simply as scribes referring to their textbooks.

The series 'If a city is set on a hill' comprises virtually all other terrestrial omens.[89] The first two tablets deal with various circumstances connected with cities; the next nineteen with building a house and phenomena connected with houses, such as funguses and moulds on the walls, cracks in the walls, devils, demons, ghosts and eerie sounds, puddles outside the door, and incidents while sinking a well. Tablets 22–41 concern the movements of animals: snakes, scorpions, lizards, insects, pigs, dogs, oxen, asses and horses. Then follow sections concerned with agriculture and with rivers and springs. Tablets 66, 67 and 79 deal with movements and sounds made by birds. The remainder contains omens from a man's behaviour while sleeping, waking up and going out to work, and miscellaneous matters connected with flames, flour on water, chance sounds and remarks overheard and family relationships.

Forerunners dealing with movements of animals and birds and a man's behaviour in sleep have survived from Old Babylonian times and in Hittite translation from Hattusas.

The following may be cited as random examples:

If on New Year's Day, before a man gets out of bed, a snake comes up out of a hole and looks at him, before anyone has seen it, that man will die during the year. If he wants to stay alive, he must [. . . . . .] his head, shave his cheeks, he will be afflicted for three months, then he will get well.
If a dog enters the palace and lies down on a bed, that palace will acquire a new possession.

A tablet from Sultantepe even describes a 'do-it-yourself' method for impetrating such omens. You sprinkle the fore-

head of a recumbent ox with water three times and observe
its reactions. Seventeen omens follow, such as: 'If it snorts
and gets up, he will attain his desire. If it snorts and does not
get up, he will not attain his desire.'[90]

Such *omina* could be counteracted by an appropriate
ritual. In so far as the presage was of a public nature, the
ritual would – at least in later times – be performed by the
kalû priest in the temple.[91] In the case of those affecting an
individual, the practitioner concerned would be the exorcist
(*āšipu* or *mašmāšu*), who would be called in to provide the
antidote in the form of a combination of ritual and incantation called *namburbi*.[92] These performances are occasionally
entered in the handbook after the relevant omen, as in the
snake example just quoted, but for the most part they are
found inscribed on separate tablets. The fact that they exist
at all shows that the omen was not, strictly speaking, a
prediction of the future, but was a sign of the ill-will of a
deity, whose anger could be averted by the appropriate rites.

The *āšipu*'s practice included treating the sick. For this
purpose symptoms of disease were listed, just as if they were
omens, and a prognosis added which usually amounts to
little more than the ascription of the disease to a particular
demon and a statement that the patient will either get well
or die. These 'Diagnostic omens' form a manual in 37 tablets
called 'Symptoms', with a prelude listing omens that the
āšipu might encounter on his way to the patient's house.[93] An
example, which surely describes an epileptic fit, is: 'If an
attack seizes him at midday and during the attack he hears
a noise to which he replies: "My father, my mother, my
brothers, my sisters, are dead"; if he goes to sleep after this
fit of weeping and does not get up and does not know, after
the attack has passed, that he has wept: it is "offspring of
Šulpae"; he will not recover.'[94]

Treatment by the *āšipu* always consisted of rituals and
incantations. Fortunately for the Babylonians a more scientific
practitioner, the *asû*, was also available, with a considerable
knowledge of drugs and even able to perform minor operations.

There was even a category of so-called 'physiognomic'
omens derived from bodily characteristics, birth-marks and

mannerisms.[95] Some of these are simply shrewd judgments of character, such as: 'If a man while speaking looks at the ground, he is telling lies.' Others purport to give a prognostic in the manner of a true omen: 'If he has a birthmark on his right cheek, his neighbourhood will give him a bad name.' These omens were finally composed into a series of twelve tablets with several sub-series. They amount to little more than fortune-telling.

Two treatises in omen form, however, have nothing to do with divination. One is a political pamphlet of protest against an unnamed tyrant.[96] Another is a moral tract in which the 'omens' consist of adages predicting rewards and punishments for good and bad conduct.[97] Here the literary form is adapted to purposes for which it was never intended.

The diviners also turned their attention to the calendar. Every month and every day of the month was defined as lucky or unlucky for various purposes. There was a royal calendar in 15 tablets called 'Fruit, lord of the month' ('fruit' being a name for the moon)[98] and another for the ordinary man in 105 short twelve-line sections (one line for each month), entitled 'He demolishes, he builds'.[99] This latter is concerned partly with various daily tasks and partly with celestial omens, in both cases using omens extracted from the two larger series. An allusion in a letter suggests that these were considered matters of elementary knowledge.[100]

To conclude this survey, we must mention two divinatory practices for which no handbook was required. One was the river ordeal, by which the guilt or innocence of an accused person was left to the verdict of 'the divine river'. If he sank, he was guilty; if he floated he was acquitted.[101] The other is the casting of lots, a popular practice hardly worthy of the dignified name of psephomancy or cleromancy.[102] Games of chance were played with astragals (*kiṣallu*). Lots were cast from early times to distribute the shares of an inheritance, and later to assign shares of temple income and to elect officials. The Sumerians, to judge from the word used, seem to have employed wooden sticks; but the Assyrians certainly used clay dice (*pūru*), one of which has actually been found, inscribed with the name of the candidate for an office and a prayer to the gods Assur and Adad that the die should show up.[103]

In retrospect, a few words must now be added on the principles on which the handbooks were constructed and the rules for their use in practice.

For the most part, if any connexion between the protasis and the apodosis can be detected at all, it depends on a naive association of ideas. Thus:

If there are two fingers on the liver, there will be rival pretenders to the throne.
If the lung is red, there will be a conflagration.
If the oil forms two drops, one big, one small, the man's wife will bear a son.
If the sun rises in a cloudbank (i.e. if it is red in the morning) the king will be angry (i.e. he will be red in the face).

Sometimes it is merely a word that suggests the interpretation:

If the gall-bladder is enclosed (*kussât*) in fat, there will be cold weather (*kuṣṣu*).
If the diaphragm(?) clings (*emid*), (there will be) divine support (*imid ili*).[104]

As already mentioned, the 'historical' apodoses are usually thought to reflect an actual conjunction in the past between a particular omen and a particular event. If so, they are more probably an intrusion into the corpus than the very basis on which it was built, for the practice of interpreting omens must be older than Sargon of Akkad (*c.* 2334 BC), the most ancient king mentioned in these omens.[105] But one begins to doubt the empirical basis of these omens when one observes that in the case of the omen of Naram-Sin who captured the ruler of Apišal by 'breaching' (*ina pilšim*), the protasis (in part) has 'If on the right of the gall-bladder there are two perforations (two *pilšu palšu*) and they go right through'. This looks suspiciously like another play on words.[106]

One important principle of interpretation, however, is explicitly laid down in the handbook: 'The right half refers to me, the left half to the enemy.'[107] This is the Roman distinction between the *pars familiaris* and the *pars hostilis* (though the classical sources do not make clear which parts these were). It means that an intrinsically good sign, if it occurred on the right, was 'favourable', if it occurred on the left, was 'unfavourable'. Similarly, a bad sign on the right was 'unfavourable', but one on the left was bad for the enemy and therefore 'favourable'. This principle is applied very consistently, at least in the static techniques such as the birth omens. However, the diviners seem to have become somewhat confused with moving phenomena. From the omens I have quoted, we may compare the following:

If the smoke moves to the right, you will prevail over your enemy.

If a sheep lashes its tail from right to left, you will overcome your enemy.

In order that a man may carry out his undertaking with success, let a bird run from right to left.

And from a text from Sultantepe: 'If shooting stars pass from right to left: favourable; if left to right, unfavourable.'[108] In the first three instances, the favourable direction is right to left; in the last one, it is left to right. These can only be reconciled by supposing that smoke is intrinsically bad, the other phenomena good (or vice versa), for which there is no evidence.

When interpreting a single omen the *barû* could read straight from his handbook. But when asked to provide an answer from his extispicy on a specific matter of policy, many of his apodoses would be irrelevant and he would have to reduce a complex of often contradictory omens to binary form, yes or no. The handbooks contain instructions for this:

If the good signs are many and the bad few, that omen is favourable.

If bad signs are many and the good few, that omen is unfavourable.

If your first inspection is confused and does not agree with its countercheck, you do it a third time and if that is good you make a statement; if your countercheck is confused and does not agree with your first inspection, you do not make a statement.[109]

Reading such texts, one is left in no doubt that the diviners at least, right to the last, took their craft with the utmost seriousness. And it is precisely some of the last kings who show the greatest interest in it. Esarhaddon organized a regular civil service to provide him with the latest astrological information. Assurbanipal boasts in his colophons of having himself acquired the lore of the diviner (*barûtu*). And no king is more zealous than Nabonidus in claiming support for his policies in divine revelation through dreams and the responses of the *haruspices*. In a moment of pique a king might occasionally 'close his ears' to an astrologer's warning and be taken to task afterwards when the chief justice suddenly died.[110] But I see no sign of any real scepticism. Divination remained to the end a revered and respected 'science'.

Notes

1   The classic account of Greek and Roman divination is A. Bouché-Leclercq, *Histoire de la divination dans l'antiquité* (4 vols., Paris, 1879–82).

2   Cf. Bouché-Leclercq, op. cit.; and J. Bottéro, 'Symptômes, signes, écritures en Mésopotamie ancienne', in *Divination et Rationalité*, ed. J.-P. Vernant (Paris, 1974), pp. 70–195.

3   A. Götze's dictum 'Orakel sind künstlich herbeigeführte Omina' (*Kleinasien*[2] [1957], 148) can lead to confusion. For the distinction between *omina oblativa* and *omina impetrativa* see below. Recent writers have expressed this distinction in different ways: 'unprovoked – provoked' (Oppenheim, *Ancient Mesopotamia* [1964], 208); 'simply seen – deliberately sought out' (E. Leichty in *XIV RAI*, 131); 'natural occurrences (unusual or normal) – processes induced by human action' (J. J. Finkelstein in *PAPS* 107, 464 n. 10); 'divination déductive de simple observation – divination déductive liturgique' (Bottéro, op. cit., 100 and 111).

4   Second Plague Prayer of Mursili II, §11 (*ANET* p. 396), with variant from the Prayer of Kantuzzili (ibid. 400; ENSI translated 'sibyl'). Cf. A. Kammenhuber, *Orakelpraxis, Träume und Vorzeichenschau bei den Hethitern* (Heidelberg, 1976), pp. 16, 19–20, 32 and 146.

5   E. Sollberger and J.-R. Kupper, *Inscriptions royales sumériennes et akkadiennes* (Paris, 1971), p. 49. Cf. A. Falkenstein in *XIV RAI*, pp. 57–8.

6   So Falkenstein, *XIV RAI*, p. 56.

7   Falkenstein, ibid. 58. A. L. Oppenheim, *The Interpretation of Dreams in the Ancient Near East* (Philadelphia, 1956), p. 211f.

8   Oppenheim, op. cit., p. 254.

9   Oppenheim, ibid.

10 See below.

11 Oppenheim, ibid., p. 250.

12 H. B. Huffmon, 'Prophecy in the Mari letters', *BA* XXXI (1968), pp. 101–24; W. L. Moran, in *Biblica* 50 (1969), pp. 15–56; G. P. Neate, *Akkadian Oracles* (thesis presented for the degree of B. Phil., Oxford University, 1973), p. 43f; E. Noort, *Untersuchungen zum Gottesbescheid in Mari* (Neukirchen-Vluyn, 1977). Another oracle of the Old Babylonian period, delivered by the goddess Nanaya at Uruk, is reported in a text translated in *ANET* p. 604.

13 Bibliography on the *muhhû apud* Noort, op. cit., p. 71 n. 8; add Neate, op. cit., p. 30f. In a few instances other persons are said to fall into a trance (*mahû*) and deliver similar messages (*ARM* X 7 and 8). The table *apud* Noort p. 74 includes these and the persons who received their messages in dreams or visions.

14 On the *āpilu* cf. Dossin in *XIV RAI*, 85; Neate, op. cit., p. 37f; Bottéro, op. cit., p. 90f; and bibliography *apud* Noort, op. cit., p. 69 n. 2.

15 Edited and discussed by Neate, op. cit., pp. 54–109, with a list of speakers p. 101. See also J. C. Greenfield, *Fifth World Congress of Jewish Studies*, I, pp. 187–9.

16 S. Langdon, *Tammuz and Ishtar*, pp. 137–40, re-edited by Neate, op. cit., pp. 70–80, col. ii 7–10. Cf. *CAD* 'S' p. 3a, and 'M' Part II p. 106.

17 Text translated *ANET*, pp. 449f and 605, with emendations (Landsberger, *JNES* 8, p. 257 n. 45(d), *CAD* 'K' p. 271a), as in Neate's edition, op. cit., pp. 55 and 64.

18 M. Streck, *Assurbanipal* II, p. 114f; *ANET* 606.

19 *ABL* 614 rev. 4, 6 (*CAD* 'E' p. 397b), now S. Parpola, *LASEA* 132.

20 Bottéro, op. cit. (n. 2) p. 97f; Oppenheim, op. cit. (n. 7), p. 223.

21 W. G. Lambert, 'Enmeduranki and related matters', *JCS*. XXI, p. 127f.

22 Bottéro, op. cit. (n. 2), p. 152f.

23 *MSL* XII (1969), p. 15 line 63 and p. 19 line 130. The verbal form *máš šu-mu-gíd* also occurs in these tablets.

24 Sollberger and Kupper, op. cit. (n. 5), p. 45, IC3d III pp. 3–6. From the use of *máš*, 'kid', in these expressions Falkenstein (*XIV RAI* 46) and Bottéro (op. cit. p. 112 n. 1) have inferred that the victim was originally a goat, though from the time of the Third Dynasty of Ur only sheep appear to have been used. Falkenstein himself, however, regularly translates 'sacrificial animal', implying a more general use of the word *máš*.

25 E. F. Weidner, 'Historisches Material in der babylonischen Omina-Literatur', *MAOG* IV (1929), p. 226f; A. Goetze, 'Historical allusions in Old Babylonian Omen Texts', *JCS* I (1947), p. 253ff; J. J. Finkelstein, *PAPS* 107 (1963), p. 462f; E. Reiner, 'New light on some historical omens', in *Anatolian Studies presented to Hans Gustav Güterbock* (1974), p. 257f.

26 *YOS* X no. 1. The translation of this text is disputed. Cf. Goetze op. cit. p. 265 ('on whom the stairs fell'), Falkenstein *BiOr* 6, p. 179 n. 5 ('on whom a stone slab fell'), *CAD* 'A' Part II pp. 96 and 335 ('on whom (the wall) buckled and fell', rejecting the reading I.DÍB.BA). However, the reading *i-díb* (rather than *kun₅*) is supported by the variant *i-dub* in 'Nungal in the Ekur', *AfO* XXIV 28, 14. I.DÍB.BA is therefore possible and 'ladder' (*simmiltu*) surely gives the best sense, as the most likely thing to fall on a man.

27 Finkelstein, op. cit. p. 465; Bottéro, op. cit. p. 149; Goetze, op. cit. p. 265; Oppenheim, *Anc. Mesopotamia*, pp. 210, 216. Many of the events recorded are actually attested elsewhere. But cf. p. 166.

28 The Mari liver models were published by M. Rutten in *RA* 35, p. 36f. On the different types of models cf. B. Landsberger and H. Tadmor in *IEJ* 14 (1964), p. 201f. For examples, see Plate 9.

29 *YOS* X no. 16, on the feature of the liver called *naplastum*.

30 Collected by Goetze, *JCS* XI p. 89f and Nougayrol, *JCS* XXI p. 219f.

31 Nougayrol, loc. cit. p. 229f; Bottéro, op. cit. p. 125f.

32 Cf. Goetze, *YOS* X p. 5ff; M. I. Hussey, *JCS* II p. 21f; Nougayrol, *JCS* XXI p. 232f; W. L. Moran, ibid. p. 178f; R. D. Biggs, *RA* 63, p. 159ff. The spleen (*ṭulīmu*, Goetze n. 66) occurs (by chance?) only in the handbooks, not in the reports.

33 Goetze, *JCS* XI, p. 95; Nougayrol, text M. In all cases only one victim is mentioned in the preamble, but it is difficult to see how a quite different finding could be obtained by rechecking the same victim.

34 W. G. Lambert in *XIV RAI* p. 119f.

35 E. G. Klauber, *Politisch-religiöse Teüte aus der Sargonidenzeit* (Leipzig, 1913).

36 Klauber, op. cit. p. 29ff.

37 Klauber, op. cit. p. 103f. The relation between prayers and reports is discussed by Klauber on p. xxiv.

38 *YOS* I no. 45 p. 13ff, translated by F. M. Th. Böhl in *Symbolae . . . Paulo Koschaker Dedicatae* (Leiden, 1939), p. 162f. Cf. C. J. Gadd in *XIV RAI* p. 32f.

39 Listed by Nougayrol, *RA* 62 (1968), p. 31f.

40 Laroche, *RA* 64 (1970), p. 127f.

41 A good example is translated by A. Goetze in *ANET*, p. 547f.

42 Laroche, loc. cit.

43 A. Archi, *SMEA* XVI (1975), p. 139f; A. Kammenhuber, op. cit. (n. 4), p. 11.

44 B. Landsberger, *WO* III (1966), p. 262f. But these creatures may fall (ŠUB), stand (GUB) or gather(?)/settle(?) (*innindu*) *eli amēli* – surely 'on' rather than 'over' a man (cf. Caplice, *Or.* 40, p. 179f). This does not sound like partridges.

45 J. Nougayrol, ' "Oiseau" ou oiseau?', *RA* 61 (1967), p. 23f. But cf. n. 62.

46 *KAR* 252 iii 23, restored and translated by Oppenheim, op. cit.

(n. 7) 340 and 301, cf. E. Reiner, *Šurpu* (1958), 54, note on 1. 10, and J. Nougayrol, *Or.* 32, 381.

47   A. Ünal, *Ein Orakeltext über die Intrigen am hethitischen Hof* (1978).

48   Cf. especially the example in *ANET*, p. 547f.

49   *YOS* X no. 47, p. 40f; Bottéro, op. cit. (n. 2), p. 113.

50   G. Pettinato, *Die Ölwahrsagung bei den Babyloniern* (Rome, 1966) and *XIV RAI*, p. 96f.

51   J. Nougayrol, 'Aleuromancie babylonienne', *Or.* 32 (1963), p. 381f.

52   Examples quoted by Bottéro, op. cit., p. 116.

53   E. Ebeling, 'Weissagung aus Weihrauch im alten Babylonien', *SPAW*, 1935; Pettinato, *RSO* 41 (1966), p. 303f.

54   *CAD* 'B', p. 122.

55   Example quoted by Bottéro, op. cit., p. 117.

56   H. Zimmern, *Beiträge zur Kenntnis der babylonischen Religion* (Leipzig, 1901), p. 96, *barû* ritual nos. 1–20, line 8.

57   See n. 45.

58   Tablet from Ur edited by D. B. Weisberg, *Hebrew Union College Annual* 40–41 (1969–70), p. 87f.

59   Cf. Nougayrol, *RA* 61, pp. 31–2; Bottéro, op. cit., p. 121 n. 5.

60   Nougayrol, op. cit., pp. 35–7.

61   E. Reiner, 'Fortune-telling in Mesopotamia', *JNES* XIX 29 and Nougayrol, op. cit., p. 32f (*LKA* 138).

62   Bottéro, op. cit., p. 73; cf. *CAD* 'I', p. 212. However, J. Renger, *ZA* LIX, p. 208, appears to think that these birds were consigned for the purpose of extispicy.

63   So *CAD* 'Z', p. 29, but the example is unique. The verb is normally used for setting free from slavery or from imposts, literally 'make clean'.

64   A. Archi, 'L'ornitomanzia ittita', *SMEA* XVI (1975), pp. 120–80; A. Ünal, 'Zum Status der "Augures" bei den Hethitern', *RHA* XXXI (1973), pp. 27–56.

65   *KUB* XVIII 5 ii, p. 1f, translated by Archi p. 128 and Ünal p. 46.

66   Ünal, ibid., p. 55f.

67   Cf. Kammenhuber, op. cit., p. 10; Archi, op. cit., p. 121.

68   A. Archi, 'Il sistema KIN della divinazione ittita', *Oriens Antiquus* XIII (1974), pp. 113–44. Cf. Kammenhuber, ibid.

69   *KUB* V 1 ii, p. 62f, translated by Archi, ibid., p. 114f.

70   Archi, ibid., p. 129.

71   E. Laroche, 'Lécanomancie hittite', *RA* 52 (1958), pp. 150–62; lines translated, ibid., p. 152, 9–12. Laroche reads ŠUM-*u-en* 'we named' (cf. his note, p. 160), but the sign is normally read TAG = *lapatu* 'to touch' when representing a verb in Akkadian.

72   Full treatment by A. L. Oppenheim, *The Interpretation of Dreams in the Ancient Near East* (Philadelphia, 1956).

73   Huffmon, op. cit. (n. 12), p. 119.

74   Oppenheim, op. cit., p. 121f; Falkenstein, *XIV RAI*, p. 52f.

75   So Falkenstein, ibid., p. 56.

76   F. Köcher and A. L. Oppenheim, *AfO* XVIII, p. 67; Oppenheim, op. cit., p. 229; Bottéro, op. cit., p. 110.

77 Kammenhuber, op. cit., pp. 32, 146.
78 For incubation cf. Oppenheim, op. cit., pp. 187f and 205, and for the Hittite evidence Kammenhuber, op. cit., p. 38f.
79 A. L. Oppenheim, *Ancient Mesopotamia*, p. 224f; Bottéro, op. cit. (n. 2), p. 101f.
80 *CAH*³ I Part 2, p. 616. Since the variant *amūt* takes the place of *ša*, the translation 'the ruler will meet the fate of Ibbi-Sin' cannot be correct.
81 *ZA* XLIII, p. 310, 8–10.
82 A. Finet in *XIV RAI*, p. 92; J. Renger, *ZA* LIX (1969), p. 207.
83 A. Goetze in *Kleinasiatische Forschungen* I (1930), p. 405f.
84 A. L. Oppenheim, 'Divination and celestial observation in the last Assyrian Empire', *Centaurus* XIV (1969), pp. 97–135.
85 A. Sachs, 'Babylonian horoscopes', *JCS* VI (1952), pp. 49–75, especially p. 54 for the Oxford tablet.
86 E. Weidner, 'Gestirn-Darstellungen auf babylonischen Tontafeln', *Sitzungsberichte der Österreichischen Akademie der Wissenschaften*, p. 254 no. 2 (1967). See Plate 10.
87 E. Leichty, *The Omen Series* šumma izbu (*Texts from Cuneiform Sources* IV, 1970).
88 *YOS* X no. 56.
89 Partly translated by F. Nötscher in *Orientalia*, pp. 31, 39–42, 51–54, and n.s. 3, p. 177f; cf. Köcher and Oppenheim, *AfO* XVIII, p. 67f.
90 E. Reiner, 'Fortune-telling in Mesopotamia', *JNES* XIX, p. 23f.
91 F. Thureau-Dangin, *Rituels accadiens*, p. 34f (AO 6472, a text of Seleucid date).
92 R. I. Caplice, 'The Akkadian *namburbi* texts: an introduction', *SANE* I. 1 (Los Angeles, 1974).
93 R. Labat, *Traité akkadien de diagnostics et pronostics médicaux* (Paris, 1951). On the title SA.GIG.MEŠ see J. V. Kinnier Wilson in *Iraq* XVIII (1956), p. 130f and XXIV (1962), p. 59f.
94 *STT*, pp. 89, 180–6, translated by E. Reiner, *Le Monde du sorcier* (Paris, 1966), p. 92.
95 F. R. Kraus, *Die physiognomischen Omina der Babylonier* (*MVAG* 40/2, 1935); *Texte zur babylonischen Physiognomatik* (Berlin, 1939) and *Orientalia* XVI (1947), p. 199f; also 'Babylonische Omina mit Ausdeutung der Begleiterscheinungen des Sprechens', *AfO* XI (1936–7), p. 219f. Cf. Bottéro, op. cit., p. 107f.
96 W. G. Lambert, *Babylonian Wisdom Literature* (Oxford, 1960), p. 110f.
97 Kraus, 'Ein Sittenkanon in Omenform', *ZA* XLIII (1936), p. 77f.
98 Landsberger, *Der kultische Kalender* (Leipzig, 1915), p. 101f. R. Labat, *Hémérologies et ménologies d'Assur* (Paris, 1939).
99 R. Labat, *Un Calendrier babylonien des travaux des signes et des mois* (*Séries* iqqur ipuš) (Paris, 1965).
100 'They have been saying like children "It is written . . . in "*Fruit, lord of the month*" ' (Landsberger, op. cit., p. 104).
101 G. R. Driver and J. C. Miles, *The Babylonian Laws*, I (Oxford, 1952), p. 63f; W. G. Lambert, *Iraq* XXVII (1965), p. 3f; G.

Cardascia, 'L'ordalie par la fleuve dans les lois assyriennes', *Festschrift Wilhelm Eilers* (1967), p. 19f.
102 Oppenheim, *Ancient Mesopotamia*, p. 208; Bottéro, op. cit., p. 102.
103 Oppenheim, op. cit., p. 100.
104 Bottéro, ibid., p. 165.
105 So Oppenheim, op. cit., p. 216.
106 Bottéro, op. cit. 164.
107 Oppenheim, op. cit., p. 366 n. 41; Bottéro, ibid., p. 164 n. 3.
108 Reiner, *JNES* XIX, p. 28.
109 *CT* XX 46 iii, p. 29f (*CAD* 'B' 41).
110 Letter to Esarhaddon quoted by Oppenheim, op. cit., p. 227.

Abbreviations

AfO	*Archiv für Orientforschung.*
ANET	*Ancient Near Eastern Texts*, ed. J. B. Pritchard (3rd ed., 1969).
ARM	*Archives royales de Mari* (Paris, 1950–).
BA	*The Biblical Archaeologist.*
BiOr	*Bibliotheca Orientalis.*
CAD	*The Assyrian Dictionary* (Chicago, 1956–).
CAH[3]	*Cambridge Ancient History* (3rd ed.).
CT	*Cuneiform Texts . . . in the British Museum.*
IEJ	*Israel Exploration Journal.*
JCS	*Journal of Cuneiform Studies.*
JNES	*Journal of Near Eastern Studies.*
KUB	*Keilschrifturkunden aus Boghazköi* (Berlin, 1921–).
LASEA	S. Parpola, *Letters from Assyrian Scholars to the kings Esarhaddon and Assurbanipal* (Kevelaer, 1970).
LKA	E. Ebeling, *Literarische Keilschrifttexte aus Assur* (Berlin, 1953).
MAOG	*Mitteilungen der Altorientalischen Gesellschaft.*
MSL	*Materialien zum sumerischen Lexikon* (ed. B. Landsberger et al., Rome 1937–).
MVAG	*Mitteilungen der Vorderasiatisch-Aegyptischen Gesellschaft.*
Or	*Orientalia* (Rome).
PAPS	*Proceedings of the American Philosophical Society.*
RA	*Revue d'Assyriologie et d'archéologie orientale.*
RAI	*Rencontre assyriologique internationale*, especially Vol. XIV, *La divination en Mésopotamie ancienne* (Paris, 1966).
RHA	*Revue hittite et asianique.*
SANE	*Sources from the Ancient Near East* (Los Angeles, 1974–).
SMEA	*Studi Micenei ed Egeo-anatolici* (Rome).
SPAW	*Sitzungsberichte der preussischen Akademie der Wissenschaften*, phil.-hist. Klasse.
STT	O. R. Gurney et al., *The Sultantepe Tablets* (London, 1957, 1964).
WO	*Die Welt des Orients.*
YOS	*Yale Oriental Series, Babylonian Texts.*
ZA	*Zeitschrift für Assyriologie.*

7

Ancient Egypt

J. D. RAY
Herbert Thomson Reader in Egyptology, University of Cambridge

> For they say that on the first day Osiris was born, and
> that as he was delivered a voice cried out that the Lord
> of All was coming to the light of day. Some say that one
> Pamyle, who was fetching water at Thebes, heard a voice
> from the temple of Zeus instructing her to cry out loudly
> that the great king and benefactor, Osiris, had been born;
> and that because of this she brought up Osiris. (Plutarch,
> *De Iside et Osiride*, 355 E).

This is Plutarch's account of the birth of Osiris. To the
Ancient Egyptians it was a uniquely important event, the
origin of almost everything they valued in their civilisation,
and therefore it was accompanied by suitable miracles. There
is little point in stressing the inaccuracies in Plutarch's story,
such as that Zeus (the Egyptian god Amun) did not have
any cult worth speaking of before the early Middle Kingdom
(*c.* 2000 BC), or that in most accounts Pamyle, who is here
Osiris' foster-mother, is a man and was probably not
Egyptian at all. The point of the story is more important than
the details: the Egyptians believed that at the beginning of
their history the divine spoke to mankind, and that he did
so from a temple, the seat of numinosity, and that he spoke
by means of an unexpected voice. On this occasion, he was
not sought. *Vocatus atque non vocatus deus aderit* – sought or
unsought, God will still be present[1]; but more often than
not, He does not reveal Himself spontaneously, at least in a
form which is beyond any doubt.

Here it may as well be said that by divination I mean an attempt by one method or another to see into the future or discern the will of the gods; a process which is essentially originated by man. By the word oracle I mean a communication from a god, however it is thought to originate. An oracle may therefore be quite unsought, although once a particular god or a particular place has acquired a reputation for communicating with men, it will probably be consulted increasingly. It is obviously difficult to make a sharp distinction between a sought oracle and the practice of divination, as the two may overlap. The use of dreams and dream-interpretation plays a similar role to divination, as a method of determining the gods' will; yet like oracles, dreams may either be spontaneous or deliberately sought. The seeking of dreams is generally known as incubation. Dreams therefore have something in common with oracles, although they may not necessarily be thought to come from the gods, and may not always be interpreted as signs of divine will. Sometimes they are held to be of no significance at all, and different cultures may place emphasis on one aspect rather than another.

This introduces us to one of the greatest difficulties in our understanding of Ancient Egypt. There was no doubt among the Egyptians' contemporaries, at least towards the end of the country's long history, that Egypt was the home of the mysterious. This image lasted down to the Renaissance, and well beyond Napoleon's expedition; indeed, any Egyptologist knows from his correspondence that, to a certain type of mind, Egypt is beyond doubt the land of dreamlike ghostliness. The Romans certainly shared this view of the Egyptians and their religion, and temples of Isis and Serapis appeared in many towns of the Empire. The novels of Apuleius and Heliodorus confirm the impression that the land of the Nile is the perfect setting for a mystic best-seller; or, more seriously, that the Egyptians had discovered the truths of religion and the real names of the gods. And these gods and their oracles persisted, in spite of the attempts of Constantine and even Theodosius to suppress them by edict.

At Abydos in Upper Egypt as late as the fifth century AD Christian monks had to be called out to exorcise a demon which haunted the empty courts of the great temple of Osiris. It was hideous, and of monstrous size, and its name was Bes.[2] Here, if not before, the Egyptologist cannot resist a smile; Bes was the dwarf god of children, happily waving his tambourine to frighten off the very sort of evil spirit he was said to be himself. There is worse: also in the fifth century, in the suburbs of Canopus, a decaying town which lay to the east of Alexandria, there were found in a private house no less than five camel-loads of pagan idols, which were promptly taken to Alexandria and burnt. According to Christian sources, the whole area of Canopus and nearby Menouthis continued to be haunted by demons for generations.[3] Islamic sources also give useful information. According to Ibn Omayl (c. AD 900), behind the village of Abusir, which lay on the fringe of the western desert to the south of Cairo, there was still to be seen the prison where Joseph had been kept on the orders of Pharaoh. It was in a cavern, and within this cavern was a seated statue of the patriarch holding on his knees an open book, covered with cabalistic signs. The author was in fact describing the burial chamber of Imhotep – part of the complex known to the Greeks as the Asklepieion of Memphis, and one of the greatest healing and oracular shrines of the ancient world.[4] The oracles had fallen silent, but the numinosity of the place remained. The gods of Egypt still haunted the margins of the desert.

A similar picture emerges if we go back in time. The prophet Jeremiah was forced to declare his indignation against Apis and the other gods of Egypt.[5] Excavations on Assyrian sites have produced figurines of Egyptian gods; the figurines themselves may have been made in Phoenicia, but the fact remains that they were Egyptian gods,[6] and a magical cippus of Horus (a sort of prophylactic stela) was even unearthed at Nippur in Babylonia.[7] Earlier than this, in the second millennium BC, Egyptian doctors (medicine being closely allied to magic in the Ancient Near East) are known to have worked at Ugarit and even in the enemy capital Hattusas (Boğazköy).[8] It is clearly no accident that when Moses wishes to overawe Pharaoh he does so by a trial of strength with his magicians,[9] among whom it is appealing to imagine Prince Kha'emwise, son of Ramesses II, whose interest in the history of his forefathers qualifies him for the title of the first Egyptologist. Joseph, too, owes his success to dream-interpretation, and it is tempting to think that he is really defeating the Egyptians on their own ground. The impression grows that Egypt, isolated between its deserts, was the home of the occult, with its animal-headed gods and its huge temples built like forests along the Nile. Even the Greeks came to feel that none of their philosophers was worthy of the name who had not studied with its priests, even when such visits are obviously fictitious; and the Greeks had the advantage that they saw Ancient Egypt as it really was.

With this in mind, let us turn to the Egyptians as we see them. A strange thing then happens: the Egyptians turn out to be a most un-Egyptian collection of people. The awful shadow of Bes shrieking in the empty colonnades at Abydos really is cast by the friendliest of little gods. The Egyptians emerge as a rather contented and extrovert race, untroubled in their perennial sunlight, and this is the sort of view which has influenced the writers of a book such as *Before Philosophy*.[10] The sources certainly bear this out; row after row of temple scenes show the king placidly offering one ritual vase after another, while the god blandly faces him and responds with a suitable cliché. The universe is then free to continue. Clearly this is the sort of image the Egyptians wished to have of themselves, and it is widely reflected in Egyptological literature, especially in English-speaking countries. The earliest Egyptologists were determined to penetrate the mysteries of the hieroglyphs, and the reaction, which occurred when the sources proved to be less esoteric, has lasted to the present.

It is therefore not surprising to find that the documentation on oracles from Ancient Egypt is meagre, and that references to divination are, with one exception, almost unknown. There are, however, two qualifications which ought to be made. The first arises from the nature of our sources. Most of the papyri from dynastic Egypt came out of tombs. The desert sands are certainly an ideal medium for the preservation of papyrus and other organic materials, but they are not the perfect setting for everyday life. There are of course exceptions, but not enough for our purpose. The most serious lack is of the contents of temple libraries, where the most systematic and theoretical texts were almost certainly housed. This is a sad contrast to the state of affairs from

Mesopotamia, whose clay tablets are readily preserved.
Some of the apologetic or even condescending tone of a fairly
recent treatment of Egyptian mathematics could have been
avoided if this point had been made; most people can be
forgiven for not taking a mathematical treatise into the next
world for casual reading.[11] The second qualification worth
making is that there seems to have been a reluctance in
Ancient Egypt to discuss arcane matters. The stela of
Iykhernofret, for example, which deals with the mysteries of
Osiris at Abydos, is more notable for what it leaves out than
what it says,[12] and Herodotus clearly encountered something
similar among his informants.

These qualifications are important, but I do not think
that they tell the whole story. The essential starting-point
must be the view that a particular society has of the world
and of the place of man within it. Homer characterises one
such view, widely held in Ancient Greece: as is the race of
leaves, he says, so is the race of men, and even the greatest
hero will shortly be sent gibbering down to Hades. The
universe, and the gods who made it, are hostile or at best
indifferent, and man by his existence cuts across the grain of
things. I believe that a similar *Weltanschauung* holds true for
Mesopotamia. Now it is a characteristic of both these
societies that they produce epic poetry (and in Greece, this
extends to tragedy); here man is shown pitting his strength
against hostile powers which are bound to overcome him in
the end. Ancient Egypt, however, is determined to see things
differently, at least on the surface. There is no epic poetry,
no 'heroic' tradition outside the figure of the Pharaoh. The
corresponding notion of *ma'at* is a conceptualisation of the
feeling that the universe is essentially in harmony, and that
man fits into this scheme; when he comes into conflict with
it, this is remediable error rather than ineradicable short-
coming. Between the world of gods and men there is, not an
unbridgeable gulf, but a gradual spectrum. The literary
talents of the Egyptians inclined towards lyric poetry and
narratives in which the elements tend to a synthesis. It is
difficult not to be reminded of two distinctions developed in
other fields: that sometimes used by anthropologists to
separate shame-conscious individuals from guilt-conscious
ones; and the two religious responses described by William

James as healthy-minded and unhealthy-minded.[13] These schemes of course apply to individuals and their reactions, but a society is composed of individuals, and we can try to keep this idea in mind as a guideline.

There are indications as early as the Middle Kingdom that the Egyptians had recognised ways of communicating with the gods, and it is not surprising to find that the medium adopted is that of dreams. The anonymous author of the *Instructions for Merikare*^c (2100 BC), in a well-known passage, says that dreams are sent by the gods so that man may know the future.[14] This idea is characteristically Egyptian in its optimism, even though the author, a ruler with a heightened awareness of his own wrongdoing, is not. He lived in troubled times, in which much of the complacency of the Old Kingdom disappeared.

Another medium adopted was written communication with the dead. The corpus of 'letters to the dead', edited by Gardiner and Sethe, gives us valuable information.[15] It is now possible to understand more of the psychological background to texts of this sort, and a new letter, recently published, shares not only the common motif of guilt following a bereavement (in this case, the death of a wife), but also shows clearly the link between appeals to the dead and incubation through dreams. The letter is from Merertifi to Nebetyotef:

How do you fare, now that the West (the abode of the dead) is taking care of your desires? I am your beloved upon earth. Fight on my behalf and intercede on behalf of my name. I have not garbled a spell before you when I perpetuated your name upon earth. Remove the infirmity of my body. Please become a spirit before my eyes, so that I may see you fighting for me in a dream. Then I will deposit offerings for you when the sun has risen. . . .[16]

This letter is quite characteristic. The writer may be ill, but he still feels that he has not done wrong, not upset the cosmic balance, and therefore that he is entitled not to suffer.

With the New Kingdom (after 1500 BC) the sources begin to improve. The Eighteenth Dynasty has given us a series of propagandistic inscriptions in which a king describes oracles by a god, usually Amun, confirming his right to the throne. Both Hatshepsut and Tuthmosis III engaged in this, since they were rivals for the same throne; and Tuthmosis IV records in a famous stela how he fell asleep in front of the Sphinx and had a dream-conversation with it.[17] These inscriptions are picturesque, but they tell us very little for our purpose beyond the fact that occasional oracles were used to confirm desirable events – or at least events which the rulers wished to portray as desirable. At the most, they testify to a vague belief in the gods' making their will known from time to time, and for the benefit of the state.

For a different picture we should turn to the village of Deir el-Medineh, the home of the workmen who carved and decorated the royal tombs in the Valley of the Kings. Here among the workmen we find for the first time a fully-developed oracular procedure.[18] The workmen of Deir el-Medineh consulted the gods of their community – notably the deified King Amenophis I and various local forms of the Theban Amun – when they appeared, carried on the shoulders of their priests, during their festival days. Questions would be put to the god, covering almost every aspect of daily life,[19] and the god would reply either 'yes' (by moving forward toward the questioner) or 'no' (by recoiling). This simple mechanism of course determines the form of the questions put, but the system was capable of some complexity, as Papyrus BM 10335 shows. A workman, Amenemwia, has been placed in charge of a storehouse. Someone has stolen several garments and Amenemwia asks the local Amun, Amun of Pakhenty, to restore the stolen items. The god moved forward and agreed. The names of all the villagers were read out, and the god moved at the mention of one. But the man indicated was uncooperative enough to protest his innocence; the god was then 'exceedingly wroth' (perhaps he recoiled twice). The accused declared 'I am in disgrace with my god. I shall go to another'. This he did, and the original represents him as bribing the second oracle; but perhaps he was just demonstrating his innocence. The case dragged on.

How did a system like this work? One possibility that suggests itself is fraud, by the priests or an interested party. Although it would be naive to assume that deception never took place, it is obviously an unlikely explanation for a technique which relied on popular consensus. Some form of auto-suggestion is far more probable, and a counterpart of this survives at Luxor today in the Muslim feast of Abu – 'l-ḥaggag. Another fruitful line would probably follow the analysis of Evans-Pritchard among the Azande: the oracle is really socially irreplaceable, and like all effective magic is properly supplied with qualifications and exceptions, so that in practice it never has to have its reason for existing questioned.[20]

Oracles could however resort to passive resistance. Papyrus Nevill is a good example. The customer complains – 'I was looking for you to tell you of certain matters of mine, but you disappeared into your sanctuary and there was no one admitted. But as I was waiting I met Ḥori, the scribe of the temple of Ramesses III, and he said to me, "I'm admitted". So I am sending him to you. Now look; you must discard mystery today, and come out in procession, and decide the case of the five garments of the Estate of Ḥaremḥab, also these two garments of the scribe of the Necropolis. . . . Now one like you, being in a place of secrecy and hidden, sends out his pronouncements; but you haven't sent me anything, either good or bad.'[21]

Clearly this speaker is not crushed beneath feelings of personal inadequacy, but there is no doubt that a change overcame Egypt in the Ramesside period (after 1200 BC), and it is a change which is one of the greatest challenges to our understanding. Essentially it is a change from extrovert to introvert, and it is marked in art (especially the decoration of tombs, which becomes funereal rather than funerary, gloomy rather than paradisal), and in literature, where writers turn to the problems caused by an all-controlling fate and the question of what validity, if any, moral actions can possess once they are determined. The causes can be debated at length – except by the school which believes that Egyptian history ends with the Ramesside period – but the main symptom looks very like what a psychologist would call 'the return of suppressed material'. It is as if the burden of a sympathetic universe had at last proved too great to bear. The self-abasing prayers of the Deir el-Medineh workmen are something new and eloquent[22]; and after the work of

Černý and Janssen it is no longer possible to ascribe them to the workmen's lowly or insecure status, and leave it at that.[23]

Whatever the explanation, it is clear that the new mentality was more conducive to the type of oracular material we find from other societies. Healing is a typical phenomenon. Most people fall sick, but to a certain type of mind it is almost invariably seen as a sign of moral failing. We have already seen, when discussing letters to the dead, a brief reference to illness, and to an optimistic sufferer; but the notion of turning in helplessness to a god to find relief is characteristic of the later approach. This is seen beyond any doubt in the letter from the high-priest Menkheperre[c] found at el-Hibeh, and this from the effective ruler of half the country.[24]

Another field ripe for exploitation was that of omens. Casual omens were probably observed and even collected at all periods of Egyptian history, but the later period clearly elevated them to a branch of learning. One of the transitional forms of literature is the oracular amuletic decree, a document issued in the name of a major god guaranteeing protection for the bearer, who is normally a child, from everything down to pains in the left knee. This is of course a violation of one of the essential rules of magic – avoidance of the specific – and it is not surprising that these decrees rapidly lose their popularity.[25] The idea of oracular prophylaxis is in itself neither pessimistic nor optimistic; it may be a sign that everything is felt to be in order, or it may act as a symptom of the sort of neurosis which prevents a man stepping on the cracks in a pavement. But few societies can escape blame one way or another, and whatever the reason we find on a day in October, 651 BC that no less than fifty prominent members of the clergy gather to witness the oracle's approval to the transfer of one priestly office.[26]

The extension of the oracle into the realms of high politics was accomplished by means of prophecy. Gifted seers appear in earlier literature, notably in the early Middle Kingdom, but they are really only fictional creations designed to serve the cause of propaganda. In the latest period of Egyptian history their place is taken by the divine oracle. Already in Papyrus Rylands IX, a document of the reign of Darius the

Persian, several utterances by the god Amun, originally made in the reign of Psammetichus I a century and a half earlier, are pressed into service to prophesy the fortunes of the writer and his family.[27] By the Hellenistic period, however, oracular prophecy of this sort has been extended to nationalistic themes. The so-called 'Demotic Chronicle' is in reality a series of prophetic (and highly obscure) utterances interpreted largely after the event; the fates of various kings are briefly described, and it is clear that in more than one case moral character is equated with length of reign.[28] The main point of the text, however, is to 'prophesy' the conquest by the Greeks and the eventual coming of a deliverer; as such the Chronicle is obviously similar to the Oracle of the Potter, a text surviving largely in Greek, but with a similar theme in which the destruction of Alexandria is foretold.[29] The tale of Pharaoh Bocchoris and the miraculous lamb, which furnished the Greeks with a sarcastic proverb, is another example of this *genre*, in which the oracle is effectively turned into literature.[30]

Far removed from entertainment, however, is the document known as Papyrus Dodgson, now in the Ashmolean.[31] In this text a rather mysterious entity, the 'Child born in Elephantine' berates a devotee for his sins (the word is appropriate here), and even imposes upon him a change of name now that his innermost nature has been made apparent. It is not a comforting text, but it illustrates aptly the connection between Egyptian oracles and feelings of personal inadequacy which I mentioned above.

The Ancient Egyptians are often accused of xenophobia, and there are good grounds for this, but there is a corresponding tendency to ignore one of their other characteristics. It is the complementary one of capacity to absorb foreign influences. Indeed, it may turn out to be true that Ancient Egypt invented little that was truly original, but that instead it showed an ability, close to genius, to adapt and perfect foreign ideas until it seemed that Egypt was their true home. No generalisation is flawless, but it is clear that in the realm of oracles and divination Egypt did precisely this. The first stage is seen in the Achaemenid period. A demotic text on eclipse- and lunar omina now in Vienna is clearly adapted from an Aramaic original[32]; the manuscript is of later date,

but an Achaemenid borrowing is quite likely, and this idea
is strengthened by the existence of a strange text in demotic
characters but at least partly in Aramaic language, containing a series of incantations. The underlying text may even
have originated in Mesopotamia.[33] In later times Egypt
'cornered the market' in material of this type. The demise
of Babylonian traditions no doubt helped, but the Egyptians
had clearly already succeeded in naturalising this sort of
text and related astrological works.

With the Hellenistic period this tendency reaches its
culmination. Epic poetry at last appears, based perhaps on
Homer, but adapted completely to an Egyptian setting. The
rich material from sites such as the Memphite Serapeum and
elsewhere introduces us to a world of oracular pronouncements, incubation, fortune-telling of all sorts, speaking
statues and nocturnal vigils.[34]

After the close of the fourth century BC, the ancient
necropolis of Memphis became the setting for a complex of
temples, dedicated to the bull-god Osiris-Apis (the classical
Sarapis) and his divine associates. His consort Isis also had
her cult, as did her father, the ibis-god Thoth, god of night,
and their companion Horus, falcon-headed god of day. They
were joined by the deified sage Imhotep, who had been
elevated to the pantheon as deity of healing and magic, and
whom the Greeks readily identified with Asklepios. Many of
the gods of the Serapeum took animal forms (and here we
have a truly Egyptian feature), but all of them were pre-
eminently givers of oracles, and as such the whole of the
Serapeum achieved fame far beyond the borders of Egypt.
The site is known to us through its rich documentation, both
in Egyptian and Greek, which covers both the daily affairs
of the various shrines and the forms which their oracles took.
The gods of the Serapeum communicated through dream-
interpretation and a medium described generally in the
texts as an 'utterance'. These 'utterances' could certainly be
enigmatic. Text 17A of the Archive of Ḥor, for example,
which dates probably from 16 April 165 BC, describes how
Ḥor the scribe, who resided at the ibis-shrine in the Serapeum,
had received an 'utterance' which he took to four different
'magicians' for interpretation. None of them was able to do
this, but the matter was finally discussed with the magician

of Imhotep, who succeeded in deciphering the oracle. This nearly induced Hor to abandon his loyalty to the ibises, but unfortunately he gives no details of the oracle or the way it was interpreted. Nevertheless, archaeological evidence from other places may help. The little-known site of Kom el- wisṭ in the northern Delta has yielded a strange bronze pedestal with holes for four feet, possibly to hold the statue of a bull. The whole was connected to a bronze pipe or tunnel, probably subterranean, which may well have served as a speaking-tube for oracular pronouncements. Similar features have been found at sites such as Karanis in the Fayum, where the temple-altar itself was hollow. The best known example of an oracle of this type is undoubtedly that of (Jupiter) Ammon in the oasis of Siwa. This belongs as much to the classical world as to Ancient Egypt, but it was certainly founded before the seventh century BC, in the period when oracles had already become an indispensable feature of life in Egypt. Here too we can see the way in which an Egyptian institution provided fertile ground for new ideas to grow.

It is at least possible that the impetus for many of these developments came from the Greek world, but it is more than likely that the Egyptians seized upon them and integrated them with their own already fabled antiquity. The presence of an increasingly irksome foreign rule no doubt encouraged the growth of transcendental concerns; and as the Greek and Babylonian religious traditions were already moribund, the Egyptians were all set to become synonymous with mysticism. The Greeks certainly thought so, and the best illustration of this is probably Papyrus Oxyrhynchus 1381, a text which deserves to be better known under a less ponderous name. Both the writer, a Greek, and his mother suffered from illness. The manuscript dates from the middle of the second century AD, but the underlying text may be as much as four centuries earlier.

It was night, when every living creature was asleep except those in pain, but divinity showed itself the more effectively; a violent fever burned me, and I was convulsed with loss of breath and coughing, owing to the pain proceeding from my side. Heavy in the head with my troubles I was lapsing half-conscious into sleep, and my mother, as a mother would for her child (and she is by nature affectionate), being extremely grieved at my agonies, was sitting without enjoying even a short period of slumber, when suddenly she perceived – it was no dream or sleep, for her eyes were open immovably, though not seeing clearly, for a divine and terrifying vision came to her, easily preventing her from observing the god himself or his servants, whichever it was. In any case there was some one whose height was more than human, clothed in shining raiment and carrying in his left hand a book, who after merely regarding me two or three times from head to foot disappeared. When she had recovered herself, she tried, still trembling, to wake me, and finding that the fever had left me and that much sweat was pouring off me, did reverence to the manifestation of the god, and then wiped me and made me more collected. When I spoke with her, she wished to declare the virtue of the god, but I anticipating her told her all myself; for everything that she saw in the vision appeared to me in dreams.[35]

The god was Imhotep – Asclepius, and the author went on to write the history of his cult. Parallels with other cultures are marked, and the simultaneous recording of both dream and waking vision raises questions, unless the whole account is merely fictitious, of the true nature of experiences of this sort.

The Egyptians finally moved into the realm of divination. The London/Leiden magical papyrus, which dates, together with related texts, from the third century AD, contains among other spells several devoted to divination by means of a lamp (lychnomancy) or various liquids, often with the aid of a boy assistant.[36]

The various spells of the London/Leiden text cover instructions for effective magical recipes, suitable formulae for medical or erotic charms, invocations to gods, mostly infernal, and the assorted material of a successful magician. Here is a typical passage:

You take a new lamp, you put a clean wick into it, brought from a temple, and you set it on a new brick, brought from the mould and clean, on which no man has mounted; you set it upright, and place the lamp on it; you put genuine

oil in the lamp, or Oasis oil, and you set two new bricks
beneath you. You place the boy between your feet; you
recite the charms aforesaid down into the head of the boy,
your hand over his eyes; you also offer myrrh upon a
willow-leaf before the lamp. Do this in a dark place,
opening to the east or south, with no cellar underneath it.
Do not allow the light to enter the place aforesaid, and
purify the area beforehand. Then push the boy's back to
the opening of the niche, and when you have finished,
recite a spell with your hand over his eyes . . . and question
him, saying 'What do you see?' Then he will tell you about
everything you ask him.[37]

Here again the Mesopotamian influence is clear, but the
whole process has been completely absorbed into an
Egyptian setting. We are already in the world described
sixteen centuries later by Edward Lane.[38] Divination too has
been assimilated.

I am tempted to think that this capacity for adaptation,
which is seen in the realm of oracles as much as in other
aspects of life and which is one of the greatest achievements
of the Ancient Egyptians, was in reality a product of the
tension created between the various tendencies within their
civilisation. It was successful for more than three centuries.
It even made money. Yet, as in the Ramesside period, one
feels that something new is about to come to the surface.
No ordinary view of the Ancient Egyptians, certainly not
the rather self-satisfied description current in much modern
writing about them, can explain why these people produced
one of the most self-lacerating forms of Christianity known.
The answer is certainly not straightforward, but it probably
involves a paradox. Oracles and divination act rather like
an addictive drug: the more the gods are sought, the more
they retreat from view. This is one reason why revealed
religion is so opposed to such practices. 'Raise the stone and
there you shall find me; cleave the wood and there I am.'
The Egyptians would have agreed with one sense of this, a
sort of pantheism. But the other sense – that God is to be
sought in the mundane – would have caused them dismay.

The only way out of this paradox is constant worship; and
already Herodotus had noticed that the Egyptians were the

most religiously observant of men. A small pebble found by
the hypogeum of the sacred bulls at Armant dates from the
first century AD, and gives a foreshadowing of what was to
come.[39] Here is a worshipper whose god confronts him with
the sort of personal demands which are characteristic of
Christianity and Islam.

> Come unto me Osiris-Buchis my great lord (O may he
> live, may he enjoy the duration of the sun) ! I am thy
> servant, my great lord. I cry unto thee; I cease not to cry.
> Unceasing are my cries by night, more than my distrac-
> tions by day. Cares are great upon me, and I am small
> against them all. I cry out to thee; I cease not to cry.
> Weary not of calling unto God. Has he his time of death
> when he will not listen? I cry unto thee, and thou hast
> hearkened to what I have said. If I call, thou hearkenest.
> . . . O good fortune, life pure and steadfast.

Notes

1   This, a Latin version of one of the Delphic responses, was written
    above the door of Jung's house in Küsnacht. On the distinction
    between sought and unsought omens cf. for example J. D. Ray,
    The Archive of Hor, London, 1976, Commentary § 3, pp. 130–136.
2   For the background to the cult of Bes at Abydos see A. H. Sayce,
    PSBA 10 (1888), 377–388; and bibliography in S. Sauneron, *Le
    papyrus magique illustré de Brooklyn*, New York, 1970, p. 14f.
3   See the literature cited in P. M. Fraser, *Ptolemaic Alexandria*, Oxford,
    1972, II, 407 nn., pp. 527–8.
4   B. H. Stricker, *Acta Orientalia* 19 i (1941), p. 101f. The whole
    question of Imhotep in Arabic sources has recently been dealt with
    by A. Fodor, *AAWG* 98 (1976), p. 155f.
5   *Jeremiah* 46: 13–17 (Revised Version).
6   There is a possibility of even greater influence; for an arguably
    Egyptian motif in an Assyrian text concerned with dreams see A.
    Spalinger *BASOR* 223 (1976), pp. 64–67.
7   J. H. Johnson in J. M. Gibson, *Excavations at Nippur, Eleventh Season*,
    Chicago, 1975, appendix, pp. 143–150.
8   E. Edel, *Ägyptische Ärzte und ägyptische Medizin am hethitischen
    Königshof*, Opladen, 1976.
9   *Exodus* 7: 10–13.

10   H. Frankfort, J. A. Wilson, *et al.*, *Before Philosophy*, London, 1949; otherwise *The Intellectual Adventure of Ancient Man*, Chicago, 1946.

11   G. J. Toomer, 'Mathematics and Astronomy' in *The Legacy of Egypt*, second edition, ed. J. R. Harris, Oxford, 1971, pp. 27–54.

12   cf. E. Otto, *Egyptian Art and the cults of Osiris and Amun*, London, 1968, pp. 42–3.

13   W. James, *The Varieties of Religious Experience* (reprinted with an introduction by A. D. Nock, London 1960), Lectures IV–VII.

14   *Merikare*[c] p. 137; A. Volten, *Zwei altägyptische politische Schriften*, Copenhagen, 1945, pp. 75, 78.

15   A. H. Gardiner and K. Sethe, *Egyptian Letters to the Dead*, London, 1928.

16   E. F. Wente, *Or. Lov. Per.* 6–7 (1975–6), p. 595f; cf. W. K. Simpson, *JEA* 52 (1966), pp. 44–5. The text dates from about 1850 BC.

17   A collection of these texts may be found in G. Roeder, *Kulte, Orakel und Naturverehrung im alten Ägypten*, Zurich and Stuttgart, 1960, pp. 191–272 and J. Černý, 'Egyptian Oracles', in R. A. Parker, *A Saite Oracle Papyrus from Thebes*, Providence, 1962, Chapter 6.

18   For a full account, see Černý, as cited in note 17.

19   J. Černý, *BIFAO* 35 (1935), pp. 41–58; *BIFAO* 41 (1942), pp. 13–24 and *BIFAO* 72 (1972), pp. 49–69; cf. also the same author in *BIFAO* 40 (1941), p. 135f. For a bibliography of later Greek and demotic versions see A. Henrichs, *Zwei Orakelfragen*, *ZPE* 11 (1973), pp. 115–19.

20   E. E. Evans-Pritchard, *Witchcraft, Oracles and Magic among the Azande*, Oxford, 1937, Part III.

21   J. W. B. Barns, *JEA* 35 (1949), p. 69ff.

22   B. Gunn 'The religion of the poor in Ancient Egypt'. *JEA* 3 (1917), p. 81f.

23   cf. among others J. J. Janssen, *Commodity prices from the Ramessid Period*, Leiden, 1975, p. 533f.

24   W. Spiegelberg, *ZÄS* 53 (1917), p. 13f; cf. also *JEA* 61 (1975), pp. 181–8.

25   For a recent bibliography see A. Klasens, *OMRO* 56 (1975), pp. 20–8.

26   R. A. Parker, *A Saite Oracle Papyrus from Thebes*, Providence, 1962.

27   F. Ll. Griffith, *Catalogue of the Demotic Papyri in the John Rylands Library*, Manchester, 1909, III, pp. 107f; 247f.

28   W. Spiegelberg, *Die sogenannte Demotische Chronik*, Leipzig, 1914; cf. also J. H. Johnson in *Enchoria* 4 (1974), pp. 1–17.

29   P. Oxyrhynchus 2332; cf. among others P. M. Fraser, *Ptolemaic Alexandria*, Oxford, 1972, II, p. 358 n. 173, and II, p. 953 n. 43; and W. J. Tait, *Papyri from Tebtunis in Egyptian and Greek*, London, 1977, pp. 45–48 (Text 13).

30   P. Wien 10.000 a-c; see the bibliography by Zauzich, *Enchoria* 6 (1976), pp. 127–8.

31   F. Ll. Griffith, *PSBA* 31 (1909), pp. 100–109.

32   R. A. Parker, *A Vienna demotic papyrus on eclipse- and lunar omina*, Providence, 1959.

33   R. A. Bowman, *JNES* 3 (1944), p. 219f.

34   Some of the considerable literature on the Memphite Serapeum is listed by J. D. Ray in *World Archaeology* 10 no. 2 (October, 1978), pp. 149–157. For Apis as an oracular god see E. Kiessling, *Archiv Pap.* 15 (1953), 26 n. 8. The text from the Hor Archive may be found in J. D. Ray, *The Archive of Hor*, London, 1976, pp. 63–66. The pedestal from Kom el- wisṭ is described by G. Brunton, *ASAE* 47 (1947), pp. 293–5; and for speaking statues in general see G. Loukianoff, *ASAE* 36 (1936), pp. 187–193. The oracle of Ammon at Siwa is dealt with among others by A. Fakhry, *Siwa Oasis*, Cairo, 1973, pp. 78–89, 153–63; add to this the remarks by Brunton, *ASAE* 47 (1947), p. 295.

35   B. P. Grenfell and A. S. Hunt, *The Oxyrhynchus Papyri* Vol. XI, London, 1915, pp. 230–31 (editor's translation).

36   F. Ll.·Griffith and H. Thompson *The Demotic Magical Papyrus of London and Leiden*, London, 1904.

37   London/Leiden XXV, pp. 8–22.

38   E. Lane, *The Manners and Customs of the Modern Egyptians*, London, 1860 version, Chapter XII; cf. J. Vergote, *Joseph en Égypte*, Louvain, 1959, pp. 172–6.

39   R. Mond and O. H. Myers, *The Bucheum* II, London, 1934, p. 56 (Text O. 167).

Abbreviations

AAWG   *Abhandlungen der Akademie der Wissenschaften in Göttingen* (Göttingen).

Archiv Pap.   *Archiv für Papyrusforschung und verwandte Gebiete* (Leipzig).

ASAE   *Annales du Service des Antiquités de l'Égypte* (Cairo).

BASOR   *Bulletin of the American Schools of Oriental Research* (Michigan).

BIFAO   *Bulletin de l'Institut français d'archéologie orientale du Caire* (Cairo).

JEA   *Journal of Egyptian Archaeology* (London).

JNES   *Journal of Near Eastern Studies* (Chicago).

OMRO   *Oudheidkundige Mededelingen uit het Rijksmuseum van Oudheden te Leiden* (Leiden).

Or. Lov. Per.   *Orientalia Lovaniensia Periodica* (Louvain).

PSBA   *Proceedings of the Society of Biblical Archaeology* (London).

ZÄS   *Zeitschrift für ägyptische Sprache und Altertumskunde* (Berlin).

ZPE   *Zeitschrift für Papyrologie und Epigraphik* (Bonn).

8

Ancient Israel

J. R. PORTER
Professor of Theology, University of Exeter

Divinatory practices in ancient Israel, and even the kind of oracles received in response to them, show many resemblances to divination and oracles in other areas of the contemporary Near East, notably in Egypt and Mesopotamia, and the parallels have long been observed by scholars and used – perhaps sometimes over-used – to elucidate the Old Testament evidence. The Israelites themselves were well aware of the wide extent of divinatory rites in the world they knew and occasionally refer to them in some detail: one may instance the famous picture of the king of Babylon about to invade Judah in the book of Ezekiel, which includes both a description of three divinatory enquiries and the responsive oracle in answer to at least one of them:

> The king of Babylon halts to take the omens at the parting of the ways, where the road divides. He casts lots with arrows, consults household gods and inspects the livers of beasts. The augur's arrow marked 'Jerusalem' falls at his right hand: here, then, he must raise a shout and sound the battle cry, set battering-rams against the gates, pile siege-ramps and build watch-towers.[1]

After this general observation, it will not be necessary to refer again to the evidence from the world of the ancient Near East, except incidentally, since Egypt and Mesopotamia are the subject of other essays in this volume. But there are two more aspects of the background to the practice of divination in Israel which necessitate a further word. On the one hand, it seems most likely that many of the characteristics which link the Old Testament evidence in this respect with practices common in the surrounding civilisations were mediated directly to the Hebrews through their closest neighbours, the peoples usually described by the term Canaanite. These groups had their own distinctive culture and religion which exercised a profound influence on their conquerors when the two became fused together, particularly with the development of an organized state from the time of David (*c.* 1010–971 BC). The surviving evidence does not provide a great deal of detailed information about the practice of divination among the Canaanites, although there are a number of striking instances, some of which will be referred to later, which justify the conclusion that much in Israelite divination has its origin in Canaan. In particular, the existence in Israel of organized groups of professional diviners and the closely related associations of prophets can probably best be understood as a phenomenon adopted and adapted from the Canaanites. Such, at least, appears to have been the understanding of some circles in Israel itself. The key passage in *Deuteronomy* xviii, 10–11, which lists the classes of divinatory practitioners known to ancient Israel, is preceded by the words: 'When you come into the land which Yahweh your God is giving you, do not learn to imitate the abominable customs of those other nations', and, after listing those customs, the whole passage is concluded with the statement: 'These nations whose place you are taking listen to soothsayers and augurs, but Yahweh your God does not permit you to do this.'

It hardly needs saying that the prohibition of a practice implies that the practice actually exists and so these verses are good evidence that divination of a distinctively Canaanite type was common among the Hebrews in Palestine.

On the other hand, it should be recognized that there are aspects of Old Testament divination which derive from a different and somewhat older background, the situation of the Hebrews as nomadic or semi-nomadic groups. This is important because it reflects a culture and religious milieu based on a tribal or clan society, in contrast to the urban and state setting from which almost all our knowledge of divinatory activities in the ancient East otherwise comes. Perhaps the most valuable tool for recognizing and elucidating this strand in the Old Testament is through a comparison with what can be known of ancient Bedouin society, particularly in records from, or about, the pre-Islamic Arabs. Previous generations of Old Testament scholars paid a good deal of attention to this material for the understanding of what we know about Israel's life, not least in its religious aspect, and although their successors have tended to neglect and undervalue it, it still remains of great importance and urgently merits fresh investigation from the side of Biblical studies.[2] Of course, such evidence can only be used with great circumspection; the time-span between our evidence for early Israel and what we have for the pre-Islamic Arabs covers hundreds of years and it would be very wrong simply to equate Israelite society, at any stage of its existence, with the society of the Bedouin. Nevertheless, there is, as compared with Egypt and Mesopotamia, a generally similar social structure and historical development in the case of these two peoples, which makes it legitimate to speak of analogies between them, and, in the course of our investigation, attention will be called to some examples of pre-Islamic and early Islamic Arab divination which, especially with regard to the prophets, are very illuminating for similar practices among the Israelites.

There is one further problem in relation to the assessment of the Old Testament material which should briefly be mentioned. As the passage quoted from Deuteronomy indicates – and there are others of similar kind[3] – there were circles in Israelite society that sought to prohibit divination entirely, or at least severely criticized, from their particular understanding of Yahwism, what they considered to be its shortcomings. This outlook in course of time came to be the dominant one and certainly the one held by the final editors and compilers of the Old Testament as we now have it, those we might call the official representatives of post-exilic Judaism. Several consequences flow from this fact.

In the first place, we can, to some extent at least, trace a development in attitudes to divination and plot a graph of its practice in Israel in a way that is hardly possible for the rest of the ancient Near East; thus there is evidence that forms of divination associated with the prophets began to supplant the priestly oracular functions in the course of the ninth century BC[4] and that in turn these characteristic forms of prophetic divination disappeared with the exile of the sixth century.[5]

Secondly, in the dominant tradition of the Old Testament, many of the religious institutions and practices have been purged of the divinatory associations which, as will be seen, we may justifiably suspect they once possessed; to mention a few instances which will be more fully discussed later, in the book of Leviticus sacrifice has no divinatory function, the Ark is a container for the tablets of the Law and the throne of the invisible Yahweh,[6] the ephod is part of the high-priest's vestments,[7] the Urim and Thummim have become merely a non-manipulative symbol of the divine justice[8] and so on. Hence we are often forced to read between the lines to discover an earlier stage when these things had a very different significance – and this is always a hazardous procedure – or to rely on incidental episodes in older narratives which later editors either themselves no longer understood or perhaps felt were too venerable to touch or which they considered to be harmless.

For, thirdly, we must always be conscious that the Old Testament has its own kind of classification and its own kind of rationale with respect to the divinatory and oracular practices which it records. Some of these could be assimilated with what came to be the dominant concept of Yahwism but some, for whatever reason, could not. The modern scholar will need to take account of all these practices in a study of the topic in Israel, because he sees them as generically similar, but this is not the standpoint of the Bible. There is an essential difference between various rites, simply because some are legitimate and some illegitimate[9]; Saul, for example, suppressed certain forms of what we should call divination but there was nothing wrong in his resorting to others, and it was only a sign of his complete rejection by Yahweh that these in fact failed him. Lastly, from what has been noted about the nature of the Old Testament in its existing form, it is not surprising that we have no material from Israel of the kind so frequent in the rest of the ancient Near East, such as collections of omens or reports of extispicy, which provide detailed pictures, and even to some extent a rationale, of divinatory and oracular techniques. Thus we are all too often in the dark when we try to interpret, and even to translate, Old Testament notices of divination which, as has already been mentioned, are frequently only brief and incidental.

Now the evidence about Mesopotamian and Egyptian divination reflects the world of the professionals; it consists of royal records, accounts of oracular responses of skilled priests, documents intended to instruct the regular practitioner in his craft. What is lacking in all the literary deposit of the ancient Near East is the presence of authentic narrative, reflecting the customs, relationships and, particularly, the speech of real life and what may be called ordinary people.[10] By contrast, it is just this which marks off the Old Testament, and what the Bible indicates for our subject is that divining was not restricted to certain professional groups, but was very widespread and a normal part of everyday life. For the Israelite, the world he lived in was a mysterious place; there was no sharp division between what we might call the natural and the supernatural, any event or object could point beyond itself and become the vehicle for more than one meaning. To divine was to be aware of the deeper significance which an apparently random phenomenon might have – the usual definitions of 'divination' such as 'a form of communication with the higher powers'[11] or 'the art of determining the purposes, will or attributes of the gods'[12] confine its reference unduly, for often it is not concerned with gods or higher powers at all. Hence, at any rate in Israel, at one level it required no organized training or skill, although it presupposes an innate mental capacity.

Let us look at a couple of examples where a chance word, as it would seem, serves as an omen, where it acts as a sign, the Hebrew word '*ôth*, which is the regular term in the Old Testament for what the practice of divination provides. In *J Kings* xx, 30f., king Ben-hadad of Damascus has fallen into the hands of the king of Israel and his servants go to the latter to beg for their master's life. The king of Israel replies with the words: 'is he still alive, he who is my brother?' Then we read 'now the men divined' or, following the excellent rendering of the Vulgate, 'they took it for an omen'; the king's use of the friendly expression 'brother' indicated that he intended him no harm. Now the Hebrew root used here is also employed for the elaborate rituals practised by the professional Mesopotamian seer, Balaam,[13] and for Joseph's leconomancy, divination by means of liquid in a cup. But it is also used in *Genesis* xxx, 26f., where Jacob is trying to persuade Laban to release him and says: 'you know what service I have done for you' and Laban expresses his reluctance to do so in the reply: 'I have divined that Yahweh has blessed me for your sake'. The term used by Laban does not, as one recent commentator has suggested, refer 'undoubtedly to inquiries by means of omens'[14] nor, as another has proposed, does it bear the merely metaphorical sense 'perceived by careful observation'.[15] The tense of the verb in Hebrew can equally well be rendered by the English present, and it may be suggested that Jacob's words about the service he has done act as a sign for Laban of the real value of that service and an omen of what he will lose if he is deprived of it.

The preceding discussion enables us to grasp the real significance of another episode, where the technical language of divination is not used – so that the real import has been missed by the commentators – but where the idea would seem to be present. In *I Kings* ii, 28f., Joab, suspecting that king Solomon has designs on his life, has taken sanctuary in Yahweh's shrine. Solomon sends his commander-in-chief to finish the fugitive off, but he is nervous of violating the right of sanctuary and tries to get him to leave the holy place. Joab refuses with the words: 'No; I will die here'. The commander returns to the king and reports what Joab has said, to which the king answers: 'Do as he has said and strike him down' and the commander promptly does so. Surely we are to understand that Solomon took Joab's words as a sign or omen that his fate was intended – he divined their deepest import just as Ben-hadad's servants or Laban did – and so knew that he would not incur any guilt that might be involved in disregarding the obligation of sanctuary.

An interesting development of this kind of popular, non-professional type of divination, as it might be called, is when, instead of relying on a chance omen, a situation is deliberately contrived so that it may provide the answer to a problem or

11. THE BEER-SHEBA ALTAR

An Israelite altar from a shrine at Beer-sheba, probably dating from before the reign of Hezekiah (714–686 BC), in the early part of which it appears to have been dismantled. It has horns at each corner and its height was originally about 157 cm., that is, approximately three 'large' cubits. It was thus of the same shape and dimensions as the altar overlaid with bronze or copper (cf. *Exodus* xxvii, 1–2; *I Kings* viii, 64; *II Chronicles* vi, 13) which stood in the Jerusalem temple and which King Ahaz used for divination (*II Kings* xvi, 14–15). A similar altar has been discovered at the Israelite sanctuary of Arad (cf. *Israel Exploration Journal* 14 (1964), p. 282). The representation of a twisting snake on one of the stones of the Beer-sheba altar attests the widespread veneration of the serpent in ancient Israel (cf. K. R. Joines, *Serpent Symbolism in the Old Testament*, 1974). From *The Biblical Archeologist* 37, no. 1, March 1974, 2–6. By courtesy of the *The Biblical Archeologist* and the American Schools of Oriental Research.

12. MEGIDDO SHRINE–*No. 2986*

One of a number of miniature temples in pottery from the Canaanite city of Megiddo in central Palestine, dating from between 1000–800 BC. Its height is about 41 cm. The oblong openings at the sides represent windows and the circular holes above them probably represent openings for the doves of the goddess worshipped at the sanctuary. Of special interest is the fact that the shrine is decorated with cherubim, figures with a human face and lion body: the two at the corners are female and those on the side male. It has been suggested that these shrine models were the prototype of the ark in Solomon's temple, both with regard to its form and function (cf. H. G. May, 'The Ark–A Miniature Temple', *American Journal of Semitic Languages and Literature*, LII (1936) 215–34). The Jerusalem ark would have been contemporary with the Megiddo shrines, like them it was portable and, above all, it was, like them, guarded by cherubim (cf. *I Samuel* iv, 4; *I Kings* vi, 23–28, viii, 6–7). From H. G. May, *The Material Remains of the Megiddo Cult*, OIP vol. xxvi, 1935, pl. xiii. Courtesy of the Oriental Institute, The University of Chicago.

indicate the right course of action. A good example is found in *I Samuel* xiv, 8f., where Jonathan is trying to decide whether or not to attack the Philistines and says: 'We will cross over and let them see us. If they say, "Stay where you are till we come to you", then we will stay where we are and not go up to them. But if they say, "Come up to us", we will go up; this will be the sign (*'ôth*, the technical divinatory term) that Yahweh has put them into our power.'

In the event, the Philistines take the latter alternative and the attack succeeds, but, as we have suggested, the outcome does not depend on a random word[16]; rather, a divinatory situation is contrived and its scope clearly defined. A similar instance occurs in *I Samuel* vi, when the Philistines are trying to determine whether or not the plagues that have afflicted them were caused by the presence of the ark, the effective symbol of Yahweh's presence. They consult their priests and diviners and are instructed to place the ark on a new wagon, drawn by two milch-cows from whom their calves have been taken away; then, they are told: 'Watch the wagon: if it goes up towards its own territory, then it is Yahweh who has done us this great injury; but if not, then we shall know that his hand has not touched us, but we have been the victims of chance.'

It has been suggested that here we have an example of a regular practice of divination by observing the action of animals,[17] such as is known in other contemporary cultures. However, in spite of the fact that the course of action was initiated by experts, the priests and diviners, it would be hazardous to conclude that it reflects a professional mode of divination recognized by the ancient Israelites. For the centre of interest is not the behaviour of the cows but the behaviour of the ark; it is a test to see whether the ark has the supernatural power to drive the animals in a certain direction against their natural inclination to return home to suckle their hungry calves. It is essentially a piece of popular folklore, although it need not be denied that concepts about divination lie in the background.

A further example of the same type is perhaps Gideon's famous test of the wet or dry fleece in *Judges* vi, 36–40, but here we cannot exclude the possibility that we have moved away from the ordinary folk-tale and that we are concerned with an actual divinatory ritual. It may be noted that Gideon directly invokes the deity to give a response by means of the fleece, the setting of the story appears to be Ophrah, which was certainly a sanctuary, while the fleece is said to have been placed on the threshing-floor which, in several cases in the Old Testament, is regarded as a sacred place and associated with divination.[18] Possibly, therefore, the story of Gideon's fleece in fact indicates a regular means of consulting the oracle at the Ophrah shrine. Similar considerations apply to the narrative in *Numbers* xvii of how Aaron's rod alone sprouted when it was presented with eleven others in the sanctuary, thus indicating that Aaron was the divinely chosen priest. Again, it has been suggested that this is an instance of divining by the observation of budding plants[19] but, although once more such an idea may be part of the background of the story, it is hardly applicable to the tale as we have it, since the rods are in no sense growing plants. Rather, we have to do with a mythological theme, known in many parts of the world,[20] and perhaps with a religious ritual, which has been adapted to provide a divinatory test of the kind which, as we have seen, was well recognized in Israel.

In the discussion so far, we have had indications of the way in which an originally spontaneous type of divination develops into something much more organized and in fact becomes virtually a technique. A similar process can be discerned if we consider the Old Testament evidence about divination through visual experiences, and especially through what are there termed 'visions' and 'dreams', which comprise perhaps the commonest form of divination in the Bible. The root meanings of the Hebrew words rendered 'vision' and 'dream' both mean 'to see' and clearly something seen, as well as heard, apparently by chance or at random, could be an omen and give information as to what was going to happen. But what we find in Israel is that this innate faculty becomes a skilled technique regularly practiced by what may be called professionals specially adept in this particular area. In the Old Testament there occurs the class of experts, who have their close parallels throughout the ancient Near Eastern world, known as 'seers'. The one English word translates two different Hebrew terms, *ḥōzêh* and *rō'êh*, but both of them mean 'one who sees' and they derive from the same roots from which come the two commonest Hebrew words which we render as 'vision'. Scholars have sometimes attempted to draw a fairly clear distinction between the Hebrew 'prophet' (*nābhî*') and the Hebrew 'seer', at least in their origins, but it is very difficult to discover any real differentiation between the persons described by these terms in the Old Testament itself[21] and it is probably safer to take these words as denoting particular *specialisms*, one or other of which an individual might make peculiarly his own or either of which he might practice on particular occasions. At any rate, the employment of a well-established divinatory visual technique is as fully, if not more fully, established for the people described as 'prophets' as it is for those described as 'seers'.

This technique, as it is found among the Hebrew prophets, can be best understood from a comparison with similar practices recounted in Arabic sources[22]; indeed, it can best be summarized in the words used in a 10th century Arabic text[23] to describe the *modus operandi* of a 9th century Bedouin diviner: 'he glanced at the first object on which his eye fell and he extracted from thence a notion which he applied to the matter about which he was to give a decision.' There are a considerable number of examples of divination by Old Testament prophets which conform very closely to this pattern and two may be selected for brief discussion.

The first occurs in the narrative about Balaam in *Numbers* xxiv. Balaam, of course, is not an Israelite, but we may take it that this particular prophecy of his is meant to be understood as typical of what was practised and regarded as legitimate in Israel, since it is preceded by the words 'he did not go and resort to divination as before.'There are three aspects or stages in the account which should be specially noted. First, Balaam sees something in a perfectly natural and ordinary way – 'he turned toward the desert; and, as he looked, he saw Israel encamped tribe by tribe': this was 'the object on which his eye fell.' Secondly, however, this sight immediately turns into second-sight and there follows a most interesting and quite unique description of the outward phenomena of the divinatory vision as the vehicle for the succeeding oracle:

> The oracle of Balaam son of Beor,
> the oracle of the man whose sight is clear,
> the oracle of him who hears the words of God,
> who with staring eyes sees in a trance
> the vision from the Almighty.

Thirdly, the opening words of the actual oracle are as follows:

> How goodly are your tents, O Jacob,
> your dwelling-places, Israel,
> like long rows of palms,
> like gardens by a river,
> like aloes planted by Yahweh,
> like cedars beside the water!

It can be seen at once that the oracle is rooted in what Balaam had previously observed in a quite ordinary way and that he does indeed extract from that a notion which he applies to the matter about which he is to give a decision, namely the destiny of Israel. Further, however, and this is another characteristic it shares with what is known of pre-Islamic Arab divination, it is in verse, it exhibits the nature and style of regular Hebrew poetry. Moreover, the link between sight and second-sight is brought out by a play on words: the consonants of the Hebrew word translated 'tents', 'ōhālîm, and that translated 'aloes', 'ᵃhālîm, are identical, the two expressions both look and sound very much alike. Now, all this reveals a sophisticated and well recognized interpretative technique of a skilled practitioner; we are far removed from a merely chance or random experience.

The second example, which can be dealt with even more briefly, is the set of five so-called visions which form the central part of the book of Amos,[24] who, it is worth remarking, is described as a 'seer'[25] as well as a 'prophet'. These visions all have a clear formal pattern, which is basically the same as what we have noted in the case of Balaam; they begin with the observation of a natural phenomenon, a swarm of locusts or a plumb-line, the resulting oracle is strongly rhythmical in character, and word-play occurs – Amos sees 'a basket of ripe summer fruit' and then Yahweh tells him 'the time is ripe for my people Israel'. But, with these visions of Amos, the natural phenomenon which is their starting-point is now itself part of the whole divinatory process; it is Yahweh directly who shows the prophet the locusts or the plumb-line or the fruit basket. This, coupled with the fact that the same features as are found in Amos occur elsewhere in the prophetical books,[26] only serves to emphasize again that we are here concerned with a well-established traditional technique of divination which the prophetic groups employed.

The Old Testament draws no sharp distinction between 'visions' and 'dreams', frequently coupling them together. Not all dreams were considered to be of significance nor were all of them necessarily sent from Yahweh. Many were, however, and they could again be received by anybody. There are numerous examples in the Old Testament of dreams which are quite straightforward and self-explanatory and where the auditory rather than the visual aspect is primary: their basic form is a clear and direct message to the recipient from God. However, it is clear that dreams were regularly employed as a method of divination by expert practitioners in them. Such a passage as *Jeremiah* xxiii, 25, to mention only one reference, shows that it was the hallmark of the prophets of his day, who are vividly depicted as crying out, 'I have had a dream, I have had a dream'. Further, not all dreams were self-explanatory and, long before Freud, the Hebrews, and indeed the world of the ancient Near East in general, were aware that they might have a symbolic character that needed to be unpacked – the Hebrew expression for interpreting dreams, *pāthar*, means to analyze or dissolve – to find out what their message really was, since they were held to presage future events. So there developed a class of persons, of whom Joseph and Daniel are, the most obvious examples, who, on the one hand, were expert dreamers themselves, but were also experts in interpreting the dreams of others. For this, they needed above all what the Old Testament terms 'wisdom', the special skill which the understanding of a dream required; hence the interpretation of dreams was a function of the distinct class of wise men, though not exclusively confined to them, and, as with all wisdom, represented a combination of innate faculty and acquired knowledge.

Finally, in this connection, we should expect that in ancient Israel there would be some methods for inducing dreams, for of course these could not always be relied upon to be available when required. There is not a great deal of information on this matter in the Old Testament but it does provide some evidence for one such practice, that is incuba- *v* tion, passing the night in a holy place with the expectation of receiving a divine revelation through a dream, a rite which is well attested in Egypt, Mesopotamia and Canaan. In the Bible, the clearest example is Solomon's dream at the hill-shrine of Gibeon recounted in *I Kings* iii; the close parallel between this and similar royal dreams of Egyptian Pharaohs strongly suggests that Solomon was following a well-recognized custom.[27] Very probably another example is the narrative of Samuel's night vision in *I Samuel* iii, where the text suggests that it was his regular practice to sleep in the temple before the ark and it is tempting to suppose that the ark was in some way the medium of revelation on this occasion. The same custom probably underlies the account of Jacob's dream at Bethel in *Genesis* xxviii, 10–22, for the details of the story show that Bethel was an ancient Canaanite sanctuary to which Jacob would resort to consult the oracle, and also his night vision in *Genesis* xlvi, 1f., at the sanctuary of Beersheba, which, as in the case of Solomon, is preceded by the offering of sacrifices.[28]

We may now turn to discuss in a little more detail some of the practitioners in ancient Israel and the methods they employed. As mentioned earlier, one of the key-passages is *Deuteronomy* xviii, 10–11, which lists a number of practitioners in divination existing in ancient Israel, but the information it supplies is unfortunately very limited. The problem is that it is very difficult to discover exactly what the terms used in this passage, or elsewhere in the Bible, really denote.[29] The Old Testament itself gives no explanation of them, scholars differ widely in the etymologies they propose for them, which is the only clue we have as to their exact sense, and probably in the Old Testament as it now exists the expressions are virtually interchangeable and have acquired a general sense, considerably wider than what was no doubt originally the case. But perhaps two observations are possible in this connection.

First, the very fact that there are a number of different terms employed to describe what may loosely be called 'diviners' itself indicates that they were once quite precise in meaning, denoting practitioners specializing in distinct and specific divinatory rites; and this emphasizes how widespread such practices were at least at the popular level of ancient Israel's religion.

Secondly, other evidence in the Old Testament refers fairly clearly to various divinatory practices, whether or not these are indicated by any of the actual expressions employed for divinatory persons in such passages as *Deuteronomy* xviii. For example, the word *me'ônēn* may originally have meant 'observers', those who divine by the observation of signs or omens, what we should call augurs. Now in *Judges* ix, 37 we hear of the terebinth of the *me'ônenîm*, that is, a tree which was frequented by an actual guild of diviners, presumably for the purpose of exercising their craft. That they did so by observing the movements or sounds made by large trees is suggested by *II Samuel* v, 24, where David is about to engage the Philistines in battle and instructs his troops: 'As soon as you hear a rustling sound in the tree-tops, then act at once; for Yahweh will have gone out before you to defeat the Philistine army.' The noise made by the trees was a sign or omen assuring victory. Again, the word *qesem*, although it is now employed in the Old Testament for various types of divination, may once have had the distinct sense of obtaining an oracle by casting arrows or rods. It certainly has this meaning when used in the description of the king of Babylon, which was quoted earlier, but there is some evidence that such a practice was known in Israel also. It is probably referred to in *Hosea* iv, 12:

> My people inquire from a block of wood,
> And their rod gives them oracles,[30]

while the shooting of arrows in *I Samuel* xx by Jonathan to indicate to David the disposition of Saul would seem to derive from the same custom. Or again, the word *nāhash* may originally have denoted someone who took omens from the movements of serpents, a practice attested in other early cultures; or, perhaps more probably, one who divined by availing himself of the great wisdom which the serpent was thought to possess by the world of the Ancient Near East and certainly by Israel, as *Genesis* iii shows, to mention only one example.

In what has just been said, we are led on to one method of divination among the Hebrews, the significance of which seems clear precisely because, in this instance, the grounds for its condemnation by Israel's official religion are also clear. What was involved was divining by consulting super-natural beings other than Yahweh, and the Old Testament is aware of two forms of this. On the one hand, it speaks of resorting to 'spirits'. The Hebrew word *yidde'ōnî* thus translated actually means 'those who have knowledge'. It has often been suggested that it implies a 'familiar' spirit, but there is no evidence that the Hebrews had a concept of the kind found in European witchcraft. Rather, the word refers to supernatural beings who possessed a knowledge beyond the human, which the diviner could extract from them by his special arts.

On the other hand, there was the widespread custom of necromancy, which was prohibited partly at least because in ancient Israel the realm of the departed was viewed as entirely outside Yahweh's concern or control. In the only place in the Old Testament where the method used for consulting the dead is described in any detail, the famous passage about the woman of En-dor in *I Samuel* xxviii, it is said to be done through the *'ôbh*, which the woman owned. Again, this Hebrew word has frequently been rendered as 'familiar spirit' and the woman has been equated with a medium. But there are other places in the Bible where the term seems rather to indicate some material object in the possession of the necromancer which he employed to make contact with the departed, although there is no certainty as to exactly what it was. One proposal is that it corresponded to a sort of 'bull-roarer', another that it was a pit through which the denizens of the underworld could reach the earth, another that it was an ancestral image. In any event, *I Samuel* xxviii shows that a person with the requisite power was considered to be able to bring up the dead in visible form and to force them to speak audibly and foretell the future.

Our discussion of the character of the *'ôbh* brings us to a consideration of divination by means of man-made objects, as contrasted with divination by the observation of natural phenomena, and on this subject we have a good deal of information, although, as will be seen, it is rarely as precise as we might wish, because practices of this kind were a regular and accepted part of the religion of ancient Israel. In the Old Testament we commonly meet the expression 'to enquire of Yahweh', a technical term for taking steps to acquire an oracle, and it frequently denotes the purpose for which people would visit a sanctuary where Yahweh was present and could be consulted. The oracle-givers at the sanctuaries were primarily the priests although, as will emerge later, they were not the only such persons at Israelite shrines, and it appears that their particular specialism was divining by means of what we have ventured to call man-made phenomena. It is perhaps worth emphasizing that in the Old Testament, as indeed the linguistic identity of the Arabic word *kāhin* and the Hebrew word *kōhēn* itself suggests,[31] the basic and primary function of the Hebrew priest was to divine and thereby to give oracles in response to enquiries. In *Deuteronomy* xxxiii, 8, we are told that 'Thou (i.e. Yahweh) didst give thy Thummim to Levi (i.e. the priestly tribe), Thy Urim to thy loyal servant.'

What the precise nature of the Urim and Thummim was is very obscure, but what is certain is that they were objects which the priest consulted in order to obtain a decision from Yahweh and that they comprised the chief official procedure by which oracles were obtained. Almost certainly they took the form of lots which the priest manipulated; perhaps, on the analogy of a Mesopotamian text, they were two stones of different colours, one giving a negative, the other a positive, response to an inquiry.[32] However, there are indications that the Urim and Thummim could return a 'no-answer' nor should we think of the process as purely mechanical, for the priest might often need to interpret the reply, as we find being done in the Mesopotamian and Hittite omen collections.

So, in a way similar to these latter, we can discern a fixed scheme of priestly oracular enquiry and response in the Old Testament,[33] which may be illustrated from *II Samuel* ii, 1.

The first element is the enquiry – 'David enquired of Yahweh, "Shall I go up into one of the cities of Judah?"'. The second element is the delivery of the oracle, through the priest – 'Yahweh answered, "Go up"'. These two elements are constant in all the occurrences of the schema, but in this case there is a further development when David asks again 'To which city?' and the answer comes 'To Hebron'. Here we see the interpretative role of the priest in giving an oracle, for David's second question obviously did not admit of a simple yes or no response.

Alongside the Urim and Thummim, there occur two other objects which had a divinatory role. The first is the ephod. There has been a good deal of dispute as to what this was and it may well be the case that in the Old Testament the word is applied to different things. One thing it certainly is is a priestly garment and so it is possible to suggest that it was the special dress which was put on to approach the deity to receive his message. Since the image of the god also wore the same or a similar garment, the effect would be to identify the officiant with him so that he spoke as the deity himself when delivering an oracle. However, there are some references to the ephod where this meaning is not very suitable and it seems more likely that, in the context of divination, the ephod was the container for the Urim and Thummim. This is suggested by the passage in *I Samuel* xiv, 18f., where, according to what is probably the original text, Saul orders his priest to bring out the ephod and he proceeds to make inquiry of God through the priest. But he is interrupted by the enemy attack and then orders 'withdraw your hand', that is, the priest had just stretched out his hand to take the sacred lots from the ephod. It should be noted that in these verses the existing Hebrew text has the word 'ark' in place of 'ephod' and, though this is rejected by the majority of scholars, it cannot be entirely disregarded. Perhaps ark and ephod could sometimes be two terms for the same object or perhaps the ark, which was originally a container of some sort, had a similar character and function to the ephod, even if not identical with it.

The second object to be considered is the *teraphim*, a word which again raises a whole range of problems. It appears to be a plural form and is commonly translated 'household gods'.[34] There is no doubt, however, that the teraphim gave oracles. They were consulted, as we have seen, by the king of Babylon and their function is plainly described in *Zechariah* x, 2:

> The teraphim make mischievous promises
> And the diviners see false signs.

But possibly the word is not a plural and denotes a cultic mask, again worn by both the officiant and the deity's image; such a practice may be reflected in the curious notice in *Exodus* xxxiv, 33f., about the covering which Moses put over his face when he came out from consulting Yahweh to give the Israelites the oracles he had received.[35] Again, the significance would be that the priest assumed the face of the god and was identified with him.

In view of all that is known of divination in the ancient Near East, we cannot leave this discussion of the Israelite priest's divinatory role without considering whether he may not also have divined by means of sacrifice. As already noted, all trace of this has disappeared from the Old Testament accounts of sacrifice, but was this always so? There are perhaps five considerations which may suggest that it was not. First, it is noteworthy how frequently the reception of divine oracles is narrated in the context of the offering of sacrifices. Secondly, there are a number of psalms where a response to an enquiry seems to be uttered by a priest or a prophet as the result of some distinct sign provided by the accompanying sacrifice. Thirdly, in *II Kings* xvi, 15, king Ahaz of Judah reserves for himself an altar in the Temple 'to make enquiry by': since an altar implies sacrifice, this was presumably the means he used for divining. Fourthly, Ahaz was probably copying Aramean rituals and here it is possible that the rather rare Hebrew word, which we have translated 'to make enquiry', has the technical sense of 'to consult the entrails', the most important means of divination for Babylonian and Assyrian kings.[36] Nor may hepatoscopy have been simply a Mesopotamian import into Israel.[37] In the ritual for the shared or peace offering in *Leviticus* iii, there are very full and detailed prescriptions for the extraction of the liver and its appurtenances. Nothing is said in the existing text about the reason for this and one is led to speculate that originally the entrails were so carefully removed for the purposes of divination.[38] Fifthly, the recent discovery of clay liver models, similar to those long known from Mesopotamia, at the city of Hazor makes it impossible to rule out hepatoscopy as a common practice among the Hebrews themselves.[39]

In conclusion, something must be said, although all too briefly, about the place of the prophet, *nābhî*, in divination, for he became the most important channel through which inquiry from God was made in ancient Israel, supplanting to a considerable degree in this respect figures like the priest or the seer, or other kinds of diviners. Not that he is to be too sharply distinguished from these, especially in the earliest days. We have seen how difficult it is to differentiate between seer and prophet, while, like priests, prophets were closely connected with sanctuaries and the distinct literary oracular pattern which we saw in accounts of priestly divining occur equally clearly in the records of the prophets. Prophets were regularly inquired of by all sorts of people and about all kinds of matters, from the whereabouts of a farmer's asses to high affairs of state, and one text suggests that they had regular consulting hours during cultic occasions.[40] They would appear to have used a wide range of divinatory techniques, appropriating those more properly characteristic of other groups; for example, as we have noted, they divined by the observation of natural phenomena, like the seer. But one method of divination seems to be especially distinctive of the prophets and they may be thought of as above all practitioners of this particular technique. Whatever may have been the original meaning of the word *nābhî*, the denominative verb derived from it, meaning 'to act as a prophet', often denotes what is generally described as 'ecstasy' – although the expression is not altogether a happy one[41] – that is, wild uncontrolled physical behaviour, such as is characteristic of Arab dervishes. The verb is sometimes employed when there is no question of divination, as of Saul flinging his spear at David, and so the prophet could be described as a madman.[42] Ecstatic behaviour was viewed as possession by the spirit of Yahweh, which changed a person's whole being, replacing him, in a sense, by the deity himself;

so Samuel told Saul: 'The spirit of Yahweh will suddenly take possession of you, and you too will be rapt like a prophet and become another man'; or we read that the spirit of Yahweh 'clothed itself' with Gideon,[43] while one of the commonest terms for a prophet is 'îš 'elōhîm, a divine man. Almost certainly, this means of divination was adopted by the Hebrews from their Canaanite neighbours, of whom it was characteristic. We may refer to the well-known passage in the Egyptian story of Wen-Amun's visit to Phoenicia where he records how, in the North Syrian city of Byblos, and significantly, on the occasion of a sacrifice, the god 'seized one of the king's pages and made him possessed', so that he gave a message about Wen-Amun in the name of the deity; the determinative of the hieroglyph of the word 'possessed' in the text shows a human figure in violent motion or convulsion.[44]

As some of the examples just quoted reveal, such possession could fall on anyone in Israel; it did not necessarily result in oracle giving – its outcome, for instance, was often a feat of military prowess – and it could be entirely spontaneous. However, the prophets formed a professional class, organized in groups known as 'the sons of the prophets'. Even those great individual prophetic figures who increasingly dis-associated themselves from such groups usually seem to have been surrounded by a body of disciples and recent study of the prophetic books has emphasized that they gave their oracles in well-defined traditional formal patterns[45] – we might say that they had learned their trade.

So it is not surprising that we should find evidence of the use of means to induce ecstasy when a prophetic oracle was required. Possibly, as in some other religions, this was some-times done by alcohol; thus we read in *Isaiah* xxviii, 7: 'The priest and the prophet reel with strong drink . . . they err in vision, they stumble in giving judgment.' Certainly, however, ecstasy was induced by the stimulus of music. The clearest example is in *II Kings* iii, 15–16, where the kings of Israel and Judah come to consult the prophet Elisha and he replies: ' "Now, fetch me a minstrel." They fetched a minstrel, and while he was playing, the power of Yahweh came upon Elisha (i.e. he was seized with ecstasy) and he said, "This is the word of Yahweh." ' Or, again, in *I Samuel* x, 5, there is a vivid description of 'a company of prophets coming down from the hill-shrine, led by lute, harp, fife and drum, and filled with prophetic rapture.'

There is one further phenomenon in relation to prophetic divinatory technique which should be mentioned. In the Elisha episode just mentioned, the oracle took the form of a sign – 'Pools will form all over this ravine'. But of course the sign points beyond itself and is immediately interpreted by Elisha as indicating Israel's victory over Moab. Here, then, we have the regular *double* aspect of divination, the production of the omen and its interpretation. To give such signs in response to enquiries was an accepted part of the prophetic function; king Ahaz was told by Isaiah to ask 'Yahweh your God for a sign, from lowest Sheol or from highest heaven'. In particular, the prophets often provided such signs themselves, when, in the grip of ecstasy, they performed strange and unusual symbolic actions which caught the attention of the public and guaranteed to them the authenticity of the interpretation of the sign, as an indication of what was going to happen. The book of Ezekiel is particularly rich in instances of these symbolic actions, but we may take a clear and short example from *Isaiah* xx to illustrate the procedure. First, we have the divinatory sign: 'Yahweh said to Isaiah son of Amoz, Come, strip the sackcloth from your waist and take your sandals off. He did so, and went about naked and barefoot (i.e. he made himself like a captive taken in battle).' Then follows the prophet's interpretation of the sign: 'Yahweh said, My servant Isaiah has gone naked and barefoot for three years as a sign and a warning to Egypt and Cush; just so shall the king of Assyria lead the captives of Egypt and the exiles of Cush naked and barefoot.'

In what has been said, the subject of divination and oracles in ancient Israel has certainly not been completely covered, as any Old Testament expert would at once recognize. But it has perhaps been possible to give some indication of the wide variety of ways in which men and women in that society endeavoured to find guidance for life's problems and to determine the divine will for them. At a first glance, the Old Testament might seem to provide much less evidence about divination and oracle-giving, compared with what is known from the surviving epigraphical and other material from the rest of the ancient Near East. It may perhaps be claimed, however, that the Israelite evidence displays two features which give it particular interest – it opens up a perspective on divination wider than that provided by professional practitioners or official rituals, and it enables us, to some degree at least, to trace a development in the understanding and practice of divination within a particular society in a way that is unique in that ancient world.

Notes

1   *Ezekiel* xxi, 21-22. The translations of Old Testament passages are generally those of the *New English Bible*, but on occasion they have been adapted to bring them closer to the Hebrew original where this seemed desirable for the following of the argument.

2   For a preliminary discussion and bibliography, cf. J. R. Porter, 'Pre-Islamic Arabic Historical Traditions and the Early Historical Narratives of the Old Testament', *Journal of Biblical Literature* lxxxvii (1968), pp. 17-26.

3   Cf. *Exodus* xxii, 17; *Leviticus* xix, 26, 31, xx, 6, 27.

4   Cf. A. Cody, *A History of the Old Testament Priesthood*, Rome, 1969, pp. 13-14, 44-48.

5   Cf. C. Westermann, 'Die Begriffe für Fragen und Suchen im Alten Testament', *Kerygma und Dogma* 6 (1960), 10-13.

6   Cf. the discussion of *Leviticus* xvi, 2, 13 in J. R. Porter, *Leviticus*, Cambridge, 1976, pp. 126, 130.

7   Cf. *Leviticus* viii, 7.

8   Cf. the discussion of *Leviticus* viii, 8 in J. R. Porter, op. cit., p. 83.

9   For a fuller discussion of this point, cf. J. R. Porter and W. M. S. Russell, *Animals in Folklore*, Ipswich, 1978, p. 71f.

10   Cf. J. R. Porter, 'Old Testament Historiography', in *Tradition and Interpretation*, ed. G. W. Anderson, Oxford, 1979, p. 130f.

11   Cf. I. Mendelsohn, *The Interpreter's Dictionary of the Bible*, *A-D*, New York, 1962, p. 856.

12   Cf. B. O. Long, *The Interpreter's Dictionary of the Bible*, Supplementary Volume, New York, 1976, p. 241.

13   Cf. S. Daiches, 'Balaam – a Babylonian *bārū*', Hilprecht Anniversary Volume, Leipzig, 1909, pp. 60-70, reprinted in S. Daiches, *Bible Studies*, London, 1950, pp. 110-119.

14   Cf. E. A. Speiser, *Genesis*, Garden City, New York, 1964, p. 236.

15   Cf. S. R. Driver, *The Book of Genesis*, tenth edition, London, 1916, p. 277.

212 ORACLES AND DIVINATION

16 It is therefore not strictly parallel to the Babylonian *egirrû* or the Greek *klēdōn*, as proposed by B. O. Long, op. cit., p. 242.

17 Cf. B. O. Long, ibid.

18 Cf. A. J. Wensinck, *Some Semitic Rites of Mourning and Religion*, Amsterdam, 1917.

19 Cf. B. O. Long, op. cit., p. 242.

20 Cf. A. Jeremias, *Das Alte Testament im Lichte des Alten Orients*, fourth edition, Leipzig, 1930, p. 444.

21 Cf. the careful discussion in J. Lindblom, *Prophecy in Ancient Israel*, Oxford, 1962, p. 93f.

22 Cf. in general, A. Guillaume, *Prophecy and Divination*, London, 1938.

23 The *Nishwār al Muḥāḍarah*, translated as *The Table-talk of a Mesopotamian Judge* by D. S. Margoliouth, *Journal of the Royal Asiatic Society* 1922, pp. 274–279.

24 *Amos* vii, 1–9; viii, 1–3; ix, 1–10.

25 *Amos* vii, 12.

26 Cf. e.g. *Jeremiah* i, 11–12.

27 Cf. S. Herrmann, 'Die Königsnovelle in Ägypten und in Israel', *Wissenschaftliche Zeitschrift der Universitäts Leipzig* 3 (1953–54), pp. 53–57.

28 The practice of incubation has also been discerned in *Psalms* iii, 6; iv, 9; xvii, 15, cf. S. Mowinckel, *Psalmenstudien I*, Kristiania, 1961, pp. 154–157, and in *Isaiah* lxv, 4, cf. C. Westermann, *Isaiah* 40–66, London, 1969, p. 401. The topic is surveyed in E. L. Ehrlich, *Der Traum im Alten Testament*, Berlin, 1953, pp. 13–57, but his argument that *I Kings* iii is the only genuine instance of incubation in the Old Testament is not convincing.

29 There is no adequate up-to-date discussion of the terms in *Deuteronomy* xviii, 10–11. T. Witton Davies, *Magic, Divination and Demonology among the Hebrews and their neighbours*, London, 1898, pp. 78–85 is still of value and reference may be made to the articles on individual words in the *Theological Dictionary of the Old Testament*, ed. G. J. Botterweck and H. Ringgren, Grand Rapids, Michigan, 1977 (in progress).

30 Cf. J. L. Mays, *Hosea*, London, 1969, p. 73.

31 Cf. J. Henninger, in *L'Antica Società Beduina*, ed. F. Gabrieli, Rome, 1959, p. 138f.

32 Cf. E. Lipiński, 'Ūrim and Tummim', *Vetus Testamentum* xx (1970), pp. 495–496.

33 Cf. B. O. Long, 'The Effect of Divination upon Israelite Literature', *Journal of Biblical Literature* 92 (1973), pp. 493–497.

34 It has, however, recently been suggested that the word is cognate with the Hittite *tarpiš* and denotes some kind of spirit, cf. H. A. Hoffner, 'Hittite Tarpis and Hebrew Teraphim', *Journal of Near Eastern Studies* xxvii (1968) pp. 61–68.

35 Cf. R. E. Clements, *Exodus*, Cambridge, 1972, p. 225f. A cultic clay mask has been discovered in the area of a Canaanite temple dedicated to the moon god at the city of Hazor in northern Israel, dating from *c.* 1450–1200 BC.: a similar mask was also found in the

vicinity (cf. Y. Yadin, Y. Aharoni, R. Amiran, T. Dothan, I. Dunayevsky, J. Perrot, *Hazor I*, Jerusalem, 1958, pl. CLXIII; *Hazor II*, 1960, pl. CLXXXIII.). They both have two holes for a string to attach them either to the head of a wearer or to another object. It has been objected that such masks were too small for a human being to wear – they are only just over 14 cm. and 16 cm. high respectively – and it has been suggested that they were intended rather to be hung up for apotropaic purposes (cf. E. Stern, 'Phoenician Masks and Pendants', *Palestine Exploration Quarterly* 108 (1976), pp. 117–8). But they do not have the grotesque form of the clearly apotropaic masks known from elsewhere and they might have been intended to be attached to the forehead, somewhat like the Jewish phylactery. In this case, the mask would identify the wearer with the deity and qualify him to speak in his name. Further, it has been proposed that the Hazor masks represent the consort of the moon god, probably Tanit who, at Carthage, had the title 'face of Ba'al', and that they could have also been attached to the statue of the moon god, so indicating the 'face of Ba'al' (cf. Y. Yadin, *Hazor*, London, 1975, pp. 55–7). Such masks may therefore perhaps be compared with the Biblical teraphim, a term which sometimes seems to denote cult masks (cf. O. Keel, *The Symbolism of the Biblical World*, London, 1978, p. 194).

36 Cf. J. Gray, *I & II Kings*, second edition, London, 1970, p. 637.

37 It has been suggested that the prophet Amos may have practised it. Cf. M. Bič, 'Der Prophet Amos – ein Haepatoskopos', *Vetus Testamentum* i (1951), pp. 293–6; A. E. Murtonen, 'The Prophet Amos – a Hepatoscoper?', *Vetus Testamentum* ii (1952), pp. 170–1.

38 Cf. A. Haldar, *Associations of Cult Prophets among the Ancient Semites*, Uppsala, 1945, p. 212f.; J. R. Porter, *Leviticus*, Cambridge, 1976, p. 30.

39 It should, however, be noted that the Hazor models probably date from the fifteenth century BC and thus before the Israelite occupation of the city. Cf. H. Tadmor and B. Landsberger, 'Fragments of Clay Liver Models at Hazor', *Israel Exploration Journal* xiv (1964), pp. 201–17.

40 *II Kings* iv, 22–23.

41 Cf. R. R. Wilson, 'Prophecy and Ecstasy: a Reexamination', *Journal of Biblical Literature* 98 (1979), pp. 321–337.

42 Cf. e.g. *II Kings* ix, 11.

43 This is the literal meaning of *Judges* vi, 34.

44 Cf. J. B. Pritchard, *Ancient Near Eastern Texts relating to the Old Testament*, second edition, Princeton, 1955, p. 26, note 13.

45 Cf. the important work of C. Westermann, *Basic Forms of Prophetic Speech*, London, 1967.

Bibliography

There is at present no completely adequate overall survey of divination in ancient Israel. Perhaps the most satisfactory is by A. Caquot, 'La divination dans l'ancient Israël' in *La Divination*, ed. A. Caquot and M. Leibovici, Paris, 1968, pp. 83–113. Shorter discussions are O. Eissfeldt, 'Wahrsagung im Alten Testament', *La divination en Mésopotamie ancienne et dans les régions voisines*, Recontre assyriologique internationale xiv, New York, 1965, pp. 141–145 and the articles by I. Mendelsohn and B. O. Long in *The Interpreter's Dictionary of the Bible, A–D*, New York, 1962, pp. 856–858 and the *Supplementary Volume*, New York, 1976, pp. 241–243 respectively.

9

Islam

R. B. SERJEANT
Sir Thomas Adams's Professor of Arabic, University of Cambridge

It will occasion no surprise that in the Islamic countries there appear to be close parallels to almost all the beliefs and practices described in this volume as manifest in other civilisations in past ages or at this present time of ours. Islam is rooted in the ancient culture of Arabia, which partakes with other Semitic cultures in a common heritage, so that much that is Arabian is also to be found in the civilisation of the Hebrews, Mesopotamians and other Semitic communities. In the extensive territories where Islam became the dominant religion – Africa, Persia, parts of the Indian sub-continent, Indonesia, etc. – numerous pre-Islamic religious beliefs and practices survive, and even flourish vigorously, whether adapted into Islam or, not infrequently, without pretence of an Islamic veneer. In the latter case they are condemned by the ulema (doctors of theology) even if they be powerless to eradicate them. It is less well known that many vestiges of pre-Islamic pagan religion are still to be found in the Arabian Peninsula itself. In its formative period Islam developed into the distinctive religious culture, more or less as we now know it, exposed to the influences of the Mediterranean world of Greece and Rome, and of converts to the faith from Christianity, Judaism, Iranian religions and others.

Most of this is common knowledge.

From the wealth of evidence of divination by various methods, omens, even certain forms of oracle – whether these exist at a high intellectual level or belong to the everyday life of ordinary folk – it is only possible here to select some limited examples by way of illustration. For a thorough systematic study the reader is referred to Taufic Fahd's excellent book, *La divination arabe. Études religieuses sociologiques et folkloriques sur le milieu natif de l'Islam* (Leiden, 1966), upon which this chapter has liberally drawn. To distinguish between diviner and prophet is not easy and the distinctive line between divination and magic is uncertain. Islam being an Arabian religion, it is logical to start with divination and oracles known from the preceding pagan age, the *Jāhiliyyah* as the Arabs call it, and trace where these have survived on into Islam, or the Islamic era, itself.

In the Ka'bah of Mecca, an idol, said to have been brought from Hīt in Iraq, and known to the pagan Meccans as Hubal, was set up in front of a well or pit inside the actual building. Before this god Hubal lay seven arrows known by the technical name *qidh*, a word also used of the arrows in the gambling game called *maysar*. On each arrow was something written; one arrow had written on it 'blood-money', and when two parties were at variance as to the person who should take the responsibility for paying it, the custodian, known as *sādin*, shuffled the arrows for them; the individual whose lot was to draw this arrow assumed the duty of payment. Another arrow had written on it, 'Yes', and, when they required an answer about some affair, if the arrow marked 'Yes' fell to their lot they acted in accordance with it. Another had 'No' and when they wanted to do something they shuffled it among the arrows, and if it fell to their lot they did not do that thing.

Another arrow had written on it, 'Belongs to you' or, as another version has it, 'Of pure descent', while another had 'Attached', and yet a third had 'Belonging to others, not to yourselves.' This was used to determine paternity in a disputed case. Affiliation is still an important issue among Arab tribes because of the responsibility of relatives for blood-money and blood revenge; furthermore, in parts of Arabia there is a custom current among the tribes of providing a woman concubine for the guest, and of course there is the case of plain fornication. Only some thirty to forty miles from Aden I came across a sort of oracle in 'the Bastard's Rock'. If an accusation of illegitimacy is made, the child of suspect legitimacy – always, I imagine, a boy – is made to crawl under a great square rock poised on stones with a small space between it and the ground, a natural phenomenon. If the child gets through he is legitimate. I was told of a case where a boy stuck under the rock and his mother burst into a fury of rage because he had unjustly impugned her honour! The mediaeval writer Usāmah ibn Munqidh tells of a rock-cleft at Petra which was used in the same way.

Another account of this type of oracle runs as follows:

An arrow had written upon it 'Waters' and when they wanted to dig for water they shuffled the arrows with that one among them, and they acted in accordance with wherever it came out. They used, when they wished to circumcise a lad, to give a woman in marriage, to bury a deceased person, or, if they doubted the ancestry of a person, to take him to Hubal along with 100 dirhams (silver drachmae) and a slaughter-camel which they would give to the man in charge of the arrows who shuffles them. Then they would bring up their man about whom they wished to ascertain – whatever it was. 'O God of ours', they would say, 'this is so and so, about whom we want to know such and such a thing. Produce the truth about him.' They would then say to the man in charge of the arrows, 'Shuffle' (literally, 'Strike!'). If 'Belongs to you' came out, he was a *wasīt*, of good quality as far as the tribe was concerned. If 'Belonging to others' came out he was an ally (*ḥalīf*); and if 'Attached' came out he was linked to them because of residing among them, but without any relationship or pact of alliance. If 'No' came out they would postpone an action for that year, until they decided to come for a second time, and they would go on with this affair of theirs until the arrows produced a positive answer. An ancient pre-Islamic verse runs:

Inna 'khtalafnā fa-habi 'ṣ-ṣirāḥā
Thalātat-an yā Hubalu fiṣāḥā
Al-maytu wa-'l-udhratu wa-'n-nikāḥā,
Wa-'l-bur' fi 'l-marḍā wa-'ṣ-ṣiḥāḥā.
In lam taqul-hu fa-muri 'l-qidāḥā.

When we are in dispute, give us rest
In three things, o Hubal, a clear (verdict),
The dead, circumcision and marriage,

Recovery for the sick and sound health.
If you do not utter it [i.e., make a sign] – command the
arrows (to do so).

These verses quite evidently represent authentically how and
why the pre-Islamic Arabians sought oracles from the gods
of paganism, and I am inclined to regard the verses themselves as actually pre-Islamic. The pre-Islamic south Arabian
inscriptions confirm the practice, in that in one there is a
question (*ms'l*) posed to the god Ilumqah, while another god,
Ta'lab, gives an indication of his wish by a sign.

Settling by lot, called *istiqsām* – which of course is what
resort to divination by the arrows is – is condemned by the
Qur'ān, yet, in affairs more or less mundane, the Prophet
himself did sometimes make a decision by lot. In ancient
Israel this was also practised and the technical term employed
comes from the same root as the Arabic *istiqsām*.

Arab tribesmen today occasionally treat their local saints,
whose shrines have taken the place of those of the pre-
Islamic gods, to demands couched in somewhat peremptory
language. So also did the celebrated prince of ancient
Arabian poets, Imru'u 'l-Qays. Sworn to avenge the slaying
of his father Ḥujr, he paid a visit to the oracle of Dhu
'l-Khalaṣah, north of Najrān, on the present-day Sa'udi-
North Yemen border, and consulted the god in the ordinary
way by drawing from three arrows entitled 'The Command-
ing', 'The Prohibiting' and 'The Waiting'. Drawing the
second, he broke the arrows in his anger and dashed them in
the face of the idol, exclaiming with a coarse imprecation,
'If *your* father had been slain you would not have hindered
me.'

In ancient and contemporary Arabia the most important
political function is that of arbitration between two contend-
ing parties. One of Muhammad's chief preoccupations
indeed at Medina was to enforce compliance with the
agreement he had made with the tribes there constituting
him the ultimate arbiter in disputes. Until that time one of
the several ways of settling a dispute was for the two parties
to a quarrel to go to a *kāhin* who settled cases by divinatory
or magic procedures. It need hardly be pointed out that
kāhin is the same word as Hebrew *cohen*, both deriving from

the common Semitic civilisation, but *kāhin* perhaps represented the function at a less developed and sophisticated stage than the Biblical *cohen*. The Arabian *kāhins* pronounced their decisions in rhymed prose of lofty style and cryptic oracular diction; this was nevertheless no mere exercise in rhetoric, for their utterances clothed verdicts concluded with professional forensic skill.

An office parallel to that of the *kāhin*, the *Ṭāghūt*, is alluded to in the Qur'ān eight times. The Believers were prohibited from seeking judgment from the *Ṭāghūt*, but must refer their differences to Allah and His Apostle. The term survives in the northern Yemen, meaning the head of a tribe who judges by customary law. I have not heard that the *Ṭāghūt* relies on oracular methods, but in some places, even today, recourse is had to supernatural means to determine a case, as will be mentioned. The ancient *Ṭāghūt* judge was called a *shayṭān* (lit. Satan) or a magician (*sāḥir*) because of his association with a familiar spirit. The Medina Jews seem to have fitted into the system, for the Aslamī *kāhin*, Abū Burdah, was invited by the Jewish Naḍīr and Qurayẓah tribes to judge between them, and the half-Jewish Ka'b ibn al-Ashraf is identified with the *Ṭāghūt*. That the *Ṭāghūt* was associated with ancient Arabian religion is apparent in the description of the *Ṭawāghīt* as 'interpreters of the idols, speaking with the people with their tongues.' 'There was one in every tribe, upon whom the *shayṭāns* were caused to descend.'

North Arabians might repair to a *kāhin* at the north Yemen city of Ṣa'dah. A noble Quraysh lady was accused of adultery by her husband and sent back to her father. To exonerate herself she took the oath that she was innocent and volunteered to go to one of the Yemen *kāhins* to put the matter to test. When, however, she and her father had nearly arrived she began to show some disquiet so he asked her if this was because she had done some unseemly thing. This the lady denied. 'But I know,' she said, 'that you are coming to a human being who both makes errors and hits the mark, and I cannot be sure that he will not mark me with a brand-mark (or, possibly, branding iron) which will be a disgrace until the Day of Judgment.'

This appears a clear allusion to trial by ordeal, known in

Arabia today as *bish'ah*, and the only classical reference to it of which I am aware. It is found in our time at Bir Sheba in southern Palestine, in Jordan, in Ḥaḍramawt and in Yāfiʿī country on the Yemen border. The best known *bish'ah* is to heat a knife red-hot; with this the *mubashshiʿ* (arbiter) flicks the tip of the tongue of the accused; if it burns his tongue, this proves him guilty. I discussed *bish'ah* with a shaykh of the Āl ʿAbd al-Wadūd, the *mubashshiʿ*-judge of Raydat ʿAbd al-Wadūd on the east Ḥaḍramawt coast. He emphasized that the professional *mubashshiʿ* – the function is hereditary in families – would spend a long time discussing with the litigants, painting a fearful picture of the red-hot knife and trying to bring them to agree to a settlement. An interesting aside is that he kept on saying that he had 'broken' the knife and when I persisted in asking to see even the pieces, someone told me that *kasara*, 'to break', here means 'to leave off.' In the Residency files I found that the local Arab Government had abolished *bish'ah* as a heathen practice contrary to Islamic *sharīʿah* (law), but one Arab official had written a defence of it as highly effective with the tribes. My theory is that while interrogating the parties the *mubashshiʿ* and his family carry on private investigations as to the guilty party and manipulate the red-hot knife appropriately.

When, in ancient times, contestants selected a *kāhin* to arbitrate between them they first tested his powers by asking him to guess at a certain object they had picked up on their way to him. To this the *kāhin* or *Ṭāghūt* would reply with high-sounding oaths, identifying it. In the case of the Quḍāʿah *kāhin* whose familiar or *shayṭān* was called *ʿUzzā* the two parties picked up a dead vulture which they concealed for him to guess. His answer typifies the rhetoric of the *kāhins*.

You have concealed for me the owner of a wing with a long neck, lengthy of leg, black mixed with white, when it hastens it soars and circles in its flight, when it swoops from the height of the sky it splits (its prey) from end to end, owner of a keen-pointed claw, living until worn out. . . . I swear by the light and the moon, thunder and fate, the winds and the creation, you have concealed for me a vulture's corpse in a saddle-cloth of hair, with the gallant lad of Banū Naṣr.

This testing of the *kāhin* was authenticated to me in a curious way, for when enquiring about trial by ordeal in Abyan in 1964, my informants told me that two parties repairing to the *mubashshiʿ* in Upper Yāfiʿ, would ask him to divine the secret thing they had brought with them – for example, they said, *a locust in a leather bag*. In this same year also was published for the first time, in Ḥaydarābād, *Kitāb al-Munammaq* and to my astonishment, when reading through it, I found that two parties going to the *kāhin* of Quḍāʿah some fourteen centuries ago, hid for him to divine and thereby test his confidence, the head of a locust in a water-skin (*raʾs jarādah fī khurbat mazādah*).

Muhammad set himself firmly against judgment by divination and seems to have disclaimed for himself power to perform magic. He opposed magic, though on more than one occasion he recognised himself as having been bewitched. Once he was asked by a Bedouin to prove he was the Apostle of Allah, as his Companions maintained, by telling him what was in the belly of his she-camel (in the same way as *kāhins* are tested), the Bedouin meaning that he should tell him whether the foetus was male or female. His request only brought him a coarse rejoinder from the Companions.

Nevertheless Muhammad in his outward manifestations appears to us like the *kāhins*. He was an ecstatic and took omens from his dreams as they did. At the beginning his dreams anticipated real events. However he did not draw revelation from *shayṭāns* but revelations were brought to him by Gabriel. Islamic Tradition has preserved evidently genuine accounts of how revelation came to Muhammad. 'When Muhammad received a revelation . . . this caused him much pain. so that we perceived it.' Even on cold days sweat appeared on his forehead. He would cover his head. He snored as one asleep or rattled like a young camel. The pagan prophet al-ʿAnsī in Ṣanʿāʾ seems to have groaned or cried out in the travail of receiving revelation as the Arab historians inform us. Ecstatic states in Arabia are associated with intense trembling or shaking and this is also found in popular forms in Sufism. However in the sources consulted it does not seem that Muhammad is recorded as trembling.

The way in which pagan gods manifested a sign may perhaps be understood in the light of an unusual experience I had in 1940 when stationed in the Ṣubayḥī tribal area west of Aden, in a village of the most farouche tribe I have ever encountered. This district had a number of ecstatics, known as *majdhūb* or *mamlūk*, possessed, associated with a saint, al-Qāḍī, and his shrine. When I questioned these ecstatics about this saint one of them stated that he was of Banāt al-'Arsh, the Daughters of the (Heavenly) Throne. I would have asked a great deal more but my more orthodox soldiers shut him up and told him this was nonsense. In fact these 'Islamic' saints function exactly as the ancient pagan tutelary deities.

We engaged some of these *majdhūbs* as tribal auxiliaries and upon an occasion one of them fell into a trance which even our regular soldiers recognised as being effected by the saint. We were at this time holding on behalf of the Lahej sultanate, several hostages from two tribal sub-sections, preparatory to judgment in an abduction case. One morning, the chief of the auxiliaries, himself a *majdhūb*, came to me, visibly distressed and trembling in every limb, with beads of sweat on his brow though it was an exceptionally cool day after the summer rains. The other *majdhūbs* present were also trembling and they knew that other *majdhūbs* with whom they had not been in contact would be trembling also. The fuss arose because our soldiers, though feeding the hostages, refused to provide them with water which was short because it had to be conveyed up the mountainside. The saint had demonstrated his displeasure at the failure to provide for hostages in their or his territory, visiting it on the *majdhūbs* and they had to discover the cause and seek to appease him.

In a northern Arabian context we seem to have a remarkable survival of pre-Islamic religion that enables us to interpret the rather bald statements of Arab genealogists and historians. These writers tell us that in such and such a section of a tribal confederation of the migratory tribes of the north lay the honour (*sharaf*) and the *bayt* – literally 'house', meaning also a 'temple' and, for Bedouin, a leather 'tent'. It is suggested that the *bayt* may have been a sort of portable temple, but I am also inclined to associate with that the family or 'house' which had charge of it. (In southern Arabia where the population is mostly settled the *bayt* would be a building.)

Now the famous scholar Alois Musil, who lived with and studied the migrating Rwalah tribes of Syria before World War I, describes what looks like a sort of camel-litter called Abu 'd-Duhūr, meaning literally 'Father of the Ages', but the name recalls *dahr* or *Manāt*, Fate, the latter being the well-known pre-Islamic goddess. Abu 'd-Duhūr is kept in the tent of the prince and is a sign of the princely authority of its holder. When the tribe goes on warlike manoeuvres, Abu 'd-Duhūr is borne on a white camel at the head of the tribal warriors. The Rwalah believe that Allah gives signs to them through the intermediary of Abu 'd-Duhūr. At times of dead calm, the ostrich feathers with which it is adorned begin to flutter; at other times the litter moves to right or left, but suddenly straightens itself. When the feathers wave, the Rwalah believe that Allah has touched it with his power. From such movements auguries are taken and it may be surmised that the *bayt* of the migrating Bedouin of ancient times had also an oracular function as Abu 'd-Duhūr has or had at any rate in very recent times.

While on the one hand Muhammad rejected the notion that he could perform miracles and denied that he was a *kāhin* (whether or not he actually considered *kāhins* had really the power of divination) it is reported by his biographers that he did pay great attention to the omen, *fa'l*, and to his dreams as has been already mentioned. Sūrat Yūsuf of the Qur'ān approves of Joseph in interpreting dreams, and Islamic Tradition sees Muhammad as an interpreter of dreams like the Prophets preceding him. Historians indeed tell that Muhammad's mission was foretold in the dream of a king of pre-Islamic Yemen – that his country would be occupied by the Abyssinians but liberated by the Yemeni leader Sayf ibn Dhī Yazan with the aid of the Persians, and that there would arrive an Arabian Prophet.

In popular Islam, the beliefs of common folk, the tradition of presage of future events or decisions made by supernatural agency through the medium of dreams seems to be universal. It figures for instance in the hagiologies of Sudanese *fiqihs*, the religious leaders and saints of the countryside, rather unsophisticated in type. The *fiqih* might be in a *khalwah*, i.e. the retreat of an ascetic which would also contain a school for teaching religion, or in the domed tomb, *qubbah*, of a departed saint, and be vouchsafed, when he falls asleep, a dream of guidance for his future actions. The Bān al-Naqā' are hereditary *fiqihs* of the districts north of Khartoum, and 'Abd al-Raḥmān wadd Bān al-Naqā' saw in a dream his grandfather flying between the Heavens and Earth, his own father flying behind him, and himself behind his father. He recounted this vision to Sharīf 'Abdullāh who said to him, 'They have indicated to you that you should occupy yourself with exoteric learning.' Yet another *fiqih* of this same family had the experience, while in a *khalwah*, of his soul departing his body in a dream and penetrating to the Heavens where he met the Prophet Muhammad who assigned Shamharūsh, the cadi of the Jinnīs, to his service, while various deceased Sudanese saints conferred on him the gifts of saintship and 'the fire of the *fiqih* Badawī.' In olden time in the Sudan fires were lighted at night so that the *fiqih* could see to study with his pupils, so that the 'fire of the *fiqih*' comes to mean his teaching circle.

The belief in familiar spirits survives into our own time and in southern Arabia it is, of all people, Muhammad's descendants, the Sayyids, who are credited with having service (*khidmah*) from the Jinnīs by even the orthodox biographical collections, as also with the power to summon (*taḥḍīr*) the Jinnīs and, one assumes, to consult them. We made the acquaintance of a Ḥaḍramī Sayyid, whose Jinnī was called Sharyūt, but his Jinnī, when willing to obey him, only performed simple tricks of white magic. It is however widely believed in the popular Islamic world that if you have a ring with the secret name of God (*khātam al-ism*), the Jinnīs will come and offer you their service.

To revert however to the question of dreams. At an early period in Islam data relating to the interpretation of dreams began to be collected, the great name associated with this activity being that of Ibn Sīrīn, who flourished in the latter part of the first *hijrah* century/7th century AD. This developed into a sort of pseudo-science known in Arabic as *ta'bīr al-ru'yā*. About the beginning of the 4th/10th century AD, the name of Artemidorus of Ephesus, and his work on dreams, starts to figure in Islamic literature, though actually the translation from Greek into Arabic took place about a century earlier. It appears to have exerted some influence on the formulation of the principles of this pseudo-science, which developed into a sort of discipline and gave rise to an extensive literature.

We are told that Ibn Sīrīn, 'When a dream was submitted to him, remained a good part of the day questioning the dreamer about his conditions, his person, his profession, his family and mode of life; in short, he neglected nothing of a kind that would supply the least indication, and he took these replies into account when pronouncing on the dream.' It will be immediately apparent that his method of ascertaining all relevant information closely resembles that of the *mubashshi‘* before he puts his client to the test of the red-hot knife.

By way of contrast to Ibn Sīrīn's rather empirical approach to the interpretation of dreams let me quote from the celebrated philosopher of history, Ibn Khaldūn, in his rationalisation of dream visions. He says:

> Dream vision is an awareness on the part of the rational soul in its spiritual essence, of glimpse(s) of the forms of events. While the soul is spiritual, the forms of events have actual existence in it, as is the case with all spiritual essences. The soul becomes spiritual through freeing itself from bodily matters and corporeal perceptions. This happens to the soul (in the form of) glimpse(s) through the agency of sleep. . . . Through (these glimpses) (the soul) gains the knowledge of future events that it desires and by means of which it regains the perceptions that (properly) belong to it. When this process is weak and indistinct, the soul applies to it allegory and imaginary pictures, in order to gain (the desired knowledge). Such allegory, then, necessitates interpretation.[1]

'Incubation' is defined for us as sleeping in the sanctuary with the formal intention of receiving, in a dream, the reply to a question asked of the god, having performed certain prescribed rites beforehand. It appears that incubation was practised in pre-Islamic Arabia since, in two inscriptions, thanksgiving offerings are recorded for visions revealed in the temples of 'Athtar and Awwam', while a third inscription alludes to a vision which is described as 'what he showed him in his slumber.'

Ibn Khaldūn maintains that the dream vision about things one desires may be induced. He says,

> It consists of saying, upon falling asleep, and after obtaining freedom of the inner senses and finding one's way clear (*sc.* for supernatural perception), the following non-Arabic words (apparently meaningless): *Tamāghis ba'dān yaswādda waghdās nawfanā ghādis*. The person should then mention what he wants, and the thing he asks for will be shown him in his sleep. . . . With the help of these words. I have myself had remarkable dream visions, through which I learned things about myself that I wanted to know.

He rationalizes this by saying that 'The dream words produce a preparedness in the soul for a dream vision.'

The Islamic practice known as *istikhārah* is by some considered a survival of incubation. *Istikhārah* is the prayer of a person who has not yet made up his mind, in order to be inspired with a sound decision regarding an enterprise he is about to undertake. In popular practice there are many forms of this *istikhārah* not sanctioned by Tradition, among which is seeking an answer through consulting the Qur'ān. The early nineteenth century Arabist Edward Lane says that in Egypt in his day the procedure was to repeat thrice the *Fātihah* of the Qur'ān, the four brief verses of Sūrat al-Ikhlāṣ, and the verse from Sūrat al-An'ām commencing *Wa-'inda-hu mafātīh al-ghayb lā ya'lamu-hā illā huwa* (With Him are the keys of the mysterious, no-one knows them but He). 'They let the book fall open, or open it at random, and from the seventh line of the right-hand page draw their answer.' This is forbidden by the Sunnī ulema but is doubtless done everywhere. In Ṣan'ā' of the Yemen in the first half of the 11th/17th century a party of notables at a banquet decided to consult the Holy Book to see whom Allah would chose as Caliph, i.e. Imām of the Yemen, and, after reciting the *Fātihah* and praying, the identical passage came up three times, 'Mention in the Book Ismā'īl.' In the event Ismā'īl son of al-Qāsim the Great succeeded in the year 1054/1644, taking the title of al-Mutawakkil.

In Persian speaking circles the Sufi *Mathnawī* of Jalāl al-Dīn Rūmī or the *Dīwān* of the poet Ḥāfiẓ are often used for the same purpose.

The means whereby presage of good or ill fortune was sought that figures perhaps most commonly in the Islamic histories is consultation of the stars. Names of astrologers or astronomers – the Arabic word *munajjim* means both – are preserved even from the pre-Islamic age; moreover a south Arabian inscription has come to light which alludes to a *kawkabān ṣ(i)dqm*, probably meaning 'a true star', in the prayer for male children of good star and fortune.

It is curious that so distinguished a scientist as al-Bīrūnī, who had spent much time and labour in studying Greek and Indian astrology and whose book on *Tanjīm*, composed in 420/1029, deals with both astronomy and astrology, should apparently have believed in the influence of the planets on the sub-lunary world and that he should even have shared the general belief in the efficacy of charms and talismans, whereas his contemporary, Avicenna, contemptuously refutes astrologers.

How general was the credence given this other pseudo-science, astrology, during the early mediaeval period can be seen from the *Qaṣīdah* of Abū Dulaf al-Khazrejī, writing, in the 4th/10th century, of tricksters and beggars, mainly in Iraq and Iran, and using the cant or argot of their professions. One of these he calls

a band of people who peer into omens (*fa'l*), auguries (*zajr*) and the meaning of the stars. They give money to a group of onlookers on the understanding that these last should come to them and ask them about their lucky stars and about their future circumstances, so that the fortune-tellers may look into their horoscopes. The customers then give back their money to the fortune-tellers. The latter usually keep it, but they may say to another person, 'We won't take your money because your star has not come out as you would like it.'; until the dupe falls into the harvest of victims ready for slaughter.

'Al-Tanbal,' he adds, 'is the simpleton who is the victim of tricks played on him and who is taken in by the fortune-tellers' returning his money to them. So he too lays out his money, fully expecting the fortune-teller to give it back to him; but the latter takes it from him, thus making him look ridiculous.' Readers of the *Arabian Nights* may also remember *The story told by the tailor*, in which the glib barber delays his exasperated victim whilst he finds with his astrolabe the precise moment auspicious for the shaving.

Recourse to astrologers was not restricted to ordinary folk in the sūq. In the fiscal and administrative survey of the Yemen under the brilliant Rasūlid dynasty, compiled at the beginning of the 9th/15th century, is included the item, among a list of other government servants, of

> the calculators of astronomical or astrological observations, experts, philosophers, who have perused the instructive books and have the reputation for sound auspicious astrological judgments and whose prognostications of propitious times to undertake a certain action coincide with auspicious movements (*sc.* of the stars, planets etc.) – what they have laid down having been (proven) sound, be it old or new. They will not leave the Royal Court (al-Bāb al-Sharīf) because of the needs of the sovereign, and the requirement of astrological observations to be made on newly-born children and the selection of (pro-pitious) movements (of stars etc.). Even if they be two, three or four persons they are indispensable.

An accusation levelled against the late Imām Aḥmad of the Yemen who died as recently as 1962 was that he consulted astrologers whom he maintained at his court.

In fact one reads in many of the histories of professional astrologers attached to the courts of Islamic monarchs, and the following is related of the 'Abbāsid period. The philosopher al-Kindī, at the court of the Caliph in early 3rd/9th century Baghdad, evidently practised astrology as part of his duties and equipment as a scholar. On a particular occasion his assertion of his superiority in the field of scholarship was challenged by a prominent *'ālim* or professional scholar who conceded however that he would admit to this if al-Kindī could show himself able to divine something that he, the *ʿālim*, would write down on a piece of paper. So they laid a wager – the *ʿālim* staked his valuable cloak and al-Kindī his mule with its expensive trappings. The *ʿālim* wrote on his piece of paper which was placed under the quilt of the Caliph. Asked to guess what he had written, al-Kindī

> asked for a tray of earth, rose up, took the altitude, ascertained the Ascendant, drew an astrological figure on the tray of earth, determined the positions of the stars and located them in the signs of the Zodiac and fulfilled all the conditions of divination and thought-reading, literally, guessing the nature of a hidden object. He then pronounced that the *ʿālim* had written something which was 'first a plant and then an animal'.

The writing turned out to say, 'The rod of Moses' – which of course turned into a snake in front of Pharaoh!

If this story from the Persian *Chahār Maqālah* or *Four Discourses* is to be considered more entertainment than historical fact, it does nevertheless contain certain points of resemblance to the testing of the *kāhin* in an earlier age.

In many countries individuals are credited with the ability to divine or to see a robbery enacted before their eyes and describe it detail by detail to the robbed so that they are able to apprehend the thief. A cynical Aden proverb runs, *Mā fāt ʿala 'l-sāriq shall-uh al-munajjim*, 'What the thief missed the astrologer has carried off.' The astrologer's fee has been so exorbitant that the owner of the stolen goods has nothing left.

The elaborate Chinese compass illustrated on Plate 4 employed in fortune-telling is to some extent to be matched by the *zāʾirajah* (fig. 11) attributed to a Moroccan scholar of Csuta about the close of the 6th/12th century. It consists of a large circle enclosing other concentric circles for the spheres, the elements, the created things, the *spiritualia*, as well as other types of beings and sciences. Each circle is divided into sections, the areas of which represent signs of the Zodiac, or the elements, or other things. The lines dividing each section run to the centre, and are called chords. Along each chord there are sets of letters that have a conventional (numerical) value. Some are *zimām* ciphers, the same as those used for numerals by government officials and accountants in the contemporary Maghrib. Others are the ordinary *ghubār*[2] ciphers. Inside the *zā'irajah*, between the circles are found the names of the sciences and topics of the created (world). On the back of the page containing the circles, there is a table with many squares.

One commences by writing down the question to be solved by the *zā'irajah* in unconnected letters and by determining the Ascendant of that day, i.e. one of the signs

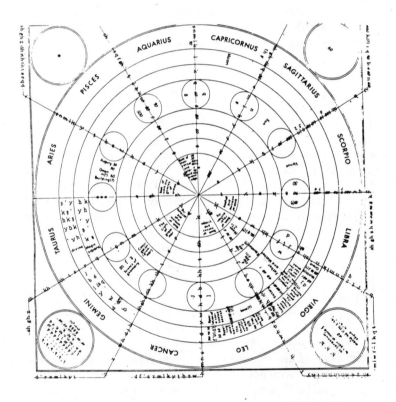

Figure 11. *The Zā'irajah*; from Franz Rosenthal, *Ibn Khaldûn: the Muqaddimah*, Bollingen series, Princeton, 1958. Reprinted by permission of Princeton University Press, and Routledge and Kegan Paul Limited.

of the Zodiac and the degree (of the sign on the horizon), so
the particular chord bordering the sign of the Zodiac of that
Ascendant is chosen. There then follows a most complicated
set of calculations involving the numerical values of the
letters of the alphabet. A very simple form of *zā'irajah* from
early 19th century Egypt is shown by Edward Lane in his
Manners and Customs of the Modern Egyptians; this is a square
table containing a hundred letters, but it has nothing in
common with the Moroccan *zā'irajah* other than the name.
It is thought that the word itself derives from the Persian
zā'ichah, horoscope, astronomical tables.

Augury by the flight of birds (*ṭīrah*) was condemned by
the Prophet as pagan superstition, but it has survived
vigorously enough among, for example, the northern Rwalah
tribe. Musil reports that two ravens flying above a raiding
party are a good omen, but a single raven or a vulture is a
bad omen. Like the ancient Arabs the Rwalah took auguries
from the movements of animals. A Rwalah Bedouin starting
on an important task considered the gazelle unlucky and
would shout at it, *'Ghazāl ghazāl, wa-sharr-an zāl!'* ('Gazelle,
gazelle, let misfortune vanish as well!'). For the ancient
Arabs, a gazelle passing from right to left was a bad omen
but, in general, the movement from left to right was considered to bring misfortune, though they do not seem to have
been consistent over this. The Rwalah carefully observe the
fox. If, on catching sight of a Rwalah raiding party, it halts,
they know they need expect no mishap but will return with
booty. A white mare, ass, camel, are good omens; a black
dog is a bad omen.

These then are a few of the forms in which divination is or
was practised in Islamic countries or some of them. I have
not dealt with geomancy or divination based on drawing
lines in sand, and many other ways of telling the future.
There is, to take a case in point, the large literature on *jafr*,[3]
which is particularly the domain of Shī'ah Muslims, its
origin being attributed to 'Alī, the fourth Caliph, himself.
It contains predictions, often apocalyptic, and covers all
methods of divination based on letters of the alphabet and
their numerical values. This category seems sometimes to be
called *ḥisbān*, and it is a lasting regret to me that on my two
tours of the former Wāḥidī sultanate circumstances prevented

me from consulting a manuscript *hisbāniyyah* in the hands of the Bā Qādir manṣab of the sanctuary at Ṣa'īd, but in the Yemen in 1966 I was able to copy a poem attributed to a semi-legendary poet, al-Ḥārith al-Rayyāshī, which was said to foretell the eventual victory of the Imām al-Badr over Nasser and the Republic. The poem was an accretion of individual verses but it looked archaic; the main interest of it however is that at the present day a poet could be held to have divinatory functions just like the ancient Arabian poets with their *hājis*, meaning muse or inspiration, who sometimes acted as oracles.

Notes

1   Franz Rosenthal, trans., *Ibn Khaldún: the Muqaddimah*, Bollingen Series XLIII, New York, 1958.
2   A form of the Arabic numerals close to that used in the west to-day.
3   Said to be a book written by the sixth Shi^cah Imām containing all that was to happen until the Last Day.

Index